New Life for Historically Black
Colleges and Universities

ALSO BY VANN R. NEWKIRK
AND FROM MCFARLAND

Lynching in North Carolina:
A History, 1865–1941 (2009)

New Life for Historically Black Colleges and Universities

A 21st Century Perspective

Edited by
Vann R. Newkirk

McFarland & Company, Inc., Publishers
Jefferson, North Carolina, and London

LIBRARY OF CONGRESS CATALOGUING-IN-PUBLICATION DATA

New life for historically black colleges and universities : a 21st
  century perspective / edited by Vann R. Newkirk.
      p.   cm.
      Includes bibliographical references and index.

  ISBN 978-0-7864-5903-2
  softcover : acid free paper ∞

  1. African American universities and colleges.   2. African
Americans— Education (Higher)   I. Newkirk, Vann R., 1962–
LC2781.N48 2012
378.1'982996073— dc23   2012011445

BRITISH LIBRARY CATALOGUING DATA ARE AVAILABLE

Front cover: Anthony Hall at Storer College, Harpers Ferry, Jefferson,
West Virginia (courtesy of the U.S. National Parks); *inset* Anthony
Hall perspective view of west rear (Library of Congress)

Manufactured in the United States of America

McFarland & Company, Inc., Publishers
  Box 611, Jefferson, North Carolina 28640
  www.mcfarlandpub.com

Table of Contents

Preface

Most contemporary literature about historically black colleges and universities is problematic in that it uses a one-dimensional framework to chronicle issues such as fund-raising challenges, leadership turnover, poor student retention, and weak graduation rates. Consequently, these studies create the belief that such problems are unique to HBCUs. In addition, using a one-dimensional approach causes chroniclers to fail to consider that historically black colleges and universities vary significantly due to doctrinal differences, types of control (i.e., public, or private), location (rural or urban), types of students served, and forms of governance (i.e., local management board or state board responsible for managing several institutions).

Another drawback of contemporary HBCU literature is a propensity to promote precise pathways that black college leaders should undertake to save or reposition their institutions. For example, in a recent issue of the *Jacksonville Times,* one of the leading proponents of this genre, Marybeth Gasman, when referring to questions about the future of beleaguered Edward Waters College, maintained that the problems "could be fixed with an institutional makeover. The first step would be to carve out a niche for the school to help differentiate it from rival colleges. If a school establishes itself as a leader in one field," she said, "potential donors and interested students will line up. It is the linchpin for every HBCU. When you think of the best HBCUs each one of them is leading the pack in a certain area."

While the strategy described may have merit, any plan that calls for

HBCUs to "first" carve out a niche is troubling. For one, niche planning is complex, requiring extensive planning and buy-in by all institutional stakeholders. It also requires revision of institutional missions and goals, extensive marketing, and sufficient financial resources to stay the course until new endeavors take hold. Unfortunately, many HBCUs, as do numerous predominately white institutions, lack sufficient financial resources to stay the course until new endeavors take hold. Many of these schools also lack modern governance structures and modes of operation to undertake such endeavors. There also is no guarantee that even if a college overcomes these issues and launches new programs, students will line up.

For example, between 1970 and 2002, Mount Senario College, a small, traditionally white institution (TWI) in Iowa, reinvented itself, several times. In the 1970s, the school's forte was its music programs. In the 1980s, it aggressively recruited Native Americans and offered degree programs in their interest. During the 1990s, the college turned its focus to its athletic programs. Unfortunately, none of the efforts worked, enrollment declined, and Mount Senario College closed in 2002.

Hence, for many small colleges, sustainability does not lie wholly in the development of niches. In many cases, sustainability requires institutional reform and the restructuring of outdated modes of operation before undertaking any attempt at niche building. For example, many HBCUs owe their existence to churches. As an outgrowth of this development, church officials made, and in many cases continue to make, most of the important decisions, including the selection of trustee, types of curriculum offered, management of daily operations, the selection of key administrators and the hiring of institutional presidents. However, this type of governance is problematic in today's society where regional accreditation and the need to connect with business leaders to raise money form key cornerstones. Another outdated mode of operation is the trend of adding new buildings, programs, and services in the belief that "if you build it they will come." However, the closures and near bankruptcies of dozens of small colleges have proven the fallacy of such beliefs.

In an attempt to overcome the shortcomings of current HBCU literature, in the winter of 2008, fifteen administrators and faculty, representing five historically black colleges universities, gathered on the campus of Fort Valley State University. Institutions represented were Livingstone College, Alabama State University, Fort Valley State University, Alabama A&M University, South Carolina State University and Bennett College. Combined, these officials averaged more than 15 years each working for, or serving on the governing boards of, historically black colleges of all types: public and private; small, mid-sized, and large; land-grant, research and small liberal-arts colleges; associate and baccalaureate degree granting institutions; as well as accredited and unaccredited institutions.

Such experiences allowed the Fort Valley group to develop a comprehensive approach for viewing HBCUs. This multifaceted approach not only identifies the challenges facing historically black colleges but places these issues within the larger framework of American higher education and the cultural context in which HBCUs operate. Through such an analysis, the Fort Valley group sought to introduce a new paradigm in the quest to ensure that HBCUs continue to play an important role in the education of Americans of all races.

Introduction

It started on a warm June morning in 1977 when authorities charged the former director of Bishop College's office of financial aid with embezzling federal funds. As reported by the *Abilene Reporter-News* over a period of months, the financial aid director, his wife and four former students made approximately 36 grant awards to themselves. "The checks ranged from less than $100 to more than $1,000."[1] The financial aid scandal triggered a federal investigation that revealed, among other things, that Bishop College improperly used $760,329 of federal funds to meet the college's operating expenses.[2]

Although the college agreed to repay the funds, the fallout from the scandal led to an enrollment decline and Bishop College defaulted on payments to bondholders and the federal government.[3] To resolve these issues, over the next few years, trustees restructured the college's debt several times. However, the problems mounted. In December 1986, the Southern Association of Colleges and Schools (SACS) revoked Bishop College's membership, and with it, their accreditation. Just two years later, Bishop College closed.[4]

The problems of Bishop College are emblematic of the difficulties faced by many of America's historically black colleges. Until the landmark decisions *McLaurin v. Oklahoma State Regents* (1950) and *Brown v. Board of Education of Topeka* (1954) which ended "separate but equal," historically black colleges and universities (HBCUs) were the only option for blacks who wanted higher education. However, after the lawsuits, colleges and universities across the nation desegregated. This made it possible for blacks to attend most institutions of higher education. Consequently, the percentage of black students enrolled in HBCUs fell from more than 90 percent in 1950 to approximately 14 percent in 2006.[5]

HBCUs also face intense financial stress brought on by a lack of corporate dollars and weak alumni support. For example, in 2003–2004, the thirty-nine members of the United Negro College Fund (UNCF) reported that 36,696 of their 261,104 alumni, 14 percent of the total, contributed $18,260,872 to their alma maters. The average per donor was $497. Unfortunately, the amount given by UNCF alumni pales significantly when compared to just one traditionally white institution, Wellesley College. During 1997, 34,000 of Wellesley College's 36,000 alumni, 94 percent of the total, raised $134,000,000. This was an average of $3,941 per donor.[6]

Additionally, with few notable exceptions, over the last thirty years the leadership at most HBCUs has been stagnant and has shown little imagination. As highlighted by Cynthia L. Jackson and Eleanor Nunn, "the observed leadership style of many HBCU presidents is grounded in the historical context in which HBCUs were established."[7] The colleges were established at the end of the Civil War with the daunting task of educating the nation's nearly 4,000,000 freedmen. Most of the schools were "created and sustained on faith, instead of generous amounts of seed money."[8] For example, throughout much of their early history, lack of resources hampered the development of black colleges. This forced black college presidents to depend upon white philanthropists, who shaped the direction and type of curriculum offered. Because of this, there was little need for presidents to be resourceful or innovative. Instead, HBCU leaders managed their schools like autocrats, tolerating no disobedience. They also frequently "favored mediocre but obedient faculty members over more gifted but independent colleagues."[9]

Such traits, however, are unsuited for today's academic landscape, which requires academic leaders to master a host of skills. These include (a) board relations; (b) fund-raising; (c) governmental relations; (d) fiscal/resource management; (e) coalition building; (f) enrollment management; and (g) regional accreditation.

Weak governing boards are another challenge for HBCUs. As with institutional leadership, the source of this problem lies in the origins of the HBCU. From the start, the primary role of the HBCU governing boards was to monitor campus life and the social actions of students and staff. There also was no expectation for board members to provide financial assistance to the institution. Financial support, and the accompanying ability to chart policy, usually lay in the hands of a few white philanthropists who often were not members of the governing board. Within such narrow constraints, HBCU governing boards actively participated in the day-to-day operation of the institution — pushing campus leaders to the brink of irrelevance. Furthermore, since most boards had only a limited understanding of higher education, they also cared little about the curriculum, philosophy and objectives of the institution. Unfortunately, these traits persist to the present. Hence, many HBCUs flounder aimlessly without guidance from the one body that is dedicated to their preservation.

Accreditation difficulties also present challenges for many HBCUs. Six regional and four national associations govern accreditation in the United States. Since most HBCUs are located in the South, and in the border states of Pennsylvania, Delaware, West Virginia, and Ohio, most HBCUs belong to the regional accrediting bodies responsible for these areas: Southern Association of College and Schools; the Middle States Commission of Higher Education; or the Higher Education Commission of the North Central Association on Accreditation and School Improvement. Each of these associations has a myriad of rules and regulations that evaluate the quality of faculty (i.e., the number of instructors teaching in a specific field holding terminal degrees), administrative competency, governance, institutional effectiveness, student performance, financial stability, and quality of library resources.[10]

For many HBCUs, difficulty in meeting accreditation standards stems from the early relationship between accreditors and black colleges. For example, until the 1930s, many accreditors refused to rate or accredit black schools. Unfortunately, the refusal of accreditors to rate or accredit black schools created an adversarial relationship that persists to the present. With membership, however, came added costs for new facilities and better-qualified faculty, as well as mandates that required HBCUs, especially church-related schools with denominational-controlled boards of trustees, to alter their traditional governing structures. Unfortunately, such mandates, especially the ones that altered governmental structures, upset traditional avenues of support, thus rendering the school vulnerable to financial difficulties and subsequent problems with accreditors.[11]

Other accreditation problems have evolved from the manner in which accrediting agencies initially reviewed black colleges. For example, from the late 1940s to 1961 the Southern Association of Colleges and Schools, in an attempt to address past discrimination and funding, used a double standard of grading institutions: one set of standards for predominately white schools and another set of weaker standards for HBCUs. Although SACS ended this process in 1961, its impact lingered as many HBCU leaders, familiar with the old weaker policies, refused to adhere to newer principles. Such intransigency caused, and continues to cause, problems with accreditors.[12]

Despite the variety of problems, scholars of HBCU studies have shown surprisingly little interest in critically examining each issue. They also have generally not advanced models for success and improvement. Only a handful of recent studies such as Carolyn O. Wilson Mbajekwe's *The Future of Historically Black Colleges and Universities* (2006) or Wilma J. Roscoe's *Accreditation of Historically and Predominately Black Colleges and Universities* (1989) even attempt to scan any of the myriad of issues that confront the modern HBCU. However, many of these studies are singular in focus or they fail to take into account the symbiotic relationship between the numerous challenges modern HBCUs face. They also continue to view HBCUs as one-dimensional monoliths with little concern for unique institutional histories or distinctive organizational challenges. As William Gray, former president of the United Negro College Fund, noted, "black colleges vary in their mission ... and situation."[13] In their book *Ebony Towers in Higher Education* (2008), Ronyelle Bertrand Ricard and M. Christopher Brown II, provide an even more salient description. According to these authors, historically black colleges "vary significantly in size, control, religious affiliation, gender composition, and available resources."[14]

Hence, any study of HBCUs must include an analysis of the distinctive institutional characteristics such as separate histories, unique academic and institutional challenges, evolutionary trends of governance structures, and resource development. Studies of HBCUs must also include an analysis of collective challenges such as technology, regional accreditation, management structures and institutional niches. This study seeks to overcome these problems by using an approach that (a) considers unique institutional histories; (b) examines the role of HBCUs on African-American advancement; (c) views historic and current operational challenges; and (d) highlights the development of unique management systems that shaped and continue to affect the development of HBCUs.

Yet, addressing these issues still does not provide a means of resolving the issues at hand. Thus, as a secondary objective, this study also identifies models of success that improve the operation and long-term viability of the historically black college. For clarity, the study is divided into two sections. The first section highlights HBCU history and the impact of black colleges on African-American social and black and economic development. Section II views current operational challenges, highlights the development of management systems, and provides models for improvement.

Notes

1. "Bishop College Official Indicted for Embezzling," Abilene Reporter-News, June 10, 1977; and "Six Indicted in Embezzlement," Corpus Christi-Times, June 9, 1977.

2. "Student Aid Embezzling is Charged," *Brownsville Herald*, June 10, 1977.

3. Handbook of Texas Online, http://www.tshaonline.org/handbook/online.

4. Ibid.

5. Ana M. Martínez Alemán, Kristen A. Renn, *Women in Higher Education: An Encyclopedia* (Santa Barbara, CA: ABC-CLIO, 2002), 267; and Kenneth E. Redd, "Historically Black College and Universities: Making a Comeback," *New Directions for Higher Education*, no. 102, Summer 1998, 35–36.

6. *Guide of the United Negro College Fund*, Fairfax, VA: United Negro College Fund, 2006, p.112; and Ernie Suggs, "The Scramble for Dollars: Begging and Thanking HBCUs Pursue Financial Security," The _Durham_ Herald-Sun, February 11, 1997.

7. Cynthia L. Jackson, Eleanor F. Nunn, *Historically Black Colleges and Universities: A Reference Handbook* (Santa Barbara CA: ABC-CLIO, 2003), 51.

8. Eric Kelderman, "Black Colleges See a Need to Improve Their Image," *Chronicle of Higher Education*, July 2, 2010, pp. 1, 17, 18.

9. Annett Woolard-Provine, *Integrating Delaware: The Reddings of Wilmington*, Wilmington: University of Delaware Press, 2003, 144.

10. A small number of HBCUs are members of the Transnational Association of Christian Schools (TRACS) and the Association of Biblical Higher Education (ABHE).

11. *Principles of Accreditation: Foundation for Quality Enhancement* (Decatur, GA: Southern Association of Colleges and Schools, 2006), and Standards for Accreditation; *Requirements of Affiliation* (Philadelphia, PA: Middle States Commission of Higher Education, 2009); and *Accreditation Manual* (Forest, VA: Transnational Association of Christian Colleges and Schools, 2010).

12. Carlos H. Vernon, "A Current History of Black Colleges," *Black World* (February 1973): 26–33.

13. Christopher Brown, Kassie Freeman, *Black Colleges: New Perspectives on Policy and Practice* (Santa Barbara CA: Greenwood, 2004), 191.

14. Ronyelle Bertrand Ricard and Lenoar Foster, *Ebony Towers in Higher Education: The Evolution, Mission and Presidency of Historically Black Colleges and Universities* (Sterling VA: Stylus, 2008).

I. HBCU History and Social Impact

1

The Origin and Development of the HBCU

The establishment of black institutions of higher education is a distinctive chapter of American higher education. Although most black colleges and universities are in the South, they encompass a wide variety of institutions. Included among the ranks of the nation's black colleges are public and private schools; land-grant and small liberal arts institutions; selective and open enrollment schools; coed and single-sex colleges; predominately black and predominately white institutions; associate and baccalaureate degree granting campuses; research, medical and professional schools; as well as a handful of church-related Bible colleges.[1]

The story of the historically black college began in 1837, when Northern philanthropists and black Church leaders established what is now Cheyney State University. At the close of the Civil War, the number and diversity of black colleges exploded as blacks and their supporters established hundreds of schools to educate the freedmen. As expressed by historian David W. Blight, "with bricks, mortar, and sometimes curriculum provided or influenced by northern white philanthropy, colleges became the mainstay of black hopes."[2]

However, many of the early schools, as were most contemporary predominately white colleges, were only colleges in name. During the post-bellum period, the organizers of black colleges realized that preparing a largely illiterate group for college would take time. For that reason, early HBCUs primarily provided elementary and secondary education, as did many contemporary white colleges. Yet, as soon as a handful of students mastered the primary curriculum, the leaders of these fledgling schools offered their pupils, normal, and theological training. Simply put, the leaders of these institutions believed that the most pressing need of freedmen was for a sufficient number of teachers, and preachers, to prepare them for life as citizens. Only as a final step, did HBCUs institute formal collegiate study for those who were ready to grasp such training. Therefore, a study conducted by the U.S. Bureau of Education in 1915 concluded that only 33 black college provided college-level instruction.[3]

Despite their limitations, early HBCUs provided an invaluable service to freedmen by educating the first generation of post-emancipation black leaders including noted educators and political figures such as Booker T. Washington, W.E.B. DuBois, and Mary McLeod Bethune; U.S. Congressman George W. White; activist and poet James Weldon Johnson; civil rights leader John R. Clifford as well as hundreds of other lesser-known personalities. By 1950, HBCUs were responsible for educating 90 percent of the African-Americans in college. They also produced more than 85 percent of black teachers, 75 percent of black Ph.D.s, and 85 percent of black physicians.[4]

However, the terrain that HBCUs operated changed in 1954 when the Supreme Court overturned the separate-but-equal doctrine and desegregated public education. This decision "called into question the overall legitimacy of educational institutions whose existence was based primarily on race." Indeed, to many it seemed that black colleges were outdated and nearly a dozen private HBCUs closed between 1955–1965.[*]

The majority of HBCUs however struggled to reposition themselves, in the wake of the Supreme Court's decision, with "poorer facilities and budgets much smaller than their white counterparts." This undoubtedly led to the departure of many of the best students and brightest faculty. Federal desegregation also seriously affected the level of financial support HBCUs received from private and philanthropic organizations as many funders questioned the continued relevancy of black colleges. For example, in the years prior to the famous *Brown v. Topeka Case*, Alabama's Talladega College annually ranked among the nation's most prestigious HBCUs and the school filled a particular niche preparing African-Amer-

[*]Notable institutions closed during this period included Storer, Leland, Immanuel Lutheran, Harbison Agricultural, Bricks Junior, Mather Junior, and Campbell colleges.

icans for careers in business, education, and the sciences. The institution was also home of the Amistad Murals and distinguished former students such as Eunice Johnson, founder and director of Ebony Fashion Fair; Geraldine Pittman Woods, renowned neuro-embryologist and special consultant to the National Institute of Health; Jewel Isadora Plummer Cobb, prominent cell biologist and first African-American president of California State University-Fullerton; and George William Stanley Ish (1905), well-known physician and founder of the first hospital for blacks in Little Rock.

However, in the years after *Brown* case Talladega College went into decline. After federal desegregation, many white supporters no longer saw a need to support a small all-black college. Therefore, Talladega College's ability to maintain its facilities or attract top students and faculty declined. With fewer top students and faculty, Talladega College's academic reputation eroded and the school's enrollment plummeted from 1,207 to 475 between 1992 and 2008. This reduced tuition revenue and created a fiscal nightmare. As a result, the Southern Association of College and Schools placed the college on "probation," the association's most serious sanction before loss of accreditation, twice, between 1999 and 2006.

Paradoxically, a handful of HBCUs such as Morehouse and Spelman Colleges as well as Claflin, Elizabeth City State, and Winston-Salem State Universities, have overcome many of the challenges facing black colleges by embracing new management and operational paradigms. For example, between 1994 and 2007, Claflin University reinvented itself by: (a) recruiting a board that contained corporate as well as influential political leaders who had experience in managing large complex entities; (b) hiring an innovative president who had ties to business and political leaders; (c) increasing the value of research grants the University received; (d) upgrading campus facilities and infrastructure; and, (e) improving the quality of the faculty. Because of these changes, Claflin University, which had an enrollment of barely 1,000 students in 1995, grew to 2,400 students in 2007. The value of the University's endowment, which stood at $7,000,000 in 1995, grew to $17,000,000 in 2007. The value of research grants won by the university tripled. However, by far the biggest transformation came from students. In 1995, the average SAT of students entering Claflin stood at approximately 680. Fifteen years later the average SAT score was 920. In conjunction with these developments, the school's graduation rate increased to 55 percent, one of the

Claflin University Administration Building, April 2009. Claflin has garnered national recognition as a premier institution. Since 1999, the university has been ranked among the top in South Carolina and number five among HBCUs by *U.S. News and World Report.*

highest among HBCUs.* When asked about the transformation, Claflin University President Henry Tisdale credits the university's success to, "a commitment to academics, which allows the University to attract high-quality students, research grants and top faculty."[5]

Another institution of note is Atlanta's Spelman College. In the early 1990s, the school's board of trustees announced what then was an unprecedented $81,000,000 capital campaign. Although many pundits

*HBCUs six-year graduation rate leaders: (1) Spelman College, 78%, (2) Howard University, 70% (3) Morehouse College, 60%, (4) Claflin University, 55%, (5) Hampton University, 54%, (6) Fisk University, 53%, (7) Elizabeth City State University, 51%, (7) North Carolina Central University, 48%, (7) Dillard University, 48%, (9) Tougaloo College, 46%; (10) Winston-Salem State University, 45%, (11) Clark-Atlanta University, 44%, (11) Oakwood College, 44%, (13) Alcorn State University, 43%, (14) South Carolina State University, 45%, (15) Johnson C. Smith University, 42%, (15) Virginia State University, 42%, (17) Albany State University, 41%, (17) North Carolina A&T, 41%, (17) Tennessee State University, 41%, (20) Savannah State University, 40%.

assumed the college could not raise the announced sum. However, the school, through a process of tapping black celebrities and corporate sponsorship, raised more than $113,000,000, which set a new standard in black college fund-raising. Spelman College President Johnetta Cole declared, "Our success has raised the bar for future Spelman fund-raising efforts as well as those of other historically black colleges and universities."[6]

Despite the success of Spelman, Claflin, and a handful of other institutions, most HBCUs continue to struggle. For example, between 2000 and 2010, 35 of the nation's 106 HBCUs (33 percent) received sanctions from accreditors or suffered embarrassing episodes that threatened the institution's future. Yet, the struggles of HBCUs vary according to location, institutional control, and historic origin. Most studies of HBCUs however fail to consider these issues. Consequently, this chapter views these distinctive issues by categorizing HBCUs into four groups. Group I consists mainly of struggling private institutions as well as one defunct institution, Storer College.* For most of these schools daily life is or was accentuated by sagging enrollment; run-down buildings; low rates of student retention; poor graduation rates; leadership turnover; accreditation problems, and the increased cost of delivering private education to students.

The second grouping of HBCUs consists of mainly mid-sized public colleges and universities with enrollments ranging from 2,000 to 5,000 students. Although most of these schools are stronger than the institutions in Group I, they nonetheless face great challenges. For instance, most of these institutions have little discretionary funding. This prevents them from implementing new programs and services with which to complete with predominately white institutions. These institutions also faced decreasing financial support from governing bodies and persistent threats of closure or merger from state legislatures grappling with huge budget deficits.

The final class of HBCUs consists of a handful of thriving institutions, that have overcome the challenges. This chapter characterizes these institutions as schools with high student achievement; stable enrollments; accreditation success; well developed fund-raising apparatuses;

---

*Storer College was selected due to its location, near the mid-point between North and South. A study of the school highlights the three issues impacting most HBCUs during the period between 1865 and the mid–1970s, namely location, white denomination support, and Black self-determination.

active and progressive governing boards; and high academic standings in relationship to similar predominately white institutions.

In light of the factors above this chapter examines the histories of six HBCUs selected as representative of each categorization. Yet, while these examples are representative of many of the historical courses taken by HBCUs this study recognizes that other pathways may exist.

Group I: A Struggle to Survive

Storer College

Dawn J. Herd-Clark

In the midst of the turmoil and pain of the Civil War, Harpers Ferry, West Virginia, became one of the many Union garrison towns where runaway slaves and freedmen sought refuge. To serve the needs of these refugees, Reverend Nathan Brackett, supported by the Freewill Baptist Church's Home Mission Society, established a grammar school in a dilapidated house. The one-room building, known as the Lockwood House, not only served as a classroom but also provided living space for Brackett and his teachers.

Despite the cramped conditions, freedmen in the Shenandoah Valley "hungered" for education. Commenting on the situation, a Union Army official maintained, "The colored people are more zealous in the cause of education than whites. They will starve themselves and go without clothes in order to send their children to school."[7] Perhaps due to this factor, by 1867, Brackett's school enrolled 2,500 students. However, with only sixteen teachers, Brackett realized that the only way to serve the masses was to train black teachers.[8]

To meet this need, New England philanthropist John Storer offered $10,000 to expand the school. The gift however came with several stipulations. First, the Free Will Baptist Church had to raise an amount equal to Storer's grant. Second, Storer required that the institution eventually become a degree-granting college. The final stipulation required officials to open the institution to everyone regardless of race, sex or religion.[9]

Raising the funds turned out to be easy, and Storer College opened on October 3, 1867, with 19 students. One year later the fledgling college obtained a campus when Congress gave the institution four dilapidated buildings that formerly belonged to the U.S. Arsenal.[10] Unfortunately, local whites disapproved of the new college. They tried everything from vandalism and violence to "pulling political strings" to close the school. Indeed, one Storer College teacher wrote, "It is unusual for me to go to the post office without being hooted at, and twice I have been stoned on the streets at noonday." In response to such harassment, Brackett allowed his teachers and students to carry guns for protection.[11]

The local hostility however did little to slow the growth of the institution. By 1874, the college enrolled 273 students. However, the rapid growth taxed the college's limited resources. As a result, college officials developed plans to reconfigure one of the old federal buildings into a residence hall for girls. Yet, in what became the norm, lack of financial resources hampered the development of these badly needed facilities. Not until 1876 were funds available to remodel the old federal building. Even then, to save money, students did most of the work.[12]

On the heels of this development, Storer College's financial picture brightened. In the mid–1880s, the West Virginia Legislature granted the school the first, of what became annual appropriations. Several years later, members of the College's Board of Trustees attempted to persuade West Virginia officials to designate the school as a land-grant college for Negroes. That such an opportunity came about was due to the passage of the second Morrill Act in 1890. This act, aimed at the former Confederate States, required each southern state to desegregate their existing land-grant colleges or to establish separate institutions for African-Americans.[13] To comply with the federal legislation, supporters of Storer College sponsored a bill to establish a land-grant college for Negroes on the campus of Storer College. However, just before the legislature voted on the matter, James Ferguson, a prominent representative from Kanawha County, opting to secure the school for his district, moved to strike the words "Storer College, county of Jefferson," and insert the words "some institution to be established in the county of Kanawha." The amendment prevailed and the state established the new West Virginia Colored Institute in Kanawha County.[14]

Despite the setback, Storer College continued to carry out its mission educating teachers to serve the blacks of the Shenandoah Valley. By 1890, nearly 500 teachers received training at the college. Their impact was immense. For example, during the mid–1890's, Storer College teachers comprised nearly 80 percent of the black teachers in West Virginia and the western part of the state of Virginia. Storer College graduates also played major roles in the development of West Virginia's other historically black colleges. For example, Hamilton Hatter, a graduate of the school's high school division served as the founding president of Bluefield State College.[15]

Storer During the Nadir

At the start of the twentieth century, conditions for African-Americans worsened. The implementation of Jim Crow laws coupled with Booker T. Washington's accomodationist policies effectively relegated African-Americans to second-class citizenship. In response, Atlanta University professor, W.E.B. Du Bois drafted a "Call" to a few select people. The Call had two aims, "organized determination and aggressive action on the part of men who believed in Negro freedom and growth." Hence, in July 1905 Du Bois invited 59 like-minded black activists to meet in Buffalo, New York, where they formed the Niagara Movement, an organization dedicated to the end of racial discrimination and the improvement of civil liberties.[16]

The second meeting of the Niagara Movement occurred on the Storer Campus. During the three day conference, held August 15 to18, 1905, African-American leaders, such as John Robert Clifford, a 1875 Storer College graduate and West Virginia's first African-American attorney; Lewis Douglas, the son of Fredrick Douglas; and publisher Freeman H. M. Murray, discussed ways to secure civil rights for blacks. As a highlight of the meeting, the attendees walked from the Storer College campus to the fort where John Brown's quest to free the slaves ended. At the fort, the crowd removed their shoes and socks to honor the "hallowed ground." Then they marched single file around the fort and sang two songs, the "Battle Hymn of the Republic" and "John Brown's Body." Following the meeting, Max Barber, editor of *The Voice of the Negro,* said, "A more suitable place for the meeting would have been hard to find."[17] Yet, the suitability of the Storer Campus and Harpers Ferry came as little surprise to those associated with the college. Storer College had a long association with civil rights. For example, in 1881 Frederick Douglas, a Storer College trustee, gave perhaps his most famous speech, "A Lecture on John Brown." In this speech, Douglas looked at the question, "Did John Brown fail?" Mary Church Terrell also visited the college in the

Storer College's Anthony Hall. From 1865 until 1955 Storer College played a vital role in educating African-Americans in Virginia and West Virginia. However, the push to provide equal education for blacks was fatal. Less than one year after the Brown v. Board of Education case ended legal segregation in public schools, the state of West Virginia withdrew its financial support from Storer College. One year later the college closed. The old campus is now part of the Harpers Ferry National Park operated by the U.S. National Park Service (courtesy of Harpers Ferry National Historical Park).

mid–1890s and gave her popular lecture "The Bright Side of a Dark Subject," in which she chronicled the achievements of blacks.[18]

Perhaps the most controversial call for civil rights however occurred in 1885 when black nationalist, Alexander Crummell delivered "The Need of New Ideas and New Aims for a New Era." Crummell's aim was to turn blacks from focusing "morbidly and absorbingly upon the servile past," and to aggressively exercise their civil rights. Hence, when Crummell delivered his Storer College address he warned students to guard against the constant recollection of slavery. Such recollection Crummell maintained would only degrade racial progress. Following the speech, Fredrick Douglas, who sat in the audience, openly expressed his displeasure. This sparked a debate among black intellects that continued throughout the late nineteenth and early twentieth centuries over how African-Americans should view slavery and their history.[19]

Yet, the college's stance in the growing quest for black civil rights did little to improve the school's financial health. In fact as a direct consequence of the Niagara Movement conference, the West Virginia legislature reduced funding for the school.[20] Consequently, college officials, in similar fashion to Fisk University, formed the Harpers Ferry Jubilee Singers. The singers, composed of graduates of Storer College, annually toured New England, Europe and South America raising funds for the school. On their most successful tour in 1898, the Singers raised $22,000.00.[21]

College officials also rented rooms to black vacationers to make ends meet. However, in the 1890s Storer College president Nathanial Brackett closed the campus to African-American visitors and instead focused solely on white vacationers. This decision launched a whirlwind of opposition from African-American professionals. Perhaps none were more vocal than noted Storer College alumnus J. R. Clifford. In his newspaper, *The Pioneer Press,* Clifford wrote a column that condemned the actions of the Brackett. "The crime of evil discrimination in the boarding department is bad enough. The crime of race prejudice and double-dealing is worse. How can students feel a pride for an institution that pretends to teach full-fledged manhood and the religion of Jesus Christ part of the year and then employs them as discriminating servants the other part?" In addition to these denunciations, Clifford also raised more serious charges, namely of illicit behavior between Brackett and female students. Clifford went on to say that such affairs resulted in numerous illegitimate children.[22] Although the Board of Trustees investigated they never revealed the results of the inquiry. Nonetheless, Brackett resigned.

Storer During the Presidency of Henry Temple McDonald

Several months after Brackett's resignation, college trustees hired twenty-six-year-old Henry Temple McDonald to lead Storer College. As a graduate of Hillsdale College, a Free Will Baptist school in Michigan, McDonald saw his work at Storer as an extension of his family's abolitionist activities, "Father worked for the physical freedom of the colored people and I am working for their intellectual freedom."[23] Unfortunately, when he arrived in Harpers Ferry, McDonald's enthusiasm for the job was dampened. Many of the college's buildings needed renovation. The college also offered no courses on the collegiate level and the treasury was empty.[24]

Despite the formidable challenges, McDonald assumed the presidency launching the longest presidential tenure, 46 years, in the college's history. To improve the school's finances he secured funding from West Virginia's legislature for the development and support of industrial education.To increase the number of African-Americans trained for Christian ministry and missionary work, McDonald expanded the Biblical and Literature Department. In the last endeavor, the college made perhaps its most lasting contribution.[25]

For much of its history, Storer college and its graduates formed a key component of Freewill Baptist's efforts to establish missions and training centers along the coast of Africa. In turn, Storer became a destination for African students seeking advanced education. Among the more notable students from Africa during this period include Joseph Walters, the author of *Guanya Pau,* the oldest surviving English-language African fictional text and Nnamdi Azikiwe, the first president of Nigeria.[26]

In large part due to the success of the college's missionary and teacher preparation efforts, in 1921 Storer gained junior college status. Seventeen years later, Storer offered its first four-year degree programs." Unfortunately, these developments occurred during a period of increased operational and financial distress which stemmed from the exodus of blacks from the Shenandoah Valley. Between 1865 and 1910, the African-American population for the region declined from 20,000 to 3,499. Indeed, a survey conducted by the American Baptist Convention, a successor to the Freewill Baptist Church, concluded that within a hundred mile radius of the college "student potential was so limited that there was no reason to continue a liberal arts college for Negroes."[27]

Due to these factors as early as 1919, Dr. Alfred Williams Anthony, a trustee of the school, convinced West Virginia officials to consider a proposal for "assuming control of the college." Unfortunately, Anthony's offer met with stiff opposition from McDonald who, in 1929, convinced the state legislature to table the plan. Although Anthony accused McDonald of sabotaging the transfer and attempted to fire the president, he failed to garner the support of the remainder of the Board. In frustration, Anthony resigned.[28]

Three years later McDonald faced another hullabaloo when the NAACP attempted to place a plaque commemorating John Brown's raid on Harpers Ferry. After getting initial approval, Storer College officials later refused to allow NAACP officials to install the plaque fearing that the inscription would offend southern sensibilities. However, one year earlier, college officials allowed the United Daughters of the Confederacy (UDC) to hold a public ceremony denouncing Brown.[29]

In response to this action, African-American newspapers condemned McDonald and the college. The *Washington Tribune* called the president and school's trustees the "White Judases of Storer College." The paper also urged blacks to boycott and ostracize the college. The *Afro-American* wrote, "it was written in every facial expression that Dr. McDonald [is an] apologist for those Southern whites, who would desecrate John Brown's memory while glorifying the slave regime, must go." Undoubtedly due to growing dissatisfaction over the plaque, the fortunes of Storer College declined and the college's enrollment plunged to an all-time low of 44 students in 1943. The next year, McDonald resigned after 46 years of service.[30]

To replace McDonald, college leaders elected Richard Ishmael McKinney, dean of the College of Education at Virginia Union University. As the first African-American president, students greeted McKinney's selection with enthusiasm. In turn, McKinney sought to improve conditions for undergraduates by forming a Student Government Association as well as a local chapter of the NAACP. He also increased the number of African-American faculty members and strengthened ties to Africa. At first, these efforts appeared to transform the fortunes of Storer College. Student enrollment, which stood at only 44 in 1943, swelled to 279 by 1947. On the heels of this development, McKinney announced, in the summer of 1948, plans for the construction of the new physical education building and the establishment of a work camp for college students.[31]

Despite these accomplishments problems remained. Throughout most of the college's 80 year history the school operated as an unaccredited institution. Although the State Board of Education granted the college accreditation on November 18, 1940, such recognition mattered little outside of West Virginia. Regional accreditation, which mattered the most to students and foundations continued to elude the college. Due to this factor, the United Negro College Fund, organized in 1944 to provide financial support to private historically black colleges, refused to issue Storer College membership.[32]

In addition to this problem, McKinney's efforts to increase ties to Africa raised concerns among members of the College's Board of Trustees that he was too militant for the school. Other factors contributing to the growing dissatisfaction with McKinney stemmed from his unauthorized attempt to construct a new gym and his inability to improve the college's finances. For these reasons, in 1950, the Board of Trustees removed McKinney from the presidency.[33]

After McKinney's departure, Storer College operated without a president for nearly two years. Finally, in 1952 the Trustees appointed Leonard Earl Terrell, a Jacksonville, Florida, minister as president. A graduate of Howard University, and Drew Seminary, Terrell assumed the school's leadership just as the college faced perhaps its greatest challenges including declining gifts, weak community support, and a total enrollment of only 88 students. To remain solvent the school borrowed heavily from its meager endowment. Officials also sold parcels of school property. Yet, these efforts failed to generate the funds needed to operate the school. Consequently, in 1953, the Board of Trustees voted to close Storer College for the 1954–1955 term. However, alumni gifts, in the amount of $5,000 kept the school open for the 1954-1955 term. Unfortunately, one year later the West Virginia Legislature voted to end its annual $20,000 appropriation. State officials reasoned that in the wake of the *Brown v. The Board of Education of Topeka, Kansas* ruling, which outlawed segregation in public education, African-American students could now attend any public school. For Storer College officials the ruling was especially damaging since State appropriations made up 21 percent of the college's annual budget. With no avenue to replace the state funds Storer closed at the end of the spring 1955 term.[34]

Trustees made several attempted to reopen the school. Each attempt failed. Following these efforts, Alderson-Broaddus College, a small Baptist College in Philippi, West Virginia, attempted to merge with Storer College. The proposal preserved Storer's name and endowed several scholarships for African-American students. The African Methodist Episcopal Zion Church (AMEZ) also issued a bid to purchase the college. The AMEZ proposal allowed the school to maintain the name Storer College. It also assumed the responsibility for the operation of the school, provided a renovation schedule, and allocated 30 percent of the Board of Trustee slots to the Free Will Baptists.[35] Unfortunately, resistance by Free Will Baptists led the Board to reject the AMEZ offer.

In the midst of these efforts several alumni filed lawsuits to reopen the school. One lawsuit attempted to stop the school's liquidation of assets to Alderson-Broaddus College as they contended it violated the school's original 1867 charter. The suit failed. As a result, in 1960, Alderson-Broaddus College and Virginia Union University divided Storer College's assets. Four years later, Storer College merged with Virginia Union University. Yet, the true strength of Storer College lay in its graduates. In its 88-year history, hundreds of African-Americans entered the doors of the school gaining the skills needed to advance African-American society. Among its notable graduates are Don Redman, the Little Giant of Jazz, and Coralie Franklin Cook, distinguished professor at Howard University. Today the old campus is part of the Harpers Ferry National Historical Park.[36]

Edward Waters College

Vann R. Newkirk

In 1870, leaders of the Tallahassee Conference of the African Methodist Church (AME) passed a resolution to establish a school for the education of freedmen. After receiving a charter, members of the conference purchased ten acres in Live Oak, Florida, and opened Brown Theological Institute. To manage the enterprise, the conference appointed Reverend Charles Pearce soliciting agent.[37]

As soliciting agent, Pearce secured a number of notable gifts such as $20,000 in state script and railroad bonds from Milton S. Littlefield, a railroad magnate; a wagon and a pair of mules from Simon Conaber, treasurer for the state of Florida; and, 640 acres of land from Live Oak landowner William Gleason. However in what would become the norm for Edward Waters College, success gave rise to intrigue and scandal. As reported in the college's official history, in 1873, a fire destroyed Charles Pearce's Tallahassee home and with it presumably the $20,000 gift from Littlefield. After the fire, Pearce's neighbors speculated as to the cause of the fire. Many maintained that the blaze was the work of an arsonist. Indeed, local newspapers echoed such sentiments, "There seems to be somebody around here who has a devilish spite against Bishop Pearce." Despite such claims, officials never identified a suspect or made any arrests for the destruction of Pearce's house. In the wake of this catastrophe, church officials hired a new soliciting agent. However, after collecting $3,000, the agent absconded with the money and the school closed.[38]

Over the next nine years, supporters tried several times to reopen the institution. Each endeavor failed. Finally, in 1883, Reverend W.W. Sampson garnered enough support to open a new school in Jacksonville named East Florida Divinity High School. Church leaders selected William Preston Ross, a graduate of the Unitarian Theological Seminary of Pennsylvania, to serve as principal. According to Bishop Daniel Alexander Payne, "Ross maintained a pure and high Christian character," which the bishop predicted, "would be of great usefulness."[39]

The appointment, however, troubled Ross. On one hand, church officials failed to inform Ross of his appointment to the school until he arrived in Jacksonville to assume the pastorate of Mt. Zion A.M.E. Church. On the other hand, Ross had no experience in managing a school. Yet, Ross worked tirelessly to get the school ready for its opening. As a result, on opening day 125 students enrolled in the fledgling institution.[40]

Yet, problems remained. The only resources available to support operations consisted of tuition payments and a few hundred dollars from Mt. Zion Church. In response, Ross issued appeals in the *Christian Recorder,* "No school can be conducted without faculty, and no faculty can work without pay or will not at least." Such appeals however garnered little financial support. To save the institution, officials opted to sell a 640-acre farm. They also borrowed heavily from Mount Zion Church. Fortunately, these efforts provided just enough financial support to sustain the School.[41]

However, for many prominent AME Church officials, the name of the school did not fit their ambitions. Consequently, in 1892 they renamed the school Edward Waters College (EWC) in honor of the third bishop of the African Methodist Episcopal (AME) Church. Unfortunately, the name change did not bring with it increased financial support nor did it stabilize enrollment. For example, in 1891 enrollment reached 190 students but in 1896 and 1898 enrollment only reached 100 and 63 students respectively. These developments led to faculty turnover as well as instability as six presidents served between 1890 and 1900.[42]

The instability at EWC however differed little from the disorder faced by many predominately white colleges. For example, at Georgia's

Brewton-Parker College six presidents and three interim leaders served between 1912 and 1922 while five presidents served Berry College between 1942 and 1945.[43]

Edward Waters College in the Early Twentieth Century

Conditions worsened for Edward Waters College at the start of the twentieth century. On May 3, 1901, sparks from a smokestack ignited cotton fibers at a Jacksonville factory. In short order, high winds fanned the flame into a roaring furor that "leaped from block to block setting fire wherever it touched." When it was over, hundreds of buildings including Edward Waters College lay in ruin. For the next seven years, the college moved from one rented facility to another. Finally, in 1908 AME church officials purchased land and constructed the first permanent building on the college's current site.[44]

In the decade following this milestone, church officials also constructed a library, theological seminary, and two dormitories. Undoubtedly, the construction of a permanent campus played a major role in stabilizing the operations of the college and student enrollment reached several hundred including such notables as James and A. Phillip Randolph. However, trouble lurked. During the Great Depression, financial problems led courts to seize the school to satisfy a debt to the Putman Lumber Company. This led college officials to resort to an unusual tactic to save the college. On the date of the foreclosure sale, Reverend George C. Curry, the treasurer for Edward Waters College, purchased the college. Then he deeded the property back to the AME Church. Such a maneuver likely reduced the school's overall indebtedness because court-ordered sales rarely brought the amount sought by plaintiffs.[45]

Six years after the Putman incident, EWC faced another crisis when a fire destroyed the college's dining hall and the girls' dormitory. Again, George Curry rescued the school. Using connections from his days as presiding elder of Florida's AME Church, Curry raised the funds and rebuilt the dining hall. He also purchased a 338 acre farm and secured $15,000 from the federal government. During this period some of the school's most notable students attended the college including the writer John Oliver Killens; baseball great John "Buck" O'Neil; and civil rights pioneer Virgil Darnell Hawkins who initiated the lawsuit that desegregated the University of Florida. The presence of talented students however did little to stem the EWC's financial problems. Hence, in 1929, the college phased out high school and baccalaureate instruction and EWC became a junior college.[46]

The world in which EWC became a junior college was vastly different from the one that gave birth to the college. At the close of World War I, American higher education underwent a major transformation — going from an "elitist experience" to one with mass appeal. In conjunction with this development between 1918 and 1941, America expanded the number of secondary and high schools. As expected, this increased the number of high school graduates and created an ever-increasing pool of college aspirants. Consequently, between the wars, enrollments in colleges and universities increased more than fivefold from 250,000 to 1.3 million. For Edward Waters College this translated into an enrollment boom — one in which the number of enrolled students enrolled grew from 79 students in 1918 to 190 students in 1940.[47]

Storm clouds again loomed. As was the case throughout much of Edward Waters College's history, setbacks usually followed progress. Hence, during World War II, the college's enrollment declined from 190 students and 31 faculty members in 1942, to 162 students and 11 instructors in 1945. To survive, the college adjusted its admission standards granting admissions to all students 15 years or older with so-called "college potential."[48]

At the close of the war, conditions improved. Perhaps the most important factor in this development was the passage of the Servicemen's Readjustment Act, better known as the GI Bill, in 1944. This act paid up to $500 annually for college tuition, books and fees. Veterans also received a small living allowance. In large part due to this act, thousands of veterans enrolled in colleges across the nation. By 1947, veterans comprised nearly 49 percent of American College enrollment. At Edward Waters College, the Servicemen's Readjustment Act resulted in an influx of new students. The Act also led college officials to restore the college's four-year curriculum and EWC again became a baccalaureate degree granting institution. By 1957 enrollment at the school reached 510 students.[49]

However, major changes were under way in American higher education. In 1950, the United States Supreme Court ruled, in the landmark case *McLaurin v. Oklahoma State Regents,* that a public institution of higher learning could not provide different treatment to a student solely because of race. Four years later the Supreme Court, in the *Brown v.*

Board of Education of Topeka case, overturned the 1896 *Plessey v. Ferguson* decision that upheld the constitutionality of racial segregation. In the face of these decisions, the Florida legislature and the Duval County Commissioners, hoping to limit calls for the integration of all-white Jacksonville Junior College, each granted Edward Waters College $25,000.[50]

Such efforts however did little to curb the enthusiasm of African-American students for improved social and educational conditions. For instance, on August 13, 1960, approximately 100 high school students, members of Jacksonville's Youth Council of the NAACP, launched the city's first sit-in. Following this initial protest, the students launched almost daily lunch-counter demonstrations that led to one of the most violent confrontations of the sit-in movement. On August 25, 1960, white vigilantes, with the complicit approval of Jacksonville police, launched the violence known as "ax-handle Saturday." When it was over more than 50 people were injured or needed medical treatment.[51]

In the days following the violence, city officials declared the sit-ins dangerous and they exerted pressure to rid the city of the students who led the protestors. Hence, when Edward Waters College offered academic scholarships to Rodney Hurst and Marjorie Meeks, the alleged ringleaders of the sit-ins, the mayor of Jacksonville, Haydon Burns, reminded the president of the college that the Jacksonville and Duval County contributed $75,000 annually to the school. Then Burns ominously warned that should Hurst and Meeks attend the college the awards the college received from the city and county "could be in serious jeopardy." Despite this threat, EWC admitted both students. More importantly, the students continued their efforts to integrate the city's lunch counters eventually forcing most major downtown stores to do so.[52]

Edward Waters College Since 1960

The period from 1960 to 1983 represents some of the best as well as some of the worst times in Edward Waters College's history. During the period, Edward Waters College gained increased federal funding for scholarships. The college also constructed a new science and mathematics building and a student center. Perhaps the greatest accomplishment came in 1979 when SACS granted Edward Waters College membership as a four-year institution. Four years later, the college became the

Edward Waters College Administration Building. Although Edward Waters College holds the distinction of being the oldest HBCU in Florida, throughout its history financial problems and administrative scandals have been a recurring problem (courtesy Metro Jacksonville).

UNCF's 42nd member institution. However, for fans of the college's athletic teams perhaps the greatest triumph occurred in 1965 when "Cannonball" Butler scored six touchdowns in a football game against Friendship College en route to EWC's 142–0 victory.[53]

In contrast to these developments, the period also saw the Southern Association of Colleges and Schools reject the college's baccalaureate degree programs several times between 1960 and 1978. These reversals caused federal officials to withhold funds that were set aside for the expansion of the college. Additionally, in 1971 a report prepared by the A.M.E. Church identified other problems. Issues identified included a failure to conduct annual audits; an inability to obtain credit in the Jacksonville community; $178,700 in short-term debt; a failure to pay payroll taxes in the amount of $200,000; operating deficits of

$200,000 to $290,000 from 1969 to 1972; and, a current fund deficit of $772,000.[54]

The results of this report made clear to members of EWC's governing board that problems permeated all facets of operation including the morale of students and faculty. In response, the Board of Trustees selected a new president and the A.M.E. Church increased its support to the beleaguered institution. College officials also reorganized the College's Board of Trustees to include Jacksonville civic and community leaders and they organized the college's first capital campaign headed by Robert Davis, vice president for financial affairs at Winn-Dixie. These milestones, however, did not end the college's troubles. For example, in 1996, Jesse L. Burns, the college's president, resigned when newspapers revealed that he falsified his credentials. According to published reports, Burns claimed an MBA from Stetson University and a doctorate from the University of South Florida. However, Stetson University revealed that Burns only received a BS degree from the institution and no MBA while the University of South Florida maintained that Burns never completed any coursework.[55]

Eight years after the Burns scandal the college faced perhaps its greatest challenge when the Southern Association of Colleges and Schools (SACS) revoked EWC's accreditation in December 2004. This action stemmed from an investigation that revealed , among other problems, that college administrators plagiarized a document submitted to the accrediting agency. To save the school, the college's Board of Trustees filed a lawsuit against SACS, claiming "Procedural errors made it impossible for Edward Waters College to have a fair hearing." School officials also maintained that employees of SACS acted as non-partisan agents thereby violating policy. To avoid a lawsuit on July 2005, the accrediting body reinstated Edward Waters College. Commenting after the decision Michael L. Lomax, president of the United Negro College Fund, said this was a case in which "David stood up to Goliath."[56]

In the years since the SACS lawsuit conditions at Edward Waters College improved. By 2008, enrollment, which had never broached 1,000, stood at approximately 900 students. The school also completed the construction of its first building in nearly twenty-five years. However, perhaps the biggest change came when the city of Jacksonville made the college one of its key players in the effort to revitalize the inner-city. Today Edward Waters College stands tall as it launches its second century of service to Jacksonville's African-American community

Arkansas Baptist College

DAWN J. HERD-CLARK

At the close of Civil War, large numbers of freedmen moved to the West in search of better conditions. Arkansas, in particular, was one of the favorite destinations of the former slaves. Unfortunately Arkansas was not the utopia and many of the freedmen had hoped for, repressive conditions found in the Deep-South also existed in Arkansas. These conditions led to the birth of Arkansas Baptist College.

Like most historically black colleges, the founders of Arkansas Baptist College organized the school in 1884 with much hope and few resources. Consequently, for most of the school's first decade, classes met in Mount Zion Baptist Church or in rented lodge halls until college officials purchased land on the corner of Little Rock's sixteenth and High Street. On the heels of this milestone, the college hired its first permanent president, Joseph A. Booker, a graduate of Roger Williams University.[57]

Born in 1859, Booker was fascinated with books and learning. After completing a course of study at a normal school at the age of 17 Booker attempted to become a teacher. However, due to his age, no jobs were available. For that reason, at the age of nineteen, Booker enrolled at Roger Williams University earning an A.B. from the school in 1886. The next year officials elected him president of Arkansas Baptist College.[58]

As leader of Arkansas Baptist College, Booker expanded the institution from a facility for the education of ministers to a normal school for teachers. During the same period, Booker raised funds and constructed the college's first buildings. By the turn of the century, Arkansas Baptist College enrolled nearly 400 students in programs ranging from grammar school to the collegiate level.[59]

The school's growth was not without problems. One such setback occurred in 1893 when fire destroyed the college's main building. Although the school had insurance it only covered $4,000 which was not enough to cover the $16,000 needed to rebuild. Fortunately the community responded by donating the necessary funds and the labor needed to rebuild the college.[60]

Another issue facing the school was the racially charged assault on Amanda Reed, an Arkansas Baptist College coed, in 1904. According to published reports, the attack occurred when Reed and her sister walked to a darkened train station. No sooner than they arrived, a pair of white men assailed them at gunpoint. After restraining the women, the assailants raped Reed and escaped into the night. The attack gained national attention and stifled enrollment growth.[61]

By 1910, the crisis had abated and enrollment rebounded. Yet, in the midst of the recovery, another controversy brewed. To support the college's operation officials at Arkansas Baptist College launched a campaign to raise $10,000.00. Although officials raised $8,500 from white Baptists and the Rockefeller Foundation, only 30 cents came from colored Baptists. This strained relations between the college and Northern black Baptist supporters. Said the school's chief fun-draiser: "if this is a measure of the sympathy felt by the Negroes of the North for the Negroes of the South, I say they had better attend to their own business instead of sending telegrams to governors and sheriffs of the Southern States expressing their indignation at the lynching of Negroes. Their resolutions of sympathy are meaningless to us."[62]

On the heels of this incident, relations grew progressively worse between college officials and black Baptist supporters. For example, in the 1930s the African-American Baptists in Arkansas split between the Arkansas Consolidated Baptist Church and the newly formed Arkansas Missionary Baptist Convention. Since both branches of the church were vying for control of the school, neither would donate the necessary funds to help sustain the school. This created additional stress.[63]

Arkansas Baptist College During the Great Depression

The Great Depression was the greatest challenge in Arkansas Baptist College's history. At the start of the Great Depression, Joseph Booker died, leaving the college with an empty treasury. On the heels of this setback a greater danger emerged. In 1937, the Ouachita River flooded the campus, causing extensive damage. College officials launched efforts to rebuild including sending the college choir on a fund-raising tour. Yet, these efforts raised few funds and it appeared that the college would close. At this dark moment, one of Arkansas' unsung African-American heroines, Eliza Miller, the wife of a former member of the Arkansas legislature and the first black woman to own a movie theater in Arkansas, came to school's rescue lending the struggling institution $30,000 to keep the doors open.[64]

The situation remained grave. Consequently, in the mid–1930s, school officials dropped upper level instruction. Arkansas Baptist College became a junior college. Unfortunately, on the heels of this decision a new controversy arose when officials hired Howard L. Johnson as the new president of the college.[65]

The decision however led to a major crisis. To many of the College's Baptist supporters Johnson lacked the requisite qualifications to lead the institution. More importantly, most felt that his role as owner of the Hotel Charmaine, which sold beer, made him unfit to lead a Christian college. Consequently, in 1955, the white Baptist church withdrew support of $15,000 annually. Despite the setback, Arkansas Baptist College limped forward into a rapidly changing world. In 1955, the Montgomery bus boycott launched the start of the American civil rights movement.[66]

The civil rights movement in Little Rock, Arkansas, garnered national attention in 1957 when nine African-American youths attempted to integrate Little Rock's Central High School. To stop the protest, Arkansas Governor Orval Faubus mobilized the National Guard. However, in response to the governor's action President Dwight D. Eisenhower called out federal troops and forced the state to integrate the school.[67]

In the midst of this fight local rowdies frequently harassed Arkansas Baptist College students. Despite this threat, ABC students continued to support Little Rock's student protestors. In this regard, the students continued a legacy that started with the school's origin. For instance, in 1890 ABC students marched on the state capital to protest the imposition of Jim Crow laws.[68]

Despite these actions for most of the ABC's history the college's leadership staunchly supported the old regime. For example, when African-American sharecroppers and farmers formed the Progressive Farmers and Household Union to improve the economic conditions for black workers, which resulted in Elaine race riot of 1919, the president of Arkansas Baptist along with the leaders of Philander Smith and Shorter Colleges wrote the governor of Kansas requesting the return of one of the alleged riot leaders for prosecution. In response, the New Orleans branch of the National Association for the Advancement of Colored People wrote a letter condemning the actions of the Little Rock leaders, stating "no language is too severe in expressing condemnation of the action of Conner, Cox, and Booker [The presidents of Philander Smith, Shorter and Arkansas Baptist Colleges] in requesting the extradition of this individual in face of the fact, especially, of the recent action of the Arkansas

courts in condemning eleven Colored men to death in less than 15 minutes for the same alleged offense."[69]

Arkansas Baptist Since the Civil Rights Movement

At the end of the civil rights movement, conditions at Arkansas Baptist College teetered on the brink. For one, the lack of resources prevented
the college from properly maintaining campus buildings. This led Little
Rock officials to condemn several campus buildings. In addition, the
Arkansas Department of Education expressed concern about the school's
faculty credentials and curriculum development. However, the biggest
weaknesses was the management of the school. Although Arkansas Baptist
College had a President and Board of Trustees, they could not make any
decisions about the institution unless the Baptist Convention Consolidated
agreed. This was disturbing to the Arkansas Baptist State Convention, as
well as many creditors, since they did not like how the Baptist Convention
Consolidated ran the school.[70]

Eventually both the Baptist Convention Consolidated and the
Arkansas Baptist State Convention agreed to raise $100,000 each to sup-
port the school. Although neither group achieved its goals, they did
resume their donations to the school. Additionally, college officials borrowed $25,000.00 from the National Baptist Convention. In response to
these countless issues school officials made one of the best decisions in
the institution's history in 1962 by hiring trustee member James C. Oliver
as president.[71]

In a tenure that spanned 20 years, Oliver improved conditions at
the college, rebuilding a gym mysteriously destroyed by fire during the
Little Rock's civil rights movement and gaining membership in the
American Association of Secondary Schools and Colleges. The last act
allowed the college to access federal financial aid which strengthened the
school's poor cash flow. On the heels of these developments, the college
constructed several new buildings and increased enrollment. Under W.
Thomas Keaton, Arkansas Baptist College continued its growth. During
his tenure, from 1985 until 2001, the school received full accreditation
from the Commission on Higher Learning of the North Central Association, and the National Council for the Accreditation of Teacher Education. Keaton also improved the infrastructure of Arkansas Baptist
College by bringing technology to the campus library, and constructing

new buildings on campus, including the W. T. Keaton Men's Residence Hall.[72]

Despite these accomplishments, Arkansas Baptist College still faced challenges. These ranged from high student loan default rates and an athletic scandal that saw the men's basketball team garner negative publicity and a visit from ESPN for splitting itself into two squads in order to play multiple games and thus garner multiple payments from their opponents for playing the contests. The new millennium has provided momentum to the formerly struggling institution. In 2000, the college reduced its student loan default rate. In 2006, officials named Dr. Fitzgerald Hill the thirteenth president of Arkansas Baptist College. As a former collegiate football coach, Hill revived the college's long dormant Buffalo football program in 2007. Today Arkansas Baptist College enrolls more than 500 students in twelve degree programs.[73]

Group II: Just Enough to Survive

Bluefield State College

VANN R. NEWKIRK

Nestled in the eastern edge of the Appalachian Mountains, West Virginia sits atop one of the largest deposits of bituminous coal in the world. The coal is so pure that, during the late 1880s, it spawned one of the last epic migrations in American history. This movement of people increased the state's population from 618,457 in 1880 to 1,221,119 in 1910.[74]

To house the influx, coal mine operators built segregated housing in scores of communities across West Virginia. Perhaps none of these settlements was more important than Bluefield. In 1880, the village consisted of little more than a few dozen houses and a church. However, with the construction of the railroad and the opening of coal mines the town's population exploded from less than 600 in 1880 to 5,000 in 1900. Included in this number were hundreds of African-American miners and their families.[75]

The movement of large numbers of blacks into West Virginia significantly altered the state's political landscape. Unlike its neighbors,

West Virginia did not disenfranchise African-Americans. Black coal miners took full advantage of this political freedom, quickly becoming a "key constituency" of the Republican Party. Due to this factor, in 1893, William M. Mahood, Republican candidate for the legislature, used black support to gain a seat in the state legislature.[76]

In recognition of this support on February 1, 1895, Mahood introduced Senate Bill #122, entitled "An Act to Establish a High Graded School at Bluefield, Mercer County for the Colored Youth of the State." The legislation also authorized a name: Bluefield Colored Institute (BCI), and $8,000 for the school's construction.[77]

On October 17, 1895, the school's board of Trustees met officially for the first time. After the election of officers and some routine conversation, the Board voted to purchase four acres on the outskirts of Bluefield. The next year they constructed a sandstone structure containing classrooms, administrative offices, and an eight-hundred-seat auditorium.

To lead the institution the board selected Hamilton Hatter, a 1888 graduate of Bates College. Born two years before the outbreak of the Civil War, Hatter possessed a natural talent for overcoming obstacles. These were skills Bluefield Colored Institute sorely needed during its early years. For one, the state's failure to provide reliable funding meant the school had few resources. In addition, the recent origin of the school meant that institution also lacked much of the physical apparatus needed for instruction. As a result, Hatter planted a fruit orchard and several produce gardens. He also used student labor to construct desks and chairs for the school.[78]

The 1900–1941 Era

For most of its first two decades, BCI offered high school and teacher education training. Indeed, it was in the latter area that the school excelled. Article 12 section 8 of the West Virginia constitution stated, "White and Colored persons shall not be taught in the same schools." For that reason, towns across West Virginia constructed small segregated schools. This created a demand for black teachers, a niche Bluefield Colored Institute filled.[79]

However, the institution's mission of training black teachers occurred amid philosophical differences between W.E.B. DuBois, who sought to educate a so-called "talented tenth," and Booker T. Washington who sought to train blacks in mechanical trades to ensure financial stability. Leaders of BCI refused to take sides in the debate, instead they developed two parallel lines of instruction — one emphasizing teacher training and leadership, and another focused on industrial education.[80]

More significant changes were on the horizon. In 1909, West Virginia officials moved control of BCI from its Board of Trustees to a Board of Regents responsible for the academic operation of all public colleges in the state. State officials also established a Board of Control to watch over the finances of the various Negro institutions in the state including hospitals, prisons, schools and colleges. Ominously, the loss of local control meant an erosion of black influence. Prior to the governance change blacks held at least one voting seat on the local board. After the change, state officials relegated black participation to a non-voting Negro advisory council which only provided advice to the Board.[81]

Nonetheless, control by the state board came with increased financial support. Consequently, in 1927 college officials authorized the construction of the school's first single-purpose classroom building and expanded the campus by purchasing 22 acres of land. In conjunction with these developments, BCI expanded its offerings, adding new programs in Business Administration, Home Economics, and Education. Due to these developments, State officials renamed the school Bluefield State Teachers College (BSTC) in 1929.[82]

In the years following the name change, BSTC gained recognition as a center of African-American culture. For that reason, during the 1920s and 1930s many of the nation's leading black celebrities including opera singers Marian Anderson and Leontyne Price, jazz musicians Dizzy Gillespie and Duke Ellington, boxer Joe Louis; poet Langston Hughes, and scholars Carter G. Woodson, John Hope Franklin, and W.E.B. DuBois, visited the campus. Perhaps due to this factor, Bluefield State Teachers College became the destination for many of the nation's best and brightest African-American students including William Gray, Sr., president of Florida A&M from 1944 to 1949, and Elizabeth Drewy, the first woman elected to the West Virginia legislature.[83]

During World War II, students at Bluefield State Teachers College aided the war effort by selling war bonds and by organizing scrap metal drives. In addition, more than 300 students enlisted into the armed forces. Included in this number were former students John L. Carter, Edward Watkins and Thomas Mayfield, who served as members of the 99th Pursuit Squadron, the famed Tuskegee airmen.[84]

Post–World War II Era

At the end of World War II, Bluefield State College's enrollment exploded as veterans enrolled in record numbers. To service this influx, school officials organized Saturday classes and established a satellite center in Beckley. College officials also purchased a number of trailers and erected three old metal barracks to house the veterans. Perhaps due to this remarkable growth, in 1949 the North Central Association of Colleges and Schools granted BSC full accreditation.[85]

On the heels of this milestone, major changes transformed American higher education. In 1950, the U.S. Supreme Court, in the landmark case *McLaurin v. Oklahoma State,* overturned segregation in graduate education. Four years later, *Brown v. Board of Education* overturned laws that established separate public schools for black and white students. In response to these decisions, West Virginia's Superintendent of Schools decreed, "all colleges operating under the jurisdiction of the Board of Education of West Virginia will admit students without regard to race effective immediately." Several months later, a handful of white students enrolled in Bluefield State College. By 1962, 40 percent of the student body was white.[86]

Further change lay ahead. In 1965, state leaders forced Dr. LeRoy Allen to resign. To replace Allen, the Board of Regents selected Dr. Wendell G. Hardway. As the institution's first white president Hardway aggressively pursued a policy of desegregation. By 1968, whites comprised 69 percent of the school's enrollment. The desegregation of faculty was even more radical as Hardway refused to hire qualified blacks. For example, in 1968 Hardway hired twenty-three new faculty members, all of them white. He also replaced most of the school's black administrators with whites.[87]

In the wake of these transitions, students and alumni alleged that Hardway conspired to discriminate against blacks. However, college officials refused to heed these calls, and the chair of the College's Student Affairs Committee said "that if students did not like the way things worked at Bluefield maybe they should seek education elsewhere." This signaled the start of an all-out war between the college's administration and black students for the future of the school.[88]

In September 1967, students launched a sit-in of the administration building. Several weeks later a protest in front of the school's gym led to a rock-throwing incident. To escape the barrage, campus security escorted President Hardway from the scene. Two days after the rock throwing incident students gathered around the president's house, where an angry shouting match developed. After this episode, Hardway suspended several students, charging that they engaged in activities that "menaced the well-being of a college official." The next day, students hanged an effigy of Hardway from a tree behind the administration building.[89]

In conjunction with these acts, Hardway received a host of threatening letters. One letter threatened to shoot Hardway in the head: "we will settle for a bullet in the head. We are going to try our dimmest (sic) to kill you. We swear this." Another letter read: "Your time is up. You have been messing with black students. You will die soon."[90]

Things grew worse the next year. On the evening of November 21, 1968, an explosion inside a bathroom in the college's gym shattered glass and bricks, causing $80,000 in damage. Officials quickly pinned the blast on black residential students. Whether the students were responsible for the bombing is unknown. However, in 1968 the assassination of Martin Luther King Jr. sparked violence and riots in cities and towns across America. King's death also spawned a spate of counter actions and bombings by racists groups such as the Ku Klux Klan. For example, between 1967 and 1968, the Ku Klux Klan committed 14 bombings against black and Jewish targets across the nation. Despite the Klan bombings, officials focused their attention solely on black residential students.[91]

Whatever the case, three days after the bombing, authorities arrested two Bluefield College students, one former student, and another man, charging them with conspiracy to inflict damage or injury as a result of the bombing. Authorities also charged the men with possession of explosives with criminal intent. Among those arrested was "self-proclaimed" black student leader Edgar James, a 26-year-old Vietnam veteran.[92]

In an interview printed in the *Bluefield Daily Telegraph,* police Sergeant Robert M. Hall "emphasized that the arrest [of the bombers] followed an intensive, around the clock investigation by both state and city police." However, this announcement covered a much more complex truth. Almost two weeks before the bombing, James delivered a list of grievances to Hardway. This list demanded, among other things, the appointment of a new president and senior administration; the hiring of black faculty; the return of student test papers after an exam; and more student involvement in making important decisions. Unfortunately, the decision to present the demands directly to Hardway provided the president with a face to blame for rising tensions and dissatisfaction among black students. "Edgar James appears to be the leader (of the disturbances) ... he is very dissatisfied and he has been the leader in promoting dissatisfaction."[93]

After the arrest of James, Hardway suspended classes and closed the campus to the public. Then in perhaps his most controversial decision, Hardway closed the college's dormitories, claiming sources had discovered dynamite and munitions. However, the basis of such a claim seems far-fetched. For one, if Hardway suspected that students had dynamite or other explosives in the residence hall, why did he fail to contact state or local police or conduct a search? Additionally, if the students possessed dynamite, what prevented them from launching attacks once the residence halls were closed?[94]

Yet, even if students possessed dynamite, Hardway's stance stood far from the norm. For example, almost two weeks before the Bluefield College bombing students at Valley State College in California took the president and several senior administrators hostage. After a prolonged siege, California officials arrested students. In the days after the hostage crisis, student arsonists attacked the administration building, causing $100,000 in damages. California officials closed the college for several days. Then they arrested a seventeen-year-old and charged him with arson but refused to close the dorms.[95]

However, at Bluefield State College, after a halfhearted attempt to reopen the dorms in 1969, the residential halls closed for good. Ironically, in the days following the closure, state officials dropped all charges against students Edgar James, Lewis Tyrone Turner and Dwight Banks. Two other men, perhaps intimidated by local authorities, confessed to the crime and received light sentences.[96]

Bluefield State College Since 1968

The closure of the dorms had a disastrous impact on Bluefield State College. As early as 1930, out-of-town students comprised almost 63 percent of the school's enrollment. Hence, on-campus housing remained a central element in maintaining the school's racial identity. Unfortunately, the reliance on out-of-town students occurred in an environment in which mechanism reduced demand for labor in West Virginia's coalmines. These changes disproportionally affected blacks. For example, in Southern West Virginia, the home of Bluefield State College, the number of black miners fell from 17,799 in 1920 to 1,439 in 1980. Due to these shifts, and the closure of the residence halls, by 1972, whites comprised 80 percent of the students attending Bluefield College.[97]

The closure of the dorms did not, however, represent Bluefield State College's greatest challenge. In 1973, Hardway endorsed a proposal to merge Bluefield with nearby Concord College. Fortunately, the proposal died when the person selected to lead the combined institutions declined.[98]

In the years since the failed merger, BSC's predominately black Alumni Association stepped up efforts return the college to its pre-1968 state. In large part due to their persistence, in 2002 the college hired Dr. Albert Walker, the school's first black president in 45 years. Following this feat, efforts to reopen the residence halls gained traction. In the summer of 2004 the college conducted a feasibility study to convert historic Mahood Hall back to its original role as a residence hall. However, when state officials refused to provide funding, the conversion plan fizzled. Nonetheless, following this setback, private developers, at the urging of the Bluefield State College Research & Development Corporation, converted a closed hotel into privately owned student housing for 160 students. Due to this effort, black student enrollment showed the first significant gains since the 1960s increasing from a low of only 8 percent in 2002 to 12.77 percent in 2009. However, Bluefield State College remains an HBCU only in name.[99]

Langston University

DAWN J. HERD-CLARK

The story of Oklahoma's Langston University arose against a backdrop of politics and resistance to growing racial prejudice, not to mention as a legacy of that state's rich but little-known African-American heritage. While the slave Turk had accompanied Francisco Vazquez de Coronado to the region as early as 1540–42 on the conquistador's search for the Seven Golden Cities of Cibola, it took until the first half of the nineteenth century before substantial numbers of black men, women, and children arrived as slaves of the Five Civilized Tribes during their forced migration on "the Trail of Tears." Indian Territory's black population thereafter increased considerably when numbers of southern blacks—faced with limited economic opportunity, black codes, and poor social conditions after the Civil War—sought refuge during the Land Run of 1889. Various African-American migration societies meanwhile heightened desires for relocation westward through recruitment efforts. These included the newspaperman H. W. Rolfe's Oklahoma Immigration Society, which looked to the creation of an African-American state. The society provided brochures, ran newspaper ads, and sent agents as ways to entice blacks to think of an Oklahoma home.[100]

The 1890 formation of the town of Langston is a product of the westward migration of African-Americans. Located between Guthrie and Stillwater in Oklahoma's north central Logan County, the community honored noted African-American attorney, educator, congressman, civil rights leader, and diplomat John Mercer Langston. Founded only one year after the territory city fathers marketed the town as "the only distinctly Negro city in America."[101]

The Formation of the Colored Agricultural and Normal University

The late nineteenth-century deterioration of race relations threatened the quality and nature of schooling for African-American children in Oklahoma. When the territory formed in 1889, racial segregation of schools had remained optional. Yet, within a short time, the legislature sanctioned racial dividing lines, and blacks understandably mobilized to protect educational opportunities. At Langston in 1892, residents formed the town's first common school. Opened in February, it held 200 boarding students. Less than one year thereafter, several townsmen including D. J. Wallace, R. E. Stewart, and Edward Robinson lobbied state officials for the construction of a college. To emphasize the need the Oklahoma Association of Negro Teachers led efforts to secure admission of African-American students to the normal school in Edmond. When they were denied, Langstonians heightened their insistence that African-Americans required their own institution of higher learning. Perhaps no African-American was more influential in this effort than Edward McCabe.

Born in 1850, McCabe emerged as one of the nation's first black political activists, eventually becoming the Cook County Treasurer. In the 1880s, McCabe — influenced by Benjamin "Pap" Singleton to believe that westward migration would provide African-Americans an escape from racism and discrimination — moved to Kansas. There, he secured election as state auditor and the distinction of being the first African-American to hold a statewide position there. However, racism in Kansas, prompted him to move to Oklahoma. In Oklahoma he quickly became the territory's most prominent African-American resident and played a major role in the establishment of a college for African-American in Langston. Particularly, he lent his support to Republicans, encouraging African-American Oklahomans to vote in 1896 for William McKinley for president and Cassius Barnes for governor. In return, he received promises that, when a college was approved, the Langston community would exercise control over its institution's administrators and teachers, as well as the curriculum.[102]

During the early 1890s, a separate initiative occurring at a distance from Oklahoma aided the quest for a college. This involved congressional passage of the Second Morrill Act. This act provided funds from public land sales and other sources "for the more complete endowment and maintenance of colleges for the benefit of agriculture and the mechanic arts ... and to the facilities for such instruction." The law specified that "no money shall be paid out under this act to any State or Territory for the support and maintenance of a college where a distinction of race or color is made in the admission of students," but it also provided that "the establishment and maintenance of such colleges separately for white and colored students shall be held to be in compliance with the provisions of this act if the funds received in such State or Territory be equitably divided." Effectively, this measure furnished the black community support for higher education similar to that already provided for many white institutions by the Morrill Land Grant Act of 1862.[103]

Oklahoma lawmakers thus faced a new reality. They must either admit black students to the territory's white land grant institution or authorize an alternate institution of higher education for African-Americans as a prerequisite to receiving federal funding. Given that Oklahoma was moving ahead in the adoption of Jim Crow measures that mandated racial discrimination by law, legislators gave little thought to integrating the state-sponsored college for whites. Hence, on February 4, 1897, they approved House Bill 151, creating a college that aided in the "training of teachers and offering agricultural, mechanical, and industrial training."

The new institution carried the name Colored Agricultural and Normal University (CANU).[104]

Unfortunately, CANU's creation involved the merger of existing schools and resulted — despite earlier commitments made to McCabe — in ambiguity regarding its curriculum. This fact, in turn, led to divergence and factionalism as the Langston community and the legislature differed on the school's mission. Langston embraced educator and sociologist W. E. B. DuBois's ideas and his liberal arts perspectives, while lawmakers endorsed Booker T. Washington's concept of emphasis on industrial education. Thus, from its inception, CANU emphasized the virtues of industrial and agricultural training by strengthening "farming, Blacksmithing, and carpentry," but it also offered a wide range of courses in the liberal arts.

Despite the controversy over curriculum, CANU prospered. By 1899, the school's success led the Oklahoma Board of Regents to purchase additional land for expansion. Yet, success did not mean that the school avoided major problems. The first two decades of the twentieth century in particular proved difficult for CANU to navigate. Upon gaining statehood in 1907, Oklahoma Democrats secured control of the newly formed state government on a segregationist platform. State leaders quickly approved a grandfather clause that restricted black voting rights. However, a challenge to the law which resulted in *Guinn v. United States* case the U.S. Supreme Court declared the law unconstitutional. The state then quickly disenfranchised many African-Americans by setting a brief period to enroll the now unregistered voters.[105]

During these challenging times, several landmarks for the college occurred. The reinforced emphasis on industrial education spawned in the 1920s a host of new disciplines including tailoring, auto mechanics, plumbing, printing, and landscaping. Of major significance for the future, in 1920 CANU managed to offer its first undergraduate degrees. New president Isaac W. Young reinstated the liberal arts curriculum in 1923, and growth continued. Perhaps due to this growth, the Oklahoma Board of Regents in 1929 rated the school as "a standard four-year college offering the degrees of Bachelor of Arts and Bachelor of Science."[106]

Politics nonetheless played a continuing and significant role in college affairs, a fact only exacerbated by economic pressures produced by the Great Depression that commenced in 1929. These factors, when coupled with the school's growth, combined to spark efforts by white

Democrats who sought to hold back black education to place CANU under Oklahoma State A&M College's control. CANU supporters in turn formed a seven-member policy and administrative board, hoping that the new panel would depoliticize the presidency and protect the school from future takeover attempts. Despite the initiative, the Board of Regents continued to assert influence in Langston. In 1939, its members engineered the presidential appointment of Albert T. Turner, a Tuskegee Institute graduate. However, opposition to his appointment led to the formation of a Board of Trustees that favored the liberal arts. Consequently, Turner resigned.[107]

Interestingly, Turner's resignation came at just the time when the emerging civil rights movement was setting the stage for major growth at CANU. In 1939, the United States Supreme Court ruled in *Gaines v. Canada* that Missouri had to provide a state-supported law school for its African-American citizens, reversing a longstanding policy of paying out-of-state tuition costs for black residents who wanted to attend graduate or professional school. States across the South, including Oklahoma, now found themselves compelled to act. By 1941, Oklahoma officials recognized new potential of CANU by designating it Langston University. Seven years later, they authorized a law school. Unfortunately, the new professional program enjoyed only a short lifespan. In 1948, the National Association for the Advancement of Colored People (NAACP) argued that the Langston University law school was not equal to the University of Oklahoma law school. Consequently, the Supreme Court ordered, in *McLaurin v. Oklahoma,* that Oklahoma University admit African-American law students. The decision foretold the demise of the Langston law school.[108]

Despite the demise of the law program, 1948 represented a watershed for the college as Langston University secured membership in the Association of American Colleges and the North Central Association of Colleges and Secondary Schools. These benchmarks added further luster to the administration of President G. Lamar Harrison. A seasoned teacher and administrator, Harrison had arrived at a time when the Langston Alumni Association was endeavoring to depoliticize CANU's presidency. Taking office in 1940, he would guide the institution until 1960.[109]

While the university enjoyed solid administrative direction and support from the Federal judiciary, the state government repeatedly questioned its purpose and funding. The school filled a vital role, but white officials challenged its continued viability. In 1958, for instance, the state legislature looking for ways to reduce the state budget threatened to downgrade the university to junior-college status. Some lawmakers considered closing the college. As such challenges persisted, new President William Henri Hale fought back. He redefined Langston University as a quality institution of higher education for all citizens in Oklahoma while implementing improvements including a new student center, new music and science and technology buildings, and new residence halls. Installation of air conditioning and an Afro-American Heritage Center helped to complete his vision. With the campus physical improvements and investment in a reading clinic and audiovisual lab, graduation rates increased. Soon, as one historian put it, "in both growth and student-retention rate Langston ranked near the top of Oklahoma colleges." She added, "The long-standing argument about industrial versus liberal-arts education seemed settled when the tailoring shop gave way to an electronics lab."[110]

President Hale fortunately could glean invaluable support for his leadership from his wife Larzette Golden Hale. A Langston graduate with a doctorate in finance and accounting from the University of Wisconsin, Hale especially applied her expertise to build the school's development foundation. Her efforts paid off as the endowment soon reached $250,000. This afforded needed financial assistance for worthy students and, in so doing, helped the student body grow. By 1968, the school reached an all-time high enrollment of 1,336.[111]

Langston University's success in depoliticizing its presidency, as seen in consecutive long-term administrations during the 1940s, '50s, and '60s, unfortunately was overshadowed in the 1970s by allegations of fiscal mismanagement. Administrative instability followed. The genesis for this instability started in 1969 and 1970 when William E. Sims accepted first an interim appointment and then the presidency. Once the band director, he had risen to the deanship of academic affairs, when, to the surprise of many, he was selected to lead the institution although he had not applied for the position. However, his skills as an administrator did not allow for effective leadership of the school. Consequently, in 1974, in the wake of a charge of financial mismanagement, Sims resigned.[112]

Thomas English assumed the institution's leadership one year after Sims' departure. Selected to bring financial stability to the school, he suffered embarrassment when, after being given the task of documenting school expenditures by the Board of Regents, "the painfully reconstructed records were accidentally thrown out during a cleaning operation." When English could not adequately answer financial questions, the Regents fired him. The Board also reprimanded the deposed executive for extending credit to students who could not pay tuition. A 1977 report found that 1,940 credit hours had not been paid for, totaling approximately $33,000. Then, Samuel J. Tucker was appointed president in 1978. The same year, Tucker was dismissed due to alleged fiscal mismanagement.[113]

At that point, the darkness over Langston could only dissipate. Ernest L. Holloway, who had served as interim president in 1977, was named president in 1978. The Oklahoma Regents, the same year, requested that Langston undertake an urban mission, an initiative that resulted in the opening of upper division branches in Oklahoma City and Tulsa. This represented a considerable turnaround for a struggling institution that nearly had been closed earlier in the decade. The student population now increased and diversified. The additional students paved the way for the creation of more program offerings and brought in more tuition dollars, which encouraged increases in the school's endowment. By the 1980s, Langston University had solidified as an effective institution of higher education for African-Americans in the western states. Holloway thereafter provided leadership stability into the twenty-first century before being replaced in 2005 by the first African-American female president in the history of Oklahoma higher education, Dr. JoAnn W. Haysbert.[114]

Langston's Impact on Oklahoma

Although not widely known, Langston University, since its founding, has served all Oklahomans, not solely African-Americans. As early as 1902, for instance, CANU faculty and staff members carried out land grant extension responsibilities by teaching area residents how to purchase farmland. Their duties soon expanded, with the assistance of the U.S. Department of Agriculture, to teaching community members how to "construct farm buildings, lay out fields, and build gates and fences." Similarly, as electrification and indoor plumbing proliferated throughout the West in the early twentieth century, the Marquess administration earned credit for "helping to bring electricity and running water to the town."[115]

Another way CANU helped the community and state involved its Normal Department, where teacher-training programs prepared students for certification to teach in Oklahoma public schools. Graduates from the program earned a "bachelor of scientific didactics." This degree could be pursued through a variety of program choices, including summer school and correspondence courses. Sad to say, the Normal Department, despite its successes, closed during the Great Depression. When it closed in 1932, it managed a stunning summer-session enrollment of over 1,600 students.[116]

With the onset of World War II, CANU carried on its tradition of service by helping the United States to secure victory. Alumnus Henry P. Milligan trained United States Army mechanics. Aviation cadet Saint M. Twine meanwhile pursued the advanced flight class at Tuskegee. Several former students made the supreme sacrifice by giving their lives. Among these, Faythe Andrew McGinnis died during a Tuskegee training exercise. Moreover, military participation in World War II was not limited solely to male students. Golda Lee Patton enlisted in Women's Army Corps (WAC) during her third year at Langston. Ultimately, she served in the capacity of a postal worker as part of the first–African-American WAC battalion stationed in England.[117] Langston attended to the home front too. One notable instance came during the school's 1942 observance of Pearl Harbor Day when English professor Nick Aaron Ford spoke about "What Negroes are Fighting For." African-American through the 1960s and into the modern era, Langston University expanded its engagement with the community. Its Head Start program provided instruction to area low-income children. Upward Bound programs were conducted during the summer months, as high school students lived on campus and took college preparation courses. Langston additionally sought to enhance skills of area educators by sponsoring conferences on various subjects, including language arts, science, and social studies. To promote education in the greater Langston community, university Work-Study students tutored at area night schools. The 1970s witnessed Langston family members helping to landscape the city park, teaching arts and crafts in the local school system, and introducing a beautification initiative to the town. To help the state, Langston University, in 1972, sent home economists to rural African-American and Native American dominated areas.[118]

Through its history, Langston University has nurtured promising students who otherwise might have gone without higher education. In closing, it is only proper to put a human face on that great achievement. Bessie Coleman, although she was able to attend the institution for only one term, went on to become the first African-American female pilot and the first American woman to earn an international pilot's license. There are many others. Robert DoQui stands out for his movie roles in *Coffy* and the *Robo-Cop* trilogy, as well as numerous appearances on television. Nathan Hare merits credit for writing the first black studies proposal in America, being the first person hired to run a black studies program, and founding and editing *The Black Scholar: Journal of Black Studies and Research.* Marques Haynes, a multisport athlete at Langston, joined the Harlem Globetrotters and was elected to the Basketball Hall of Fame. In addition Opio Toure served as an Oklahoma Democratic State Representative from 1994 until 2006, when term limits ended his legislative career. Thus begins the list of distinction and the roll of service at Langston University. They reflect a heritage of true distinction.[119]

Group III: The New Elite

Claflin University

Dawn J. Herd-Clark

South Carolina's Claflin University, the state's first institution of higher education for African-Americans, originated in 1869 from the desire of clergy and laymen in the Methodist Episcopal Church to provide trained teachers to bring the bounties of education to state residents who otherwise would not be served. As one church publication observed, the school, "hopes to do, in the educational work of the freedmen at the South, what our academies and seminaries of learning do at the North among the multitudes of the rising generation." Much credit goes to the Reverend T. Willard Lewis, city pastor at Charleston, and his district presiding elder Dr. Alonzo Webster, northern missionaries who assisted freedmen. Thanks to the generosity of philanthropist Lee Claflin and his son, Massachusetts Governor William Claflin, the men purchased buildings previously occupied by the Orangeburg Female Academy. Dr. Webster, the school's first president, secured its charter from the state legislature. Among other provisions, the measure forbade racial or religious discrimination. "No instructor in said University shall ever be required by the Trustees to have any particular complexion or to profess any particular religious opinions as a test of office," it read, "and no student shall be refused admission to, or denied any of the privileges, honors or degrees of said University on account of race, complexion or religious opinions which he may entertain."[120]

Claflin's early years demonstrated ambitious hopes and produced frustrating challenges. The Claflin board of trustees—initially balanced racially with four African-American and four white members—merged the school in 1870 with Charleston's Baker Biblical Institute. In so doing, the university secured additional resources while expanding its mission. The school strove, as well, to move ahead with its collegiate curriculum, but, despite advertising throughout the state, it could not initially attract sufficient numbers of students above the basic grammar level.[121]

Claflin's success during the period depended on securing sources of funding. Webster saw the state and federal governments as the main possibilities to enlarge the university's meager finances. Consequently, he lobbied for the creation of a state-supported institution of higher education that focused on agricultural and industrial education. Through affiliating that institution with Claflin, he hoped the school would receive a portion of the 1862 Morrill Land Grant Act funds appropriated to South Carolina. Webster's efforts paid off in 1872 when the legislature mandated that a "College and Institute of Mechanical Arts be established at Orangeburg, in accordance with the provisions of the Act of Congress, passed July 2, 1862, and all Acts amendatory thereto." The lawmakers further provided, "The design of the Institution shall be to afford instruction in practical and theoretical agriculture, mechanical art and military tactics and training."[122]

The new educational facility was, as Webster had desired, associated with Claflin University. Not only did both schools at first have Webster as president, but beginning in 1878, they boasted nearly the same name when the South Carolina legislature designated their institution as Claflin College. Although Webster's lobbying succeeded, his efforts unfortunately fell short in securing adequate funding. Accordingly, his struggles and those of his successor Dr. Edward Cooke (president, 1872–1884) continued as they endeavored to keep student fees at a minimum in order to address the mission of educating freedmen and their children while also assuring the survival of the schools. Then, in 1876, disaster struck when a devastating fire hit the campus and $20,000 in property was destroyed.[123]

The great labor of resurrecting Claflin from the fire fell to University President Cooke. Cooke, a northern Methodist Episcopal minister, came to Claflin with educational administrative experience at all levels; he had most recently served as president of Lawrence College in Wisconsin. It was during Cooke's administration that the first college class graduated from Claflin in 1879. To secure funds for the school Dr. Cooke arranged for a meeting between the South Carolina Governor Wade Hampton, and State Superintendant of Education Hugh Thompson, and members of the Claflin faculty including Jonathan Wright, a former South Carolina Supreme Court judge. [124] Many South Carolinians were appalled that white elected officials would eat with African-Americans. Although the event caused a statewide scandal, Claflin continued to receive state funding.

Even when the state began to provide funding, its receipt proved erratic. In 1890, under President Lewis M. Dunton (1884–1922), further financial woes threatened when a legislator suggested elimination of the school's $5,000 state appropriation. Fortunately, Claflin had proven its worth, and only nine of 108 members of the legislature voted for the cut. Then, in 1891, Claflin found a friend in United States Secretary of the Interior, John W. Noble, who successfully pushed South Carolina to divide its land grant funds more equitably in favor of the school, because at the time, 63.3 percent of the state's population was black. Claflin unfortunately continued to suffer from underfunding even as need among the state's African-American population grew. For example, in 1891, South Carolina allocated $99,887 for educating its African-American population. Of this total, $5,000 went to Claflin. That year, black South Carolinians paid $280,000 in taxes.[125]

Nonetheless, a little financial sun did shine on Claflin during the 1880s with introduction and brief operation of a law program. The Claflin University Law School, along with a program at Allen University, were responsible for educating African-American attorneys in South Carolina. This state of affairs came about because of the implementation of Jim Crow practices at the University of South Carolina, which ended the enrollment of blacks. [126]

As the decade of the 1890s opened, legal issues swirling out from African-Americans' desires to play more-active roles in their educational institutions brought national attention to Claflin. The chain of events included the caning of African-American college chaplain J. N. Cardozo, who was also an English and biblical studies professor, by W. J. De Treville, Jr., a white professor of mathematics, after the two men heatedly debated the desirability of "noisy" revival meetings. Simmering racial tensions lay at the heart of the matter. Cardozo, and a fellow African-American faculty member named Townsend, resigned and Claflin College students boycotted classes and talked of leaving the institution. The mayor of Orangeburg, meanwhile, threatened to call out the militia if De Treville was assaulted and President Dunton appealed for protection to the governor.[127] In the end, Dunton persuaded De Treville to depart from the school.

This dispute erupted during a troubling period that brought sudden and unforeseen consequences to Claflin. Black South Carolinians were seeing Reconstruction-era civil rights gains, including voting rights, eroding. In response, many black leaders strove to secure control of the race's educational future through the formation of state-sponsored institutions of higher education. When Thomas E. Miller and other black legislators achieved creation of a state-funded institution of higher education in 1896, funds previously allocated to Claflin for Claflin College were redirected to fund the Colored, Normal, Industrial, Agricultural, and Mechanical College of South Carolina. When the schools were separated Claflin's claims to land grant and state funding suffered as the school — now known as South Carolina State University — evolved and grew.[128]

Despite separation of the schools, Claflin University endeavored to keep an industrial component in its curriculum. Architecture comprised one of Claflin's key industrial programs. Acclaim had come to the program by the late 1800s when *Builder's Exchange,* a national architecture magazine, recognized alumnus and superintendant of carpentry Robert C. Bates for successfully solving the puzzle involved in finding "the diameter of a circle when the Chord and Spring are given." For a small, rural, private black school, Bates' accomplishment resounded. When yet another fire destroyed the school's main building in 1899, Claflin alumnus William Wilson Cooke designed the new main building while also serving as the school's superintendant of vocational training. Cooke's talents subsequently were called upon for most Claflin buildings erected during the early twentieth century. He, too, garnered national attention when he was named the first African-American senior architectural designer for the United States Supervising Architects Office in Washington, D.C.[129]

In one key area, Claflin's experience differed from that of most other HBCUs during the early twentieth century. The institution did not wrestle with the direction of its curricular focus. In 1906, administrators touted the fact that, by combining liberal arts and industrial education, the school provided the best foundation for its students. "Through a series of years it has been demonstrated at Claflin," it was asserted, "that a college course can be adjusted so as to secure the successful acquisition of some trade, together with a mastery of some literary and other essential studies; thereby combining in advantageous portions, the training of both Head and hand." Such assertions articulated Claflin's pride in its industrial department, but as race relations deteriorated in the state it became increasingly difficult for African-American students to find apprenticeships outside the campus.[130]

Claflin at the Turn of the Century

Despite Claflin's record of combining industrial and liberal arts curricula successfully, many onlookers wondered whether the school could financially survive at the turn of the century. Its separation from the South Carolina Colored, Normal, Industrial, Agricultural, and Mechanical College denied it critically needed funding.[131] To obtain badly needed funding the college solicited increased funding from the Methodist Episcopal Church and from the John F. Slater Fund. In addition, officials approached Andrew Carnegie and Everett O. Fisk to provide additional resources. Students were also called upon to use their talents through the formation of the Claflin Quintet. During their summer 1899 tour the group performed on the school's behalf in Massachusetts and in the cities of Cleveland, Indianapolis, and Des Moines. By 1913, "The Jubilee singing troupe of Claflin university are said to have 'sung up' four large brick buildings for their college during their 15 vacations." These efforts, it should be noted, became ever more important in 1913, when Claflin's main building again caught fire. The structure had housed a girls' dormitory, classrooms, and administrative offices. Fortunately, no students were harmed. Unfortunately, school insurance ran only to $50,000 on a building valued at nearly $100,000. Worse, to adequately replace the structure, $125,000 was needed because of the school's growing population. Once more, the school and community rallied to support the institution, especially with the selection in 1922 of Dr. Joseph B. Randolph, the first African-American to head the school. He stayed in office through 1944.

Randolph, the former president of Samuel Houston College, was a professional administrator.[132] Upon assuming the presidency, he sought a more active role for blacks in the administration of Claflin. He also sought to transform the school into a fully accredited collegiate liberal arts institution. In line with this objective, he phased out lower level programs and improved the quality of the faculty. He also improved the quality of buildings and grounds. Randolph's successor John Seabrook continued the movement forward by increasing salaries and improving the quality of the library.[133]

Undoubtedly, due to these efforts Claflin received an A rating from the Southern Association's Committee on Approval of Negro Schools of the Southern Association of Colleges and Secondary Schools (SACS) in 1948. Four years later, it again received an A rating from SACS. This distinction stood out as even more impressive because 1952 was the first year during which HBCUs and predominately white institutions were ranked by SACS according to the same standards.[134] Once Claflin secured accreditation it became harder to maintain it. In 1953, SACS placed the school on probation when the endowment proved insufficient. As a result, college officials launched a fund-raising effort that secured $300,000. This allowed officials to remove the school from SACS probation.[135]

With accreditation secure, Claflin College soon found itself at the forefront of the modern civil rights movement. Orangeburg residents grew sensitive during the post–World War II years to the emerging social revolution. When the United States Supreme Court found racial segregation in public education unconstitutional in 1954, Claflin family and community members prepared to enforce the *Brown* v. *Board of Education of Topeka, Kansas* decision locally. Accordingly, in 1954 Claflin College trustee Thaddeus Kinloch Bythewood, along with several alumni, petitioned to desegregate the Orangeburg school system. When the local newspaper published the names and addresses of those involved, there was retaliation. Some Claflin alumni lost their jobs, while others were denied credit with local merchants. Area whites meanwhile formed South Carolina's first white citizens' council. Although some petitioners succumbed to the intimidation and retracted their desegregation requests, Claflin students supported those who remained resolute. When the students speculated that the local Sunbeam Bread Company, which held a college contract, used economic intimidation to stop its employees from exercising their civil rights, they demanded that the school find another vendor.[136]

This constituted the first steps into Claflin's civil rights activism, and, if anything, the 1960s brought even-higher visibility to the college's contributions. After North Carolina Agricultural & Technical State University students launched the sit-in movement in 1960, students at Claflin and South Carolina State College attempted to desegregate the local Kress Department Store. Kress initially closed the lunch counter so that students could not request service. However, after three weeks of sit-ins and protesting, Claflin Student Council President Tom Gaither, along with South Carolina State College's Charles "Chuck" McDew, led nearly 1,000 students on a peaceful march downtown calling for desegregation. On March 15, 1960, local police officers attacked the student protesters with clubs, tear gas, and freezing water from fire hoses. The police incarcerated nearly 400 of the protesters, which made the Orangeburg incident the largest civil rights mass arrest up to that time. Two years later, the United States Supreme Court overturned the students' "Breach of the Peace" convictions. However, this event galvanized many student activists on the Claflin and South Carolina State campuses, leading them to withdraw from school and become full time civil rights activists. Claflin's Tom Gaither became a field secretary for the Congress of Racial Equality.[137]

Soon, the "Orangeburg Movement" had coalesced. Comprised of local community activists, the group included student representatives Thomas Gaither of Claflin and Charles McDew of South Carolina State. When the Congress of Racial Equality used Freedom Riders to test the Supreme Court's *Boynton v. Virginia* decision that interstate transportation facilities could not segregate based on race, Claflin students James K. Davis and Glenda J. Gaither, the sister of Tom Gaither, volunteered and later endured arrest at Jackson, Mississippi. Dr. Martin Luther King, Jr., visited the campus to recruit members for the Southern Christian Leadership Conference, and, in subsequent efforts to desegregate downtown Orangeburg in 1963, almost 1,500 people, many of them Claflin students, were jailed.[138]

Of Claflin's many contributions to the civil rights movement, the most important occurred when its students helped to test implementation of the Civil Rights Act of 1964, which banned discrimination in public accommodations. Despite the law, Orangeburg's All Star Bowling Lane refused to serve African-American patrons. On February 5, 1968, student protesters, attempted to desegregate the facility. Three days later local law enforcement officers, aided by members of the South Carolina National Guard, fired at the protesters on the campus of South Carolina State in what has been labeled the Orangeburg Massacre. Three students lay dead, while twenty-seven others—six of them Claflin students— were wounded. A human relations council was created in the aftermath, and several Claflin faculty members actively participated.[139]

As civil rights struggles commanded attention and commitment, Claflin continued to grow. Donations from the Methodist Church and Danforth Foundation grants furnished a portion of the means, as did resources derived from federal initiatives enacted during the period. These ranged from student loans to programs that supported facilities construction and repair. In the late 1960s, the college also joined the United Negro College Fund, granting the school access to even more funding. The enhanced funding had significant impacts. More students now could afford a college education, but this worked in two directions. Desegregation meant that students enjoyed more options to choose from, including majority institutions. HBCUs such as Claflin at the same time began getting greater numbers of students who required additional academic preparation. To meet the challenge, Claflin developed an innovative curriculum aimed at supporting retention. The Methodists meanwhile launched the "Claflin Challenge," a $1.9 million effort to help Claflin survive the tremulous 1970s and alarming rates of declining enrollment. To increase the student pool, diversity scholarships were awarded and a Department of Business Administration was added.[140]

Tumult persisted into the 1980s when financial problems again plagued the school. In 1982, the United States Department of Education ruled Claflin ineligible to participate in the National Direct Student Loan program due to high default rates. Additionally, as funding for minority-serving institutions began to be shared with tribal colleges and Latino schools, HBCUs such as Claflin found it ever more difficult to secure funding. The school soon lacked adequate financing, student enrollment again declined, some faculty members resigned due to unsatisfactory working conditions, and school facilities urgently needed routine maintenance. An upcoming SACS reaffirmation process highlighted these conditions. The lack of an honors program, a paucity of faculty research, and the absence of a career placement program offered additional concerns.[141]

To find resources for needed initiatives, new and energized leadership emerged to light the way. President Oscar Allan Rogers, Jr., (1984–1994) launched an ambitious fund-raising campaign to increase the school's endowment. Through this effort, increased alumni giving, and the federal Title III Matching Grant Program, in 1985 and 1986 the necessary foundation for securing the school's future was achieved. With financial stability gained, Rogers oversaw revision of Claflin's academic programs to emphasize math and English. Succeeding President Rogers in 1994, Claflin alumnus Henry Tisdale carried on with the same spirit of leadership. Particularly, the new president immediately sought grants to further aid institutional growth and articulated academic excellence

New residential facilities at Claflin University. These buildings are just two of nearly two dozen new classroom and residential facilities. As a result of these upgrades and other new initiatives, the institution — which had an enrollment of barely 1,000 students in 1995 — grew to 2,400 students by 2007. However, by far the biggest transformation came from students. In 1995, the average SAT of students entering Claflin stood at approximately 680. Fifteen years later the average SAT score was 920. In conjunction with these developments, the school's graduation rate increased to 55 percent, one of the highest among HBCUs and among all colleges in South Carolina.

as his top priority. Subsequently, he established an Honors College and a Center for Excellence in Science and Math and secured national accreditation for most academic programs. Under the Tisdale Administration, Claflin has added graduate programs in Business Administration, Biotechnology, and Education. It further has resumed the name Claflin University.[142]

In the twenty-first century, Claflin University has emerged as a solid and stable educational institution. In 2005, the college and the University of South Carolina secured a $7.5 million federal grant to eliminate health disparities in HIV/AIDS and cancer in South Carolina. The next year, the university formed the Jonathan Jasper Wright Institute for the Study of Southern African-American History, Culture and Policy, helping to shape public policy in issues affecting the African-American community. By 2009, Claflin was noted for increasing enrollment without reducing academic standards, a graduation rate of 55 percent, and raising its endowment from $10 million to $17 million. Most recently, it opened a $5 million, 14,000-square-foot molecular science research center. Due to his visionary leadership in education, Tisdale was appointed to help newly elected South Carolina Governor Nikki Haley's executive transition committee.[143]

The Claflin University of the twenty-first century is continuing educational traditions established over 140 years ago. Noted Claflin alumni include, among countless others, Robert Abbot, founder and longtime editor of the *Chicago Defender;* Reverend Dr. Clyde Anderson, Executive of the United Methodist Church Global Ministries; the Honorable Ernest A. Finney, the first African-American Chief Justice of the South Carolina Supreme Court since Reconstruction; and artist and educator Dr. Leo Twigs, the first African-American to earn a Doctorate of Arts from the University of Georgia.[144]

Notes

1. United States Department of Education, "Historically Black Colleges and Universities: 1976 to 1994," National Center for Education Statistics, 1996.

2. David W. Blight, "The Age of Emancipation," in *A History of the African-American People*, James Horton, ed. (London: Salamander, 1995), 89.

3. Ibid.

4. Historically Black Colleges and Universities: The Development of HBCUs, Academic and Social Experiences at HBCUs, http://www.education.stateuniversity.com/pages/2046/Historically-Black-Colleges-Universities.html.

5. "Claflin College is a Private Black College That is Weathering the Economic Storm," *Journal of Blacks in Higher Education*, July 23, 2009.

6. Donald E. Winbush, "Spelman Mission Was Not Impossible: How College's Fund-Raising Drive Netted $113 Million," *Diverse*, June 23, 2007.

7. Paul H. Bergeron, Stephen V. Ash and Jeranette Keith, *Tennesseans and Their History* (Knoxville: University of Tennessee Press, 1999), p. 170.

8. Dolly Nasby, *Harpers Ferry* (Charleston, S.C.: Arcadia, 2004), p. 115; Nancy C. Curtis, *Black Heritage Sites: An African-American Odyssey and Finder's Guide* (Chicago: American Library Association, 1996), p. 261–262.

9. Nasby, *Harpers Ferry*, p. 115; and A.R. Whitehill, *History of Education in West Virginia* (Washington: Government Printing Office, 1902), p. 115. Storer was never able to see his dream come to fruition; he died from complications due to typhoid fever in 1867.

10. A.R. Whitehill, *History of Education in West Virginia* (Washington: Government Printing Office, 1902), pp. 115–116.

11. Nancy Curtis, *Black Heritage Sites: An African-American Odyssey and Finders Guide*, p.262.

12. Whitehead, p. 116.

13. B.S. Morgan and T. F. Cork, *History of Education in West Virginia* (Charleston, WV: Moses W. Donnally, 1898), pp. 189–194.

14. Ibid.

15. Carter G. Woodson and James L. Conyers, *Carter G. Woodson: A Historical Reader* (New York: Garland, 2000), pp. 152–153; and Dawne Raines Burke, *An American Phoenix: A History of Storer College from Slavery to Desegregation, 1865–1955* (Pittsburgh: Geyer, 2006), p. 93.

16. "Harpers Ferry: Storer College," National Park Service of the U.S. Department of the Interior, 1999; and W.E.B. DuBois, *The Autobiography of W.E.B. Du Bois: A Soliloquy on Viewing the Last Decade of Its First Century* (New York: International, 1968); and David L. Lewis, *W.E.B. Du Bois: Biography of A Race* (New York: Holt, 1993).

17. Burke, *An American Phoenix*, 97; Jesse J. Holland and J. R. Oldfield, ed., *Civilization and Black Progress: Selected Writings of Alexander Crummell on the South* (Charlottesville: University of Virginia Press, 1995), pp. 120–121; "Niagara Movement," *Washington Bee*, August 25, 1906, 1; Lerone Bennett Jr., "The Niagara Movement," *Ebony*, May 1976, pp. 130–134.

18. Burke, *An American Phoenix*, 97.

19. Burke, *An American Phoenix*, 97; Holland and Oldfield, pp. 120–121; "Niagara Movement," *Washington Bee*; Bennett, "The Niagara Movement."

20. Andrew W. Kahrl, "The Political Work of Leisure Class, Recreation, and African-American Commemoration at Harpers Ferry, West Virginia, 1881–1931," *Journal of Social History* (Fall 2008), Vol. 42, Issue 1: 71.

21. "Storer College: Harpers Ferry WVA: Its History and Promise," *Daily Kennebec Journal*, September 22, 1894; "Tiverton," *The Newport Mercury*, July 22, 1893; "Items-Church Doings," [Indianapolis] *Freeman*, September 24, 1898, 7.

22. "General News Pertaining to the Race, as Gathered from Several of Our Most Reliable Negro Exchanges," [Topeka, Kansas] *Plaindealer*, June 30, 1899, 1; "Letter to Editor," *Cleveland Gazette*, June 17, 1899.

23. Burke, *An American Phoenix*, p. 109.

24. Ibid., p. 110.

25. "Mountain View Notes," *Washington Bee*, August 15, 1914; Burke, 111. McDonald also reversed Brackett's policy of refusing to rent to black vacationers. As a result Harpers Ferry and a nearby island in the Potomac known as Mountain View again became a vacation destination for African Americans. Additional funding for the college was secured once it began to accept African American summer boarders. During the first part of the twentieth century even more blacks came to the area. Known as Mountain View, some of the area's most prominent African American vacationed there. The Storer College orchestra was a constant feature at Mountain View, as well as Island Park, "which no

State claims," indicating Jim Crow laws were not enforced. Badly needed finances also came from African American conferences on the campus, including the West Virginia Teachers Association and the Young Men's Christian Association, which held retreats there. The funds from outside rentals became more important in the twentieth century as the Free Will Baptist Church began to reduce their support of the school.

26. Joseph Jeffrey Walters, Garreth Griffiths, and John Victor Singler, *Guanya Pau: A Story of An African Princess* (Orchard Park, NY: Broadview Press, 1891), pp. 42–54; American Colonization Society, *The African Repository* (Washington, DC: American Colonization Society, 1889), p. 131; Bates College, *General Catalog of Bates College and Cobb Divinity School 1863–1915* (Lewiston, ME: Bates College, 1915), p. 255; Burke, *An American Phoenix*, p. 137.

27. "Storer College Use Uncertain," *The Fredrick Post*, May 24, 1955; Burke, *An American Phoenix*, p.125.

28. Burke, 133.

29. "Anti-John Brown Memorial Draws Harsh Protest," [Topeka, Kansas] *Plaindealer* October 16, 1931, 1. During the ceremony the director of the college choir, Pearl Tatten, offended many UDC members when she stated: "I am the daughter of a Connecticut volunteer, who wore the blue, who fought for the freedom of my people, for which John Brown struck the first blow. Today we are looking to the future, forgetting those things of the past. We are pushing forward to a larger freedom, not in the spirit of the black mammy, but in the spirit of new freedom and rising youth."

30. Burke, 134; Paul A. Shackel, *Memory in Black and Whites: Race, Commemoration, and the Post-Bellum Landscape* (Walnut Creek, CA: Alta Mira, 2003), 103.

31. "Quaker Work Camp to Be Located at Storer College," [Charleston, WV] *Farmer's Advocate*, July 1, 1948.

32. "Storer College is Fully Accredited," [Charles Town, WV] *Farmer's Advocate*, November 29, 1940; Faustine Childress Jones-Wilson, *Encyclopedia of African-American Education* (Westport CT: Greenwood, 1996), p.484.

33. Burke, 136.

34. Ibid., 141.

35. Ibid., 143.

36. Ibid., 149.

37. Samuel J. Tucker, *Phoenix From the Ashes: EWC's Past, Present, and Future* (Jacksonville, FL: Convention, 1976), p. 11.

38. Ibid., p. 11.

39. Larry Eugene Rivers and Canter Brown, *Labor In the Vineyard of the Lord: The Beginnings of the AME Church in Florida* (Gainesville: University of Florida Press), p. 137.

40. Ibid.

41. Ibid., p. 150.

42. Tucker, p. 37; David H. Jackson and Canter Brown, *Sound the Trumpet: Selections in Florida's African-American History* (Tampa: University of Tampa Press), p. 142; and William N. Sheets, *Report of the Superintendent of Public Institution* (Tallahassee, FL: Tallahaseean Book and Job Plant, 1899), p. 341.

43. "History of Brewton-Parker College," http://www.bpc.edu/administration/institution_research/factbooks; and Berry College-Oak Hill and Martha Berry Museum, http://www.berry.edu/oakhill/history.asp.

44. Charles Sumner Long, *History of the AME Church in Florida* (Philadelphia: AME Book Concern, 1939), pp. 120–125; and M.M. Holloway, *A Daughter's Memento* (Jacksonville, FL: Edward Waters, 1920), p. 44; and Tucker, pp. 12–14.

45. Long, *History of the AME Church*, pp. 120–125; Holloway, *A Daughter's Memento*, p. 44; and Tucker, pp. 12–14.

46. Long, 125–125; Hugh Ruppersburg, *The New Georgia Encyclopedia: Companion to Georgia Literature* (Athens: University of Georgia Press, 2007), p. 258; "A Tribute to an Invincible Civil Rights Pioneer," *Jet*, July 1994, p. 42.

47. *Sound the Trumpet*, p. 14; John R. Thelin, *A History of American Higher Education* (Baltimore: Johns Hopkins University Press, 2004), p. 205.

48. Walter Crosby Eells, "Junior College Directory 1942: Summary of Students 1940–1941," *Junior College Journal*, vol. 13, American Association of Junior Colleges, 1942; Jesse P. Brogue and Shirley Sanders, "Junior College Directory 1948: Summary of Students 1946–1947," *Junior College Journal*, vol. 13, American Association of Junior Colleges, 1948

49. Edward Humes, *Over Here: How the G.I. Bill Transformed The American Dream* (Orlando: Harcourt, 2004), p. 124; Marybeth Gasman and Christopher L. Tudico, *Historically Black Colleges and Universities: Triumphs, Troubles and Taboos* (New York: Macmillan, 2008).

50. "Edward Waters College Gets $25,000 From Duval," [Fort Pierce] *News Tribune*, May 22, 1955.

51. Hurst 70–83; 125; 160.

52. Hurst 160.

53. Tucker, 12; and "Cannonballing to Success," *Pacific Stars and Stripes*, September 7, 1965.

54. Tucker, 18

55. Tucker, 19, 16–22; "Jesse L. Burns Has Resigned as President of Edward Waters College Amid Reports that He Had Falsified His Resume," *Chronicle of Higher Education*, February 2, 1996.

56. "College in Florida Sues Its Accreditor," *Chronicle of Higher Education*, March 11, 2005. "Settlement of College's Accreditation Lawsuit Could Spur Changes in the Process," *Chronicle of Higher Education*, July 1, 2005; "Florida College Loses Accreditation," *Chronicle of Higher Education*, December 17, 2004; "String of Jobs Paralleled Trail of Accusations," *Florida Times Union*, September 12, 2008; "Former EWC Exec Gets Prison," *Florida Times Union*, October 21, 2005; "Week in Review: April 25–30," *Florida Times Union*, May 1, 2005; "Ex–EWC Administrator Pleads Guilty," *Florida Times Union*, June 1, 2005; "Second Ex–EWC VP Admits Guilt," *Florida Times Union*, July 13, 2005; "College Leader Accused of Fraud," *Florida Times Union*, March 5, 2005. Resolution of the college's accreditation problem unfortunately failed to put an end to the spate of recent scandals. In the summer of 2005, authorities charged the college's executive vice president and a former vice president for academic affairs with conspiring to defraud the government by passing off relatives as black farmers to collect approximately $550,000.00 in settlement payouts. According to the *Florida Times Union*, prior to accepting employment at Edward Waters College the former vice president of academic affairs, the alleged ringleader of the crimes, was involved in a host of crimes such as forgery, theft, shoplifting, embezzlement, credit card fraud, and misappropriation of state funds. In the wake of this scandal Edward Waters College implemented stronger background checks on all potential hires.

57. "Texarkana, Ark.," *Freeman*, September 12, 1891, 2; *Freeman*, March 15, 1902, 4; and I. Garland Penn, *The Afro-American Press and its Editors* (Springfield, MA: Wiley and Company, 1891), p. 260. Booker began working with the paper when it was initially called *The Arkansas Baptist*, however, a name change occurred in 1889 when the when Arkansas' White Baptists named their publication *The Arkansas Baptist*.

58. *Freeman*, March 15, 1902, 4; and Penn, p. 260.

59. "Arkansas Baptist College," *Plaindealer*, January 26, 1906, 7; "The Arkansas Baptist College: President Booker Has Built an Institution That is an Honor to the State," *Plaindealer*, July 26, 1918, 1; and G. P. Hamilton, *Beacon Lights of the Race* (Memphis: E. H. Clarke and Brother, 1911), p. 171. To assist with the industrial component of the school Arkansas Baptist College acquired one hundred acres, called Griggs Farm, for those majoring in agricultural education. The land for the farm was purchased by Miss Helen Griggs, and she continued to give the school $100 annually towards the operation of the farm. The farm was also used to grow food for the boarding department and provided jobs for male students in order to defray their tuition expenses. The farm also had a four-room tenant house, store, barn, and cotton gin.

60. *Freeman*, May 27, 1893, 4; "Baptist Young Men's Convention," *Freeman*, March 3, 1894, 2.

61. "Revolting Crime Of Burly White Brutes," *Cleveland Gazette*, September 17, 1904, 2.

62. "Result of an Appeal for Arkansas College," *Washington Bee*, August 13, 1910, 4; Hamilton. *Beacon Lights of the Race*, p. 169.

63. "Result of an Appeal for Arkansas College," *Washington Bee*, August 13, 1910, 4

64. "Widow of Former Arkansas Solon Dies: Races Mourn Death of Mrs. Eliza Miller; Was Noted As Pioneer Businesswoman And Philanthropist," *Chicago Defender*, September 10, 1938; "Ex-College Prexy Heads High School," *Chicago Defender*, July 14, 1934; "Arkansas: Little Rock, Ark.," July 25, 1936, 23; "Camden, Ark.," *Chicago Defender*, February 6, 1937; "Arkansas State News: Camden," *Chicago Defender*, March 13, 1937. Nelson resigned when the Arkansas Baptists would not help financially maintain the buildings, pay faculty salaries, or assist with the school's debt payments; additionally there was dissention among the state's Baptists. In the 1930s the African American Baptists in Arkansas split between the Arkansas Consolidated Baptist Church and the newly formed Arkansas Missionary Baptist Convention; both branches of the church were vying for control of the school.

65. "Name Johnson Head of Ark. Baptist College," *Chicago Defender*, May 7, 1955, 2.

66. "Arkansas Teachers Close Conference," *Chicago Defender*, May 6, 1944; "Baptists Ask Resignation Of Dr. Coggs," *Chicago Defender*, December 5, 1953; "Name Johnson Head of Ark. Baptist College," *Chicago Defender*, May 7, 1955. After the 1954–1955 term Coggs was to become president emeritus. In 1953 the Arkansas Baptist State Convention, Consolidated, voted to remove Coggs from the Arkansas Baptist College presidency twice, while the Arkansas Baptist Board of Trustees voted to keep him in his position. The board felt they had more control over the administration of the school than the church conference. In response the convention fired some of the board members who did not consent to their wishes, which resulted in a lawsuit. The Pulaski County Circuit Court ruled that the convention, not the Board of Trustees, had the ultimate authority over the school and that board members could be fired before their terms ended, thus Coggs' fate was sealed.

67. Alex Wilson, "Wilson Marooned In Bates' Home By 25 Cars of Hoods," *Chicago Defender*, September 14, 1957

68. Alex Wilson, "Wilson Marooned In Bates' Home By 25 Cars of Hoods," *Chicago Defender*, September 14, 1957; "Texarkana, Ark.," *Freeman*, September 12, 1891, 2; and "Arkansas Black History: Blacks Protest Segregation Bill, " *Homeland*, February 1, 1993.

69. *Chicago Defender*, April 10, 1920, 1.

70. Vertie L. Carter, *Arkansas Baptist College: A Historical Perspective, 1884–1982* (Houston: D. Armstrong, 1981), pp. 91–100.

71. "Dr. Jackson to Address Baptists in Beloit," *Milwaukee Star*, August 9, 1969, 6.

72. Ibid.

73. "HBCU's Making Major Progress in Curbing Loan Defaults," *Black Issues in Higher Education*, November 9, 2000, 8–9; "Notable Minority-Related Grants to Institutions of Higher Education," *Journal of Blacks in Higher Education* 67 (2010): 90–92. Throughout the 1990s many HBCU default rates increased.

74. Joe William Trotter Jr., "The Formation of Black Community In Southern West Virginia Coalfields," in John C. Inscoe, *Appalachians and Race: The Mountain South from Slavery to Segregation* (Lexington: University of Kentucky Press, 2005), pp. 284–285; and Ronald L. Lewis, *Black Coal Miners in America: Race Class and Community Conflict 1780–1980* (Lexington: University of Kentucky Press, 1987), pp. 121–130.

75. Trotter, p. 286.

76. Lewis, pp. 9, 152.

77. C. Stuart McGehee and Frank Wilson, *Bluefield State College: A Centennial History 1895–1995* (Bluefield WV: Bluefield State University, 2006), pp. 6–7.

78. Ibid., p. 12.

79. Ibid., p. 14.

80. Ibid., pp. 15–16.

81. Ibid., p. 25.

82. Ibid., pp. 61–65.

83. Ibid

84. Ibid.

85. "Large Student Body," *Bluefield Daily Telegraph*, September 29, 1946; and *Bluefield State College A Centennial History*, pp. 100–102.

86. *Bluefield State College A Centennial History*, p. 114.

87. Ibid., pp 130–131; "West Virginia College Closes Dorms After Bombing," *Jet*, December 12, 1968.

88. "Governor Announces Second Meeting on Bluefield Issue," [Beckley, WV] *Raleigh Register*, February 16, 1963.

89. C. Stuart McGehee, p. 132.

90. "Bomb Explodes at Bluefield State College," *Bluefield Daily Telegraph*, November 17, 1968; and "Five Bluefield State Officials Are Threatened," *Raleigh* [WV] *Register*, November 13, 1968.

91. Christopher Hewitt, *Political Violence and Terrorism in Modern American a Chronology* (Westport, CT: Praeger), 2005.

92. "Bomb Explodes at Bluefield State College," *Bluefield Daily Telegraph*, November 17, 1968; and "Five Bluefield State Officials Are Threatened," *Raleigh Register*, November 13, 1968.

93. "More Than Right's Report Behind Bluefield Disorder," Charleston *Daily Mail*, November 16, 1968; *Bluefield State College A Centennial History*, p. 135; "Bomb Explodes at Bluefield State College," *Bluefield Daily Telegraph*, November 25, 1968; and "One Beckleyan Believes Hardway Doing Excellent Job at Bluefield," *Raleigh Register*, November 26, 1968. Several days later officials arrested two other students and charged them in the crime.

94. After a halfhearted attempt to reopen the dorms in January 1969, the dorms closed for good.

95. Pamela Moreland, "Legacy of Turmoil: CSUN Looks Back at Years of Activism at Former Valley State College," *Los Angeles Times*, April 22, 1988.

96. "Bombing Case Halts with Pair's Release," [Beckley, WV] *Post-Herald*, August 12, 1969.

97. Lewis, p. 191–193; Robert P. Stuckert, "Black Population of Southern Appalachian Mountain," *Phylon*, vol. 18. No.2 (2nd Quarter, 1987), pp. 141–151.

98. *Bluefield State College A Centennial History*, pp. 114–119.

99. Ibid.

100. Albert B. Reagan, "The Coronado Expedition," *Southern Workman* 45, no. 11 (1916), 420–22; Quintard Taylor, *In Search of the Racial Frontier: African-Americans in the American West, 1528–1900*, New York: W. W. Norton, 1999, 27–32, 67–75; Arrell Morgan Gibson, *Oklahoma: A History of Five Centuries* (Norman: University of Oklahoma Press, 1981); W. David Baird and Donney Goble, *Oklahoma: A History* (Norman: University of Oklahoma Press, 2008).

101. Zella Black Patterson, *Langston University: A History* (Norman: University of Oklahoma Press, 1979), p.3; Kenneth M. Hamilton, "The Origin and Early Developments of Langston, Oklahoma," *Journal of Negro History* 62, no. 3. (1977), 270.

102. "The Origin and Early Developments of Langston, Oklahoma," *Journal of Negro History* 62, no. 3 (1977), 276; Janie M. McNeal-Brown, "Oklahoma's First Comprehensive University: Langston University, The Early Years," *Chronicles of Oklahoma* 74, no. 1 (1996), 34; Helen M. Stiefmiller, "David J. Wallace," http://digital.library.okstate.edu/encyclopedia; Spivey, "Crisis on a Black Campus," 433–434; "Second Morrill Act of 1890," http://www.csrees.usda.gov/about/offices/legis/second morrill.html; Willis Rudy, *Building America's Schools and Colleges: The Federal Contribution* (Cranbury, NJ: Cornwall, 2003). David J. Wallace, a former South Carolina slave, was educated at Wiley University. In 1891 he and his family moved to Langston, where he became the first attorney and served

in that capacity for the town. In addition to helping secure Langston University, he also became the second African American elected to the Oklahoma Territorial Legislature. After leaving Langston, Wallace relocated to Enid, Oklahoma, where he served as a school administrator and formed a law practice. In 1920 he worked with the Oklahoma Interracial Commission to end the practice of lynching in the state.

103. United States Department of Agriculture, "Second Morrill Act of 1890," http://www.csrees.usda.gov/about/offices/legis/secondmorrill.html. See also Willis Rudy, *Building America's Schools and Colleges: The Federal Contribution* (Cranbury, NJ: Cornwall, 2003).

104. John R. Wennersten, "The Travail of Black Land-Grant Schools in the South, 1890–1917," *Agricultural History* 65, no. 2 (1991), 55–56; Patterson, *Langston University*, 195.

105. Willis L. Brown and Janie M. McNeal-Brown, "Oklahoma's First Comprehensive University: Langston University The Early Years," *Chronicles of Oklahoma*, 30; Patterson, *Langston University*, pp. 37, 45–46, 253; "Principal of Sumner High School Elected President Langston University," *Kansas City Advocate*, March 10, 1916; "Marquess Appointment Pleases Oklahomans," [Topeka] *Plaindealer*, April 28, 1916; "People of Oklahoma Give Their New Moses A Great Ovation," *Kansas City Advocate*, June 6, 1916.

106. Patterson, *Langston University*, 40, 42, 146; "Col. Midnight Says Tell the World He is Better: Has Not Wanted for Anything," *Kansas City Advocate*, January 16, 1925; "Col. J.O. Midnight Writes His Last Letter: Pray for Me That I May Stay a Little Longer," *Kansas City Advocate*, July 17, 1925.

107. "Negro Board of Regents to Control Langston University in Oklahoma," [Topeka] *Plaindealer*, May 7, 1937; "Langston U. Prexy Quits After a Day," October 20, 1939; Spivey, "Crisis on a Black Campus," 440–441.

108. Patterson, *Langston University*, 234.

109. Ibid., 48–52.

110. Ibid., 54–58; "Regents Make Move That May Close Langston U.," [Topeka] *Plaindealer*, July 4, 1958; Spivey, "Crisis on a Black Campus," 442.

111. Patterson, *Langston University*, 54, 58, 115.

112. "Financial Struggle Seen at Langston," *Wichita Times*, September 19, 1974; Patterson, *Langston University*, 62, 64.

113. Patterson, *Langston University*, pp. 69, 72; and "English Named President of Langston U.," *Wichita Times*, June 5, 1975.

114. Currie Ballard, "Langston University," http://digital.library.okstate.edu/encyclopedia/entries/l/la021.html; "JoAnn W. Haysbert Named President of Langston University," *The Journal Record*, May 27, 2005.

115. Patterson, *Langston University*, p. 195.

116. "Commencement at Langston University," [Topeka] *Plaindealer*, May 29, 1925; Patterson, *Langston University*, 75–76.

117. "Yes the Army," *Los Angeles Tribune*, October 25, 1943; "Saint Twine Finishes Tuskegee," *Los Angeles Tribune*, November 29, 1943; "Tuskegee Flyer Killed in Airplane Crash," [Topeka] *Plaindealer*, September 25, 1942; "Langston Celebrates Pearl Harbor Day: For Speaks," *Negro Star*, January 1, 1943; "Kansas WAC in Service in England," [Topeka] *Plaindealer*, April 6, 1945.

118. Patterson, *Langston University*, 200–201.

119. Henry Louis Gates, Jr., and Cornel West, *The African-American Century: How Black Americans Have Shaped Our County* (New York: Touchstone, 2000, p. 90); Robert C. Smith, *Encyclopedia of African-American Politics* (New York: Facts On File, 2003), p. 168; Nelson George, *Elevating The Game: Black Men And Basketball* (New York: HarperCollins, 1999), pp. 51–56; Juan Williams and Dwayne Ashley, *I'll Find A Way Or Make One: A Tribute To Historically Black Colleges and Universities* (New York: Amistad, 2007), p.363.

120. Blinzy L. Gore, *On a Hilltop High: The Origin and History of Claflin College to*

*1984,*Spartanburg, SC: Reprint Company, 1994, pp. 25–27, 39, 45; *Cincinnati Daily Gazette,* October 30, 1869; *Minutes of the Seventy-Seventh Session of the New England Conference of the Methodist Episcopal Church* (Boston, MA: James P. Magee, 1876), p. 21; R.V. Lawrence, *The Centenary Souvenir, Containing a History of Centenary Church, Charleston, and an Account of the Life and Labors of Rev. R. V. Lawrence* (Charleston, SC: n.p., 1885), p. xvii; *Acts and Joint Resolutions of the General Assembly of the State of South Carolina Passed at the Regular Session of 1869–70, Part 1,* Columbia: John W. Denny, State Printer, 1870), p. 301–303; *Flake's Bulletin* (Galveston, TX: March 2, 1870).

121. Charlestine Romelle Fairley, "A History of Claflin College, 1869–1987" (Ph.D. dissertation, University of South Carolina, 1990), 22; Gore, *On a Hilltop High,* pp. 45, 96.

122. *Acts and Joint Resolutions of the General Assembly of the State of South Carolina, Passed at the Regular Session 1871–72* (Columbia: Republican Printing Company, State Printers, 1872), p. 172.

123. Gore, *On a Hilltop High,* p. 60; Washington, D.C., *Daily Critic,* January, 7, 1876.

124. Rod Andrew, Jr., *Wade Hampton: From Confederate War Hero to Southern Redeemer* (Chapel Hill: University of North Carolina Press, 2008), pp. 191–192.

125. United States Bureau of Education, *Industrial Education in the United States* (Washington, D.C.: Government Printing Office, 1883), pp. 226–27; *Cleveland Gazette,* January 4, 1890, April 18, 1891; *Savannah Tribune,* August 20, 1892.

126. "Jonathan Jasper Wright, Associate Justice of the Supreme Court of South Carolina, 1870–1877," *Journal of Negro History* 18 (1933), 114–31; W. Lewis Burke and Belinda F. Gergel, eds., *Matthew J. Perry: The Man, His Times, and His Legacy* (Columbia: University of South Carolina Press), 2004, pp. 17–18.

127. *Boston Daily Advertiser,* March 10, 1890; [Fort Worth, TX] *Daily Gazette,* March 6, 1890; James M. McPherson, *The Abolitionist Legacy: From Reconstruction to the NAACP* (Princeton, NJ: Princeton University Press, 1975), pp. 280–83; [Springfield, MA] *Republican,* April 13, 1890.

128. Philip G. Grose, *South Carolina at the Brink: Robert McNair and the Politics of Civil Rights* (Columbia: University of South Carolina Press, 2006), p. 177; "Doings of the Race," *Cleveland Gazette,* February 22, 1896, 2. The new school would have an African American president, faculty and staff members. Miller resigned from the South Carolina Legislature to become the first president of South Carolina State University.

129. "Building Excellently," *Plaindealer,* May 1, 1891, p.1; Beth L. Savage, *National Register of Historic Places: African American Historic Places* (New York: John Wiley, 1994), p. 447.

130. Thompson's Weekly Review," *The Freeman,* September 1, 1906, 1; "Negro Industrial Education Reviewed U.S. Commissioner of Labor Discusses Subject in His Annual Report," *Savannah Tribune,* January 6, 1912, 2.

131. Charlestine Romelle Fairley, "A History of Claflin College, 1869–1987" (Ph.D. dissertation, University of South Carolina, 1990), 36.

132. Charlestine Romelle Fairley, "A History of Claflin College, 1869–1987" (Ph.D. dissertation, University of South Carolina, 1990), 40. Smyrl was a member of the Claflin musical group used to raise funds for the school; "Notes of Local Churches: North Church Benevolent Society's Election," [Springfield, MA] *Republican,* June 1, 1899, p. 4; "Mr. F.P. Carey; Detroit; Cleveland; Ohio; Mr. W. R. Harris," *Cleveland Gazette,* July 1, 1899, p. 3; "The Epworth league: The Fourth International Epworth League Convention, at Indianapolis, Ind., July 20–23 the Prevailing Religious Topic," *Plaindealer,* July 7, 1899, 1; "Colonel Duncan; Claflin University; Orangeburg; Solicited; Congenial," *Iowa State Bystander,* August 25, 1899, 1; "Afro-American Cullings," *Cleveland Gazette,* February 22, 1913, 1; *Cleveland Gazette,* February 10, 1906, 3; "Claflin University Suffers Loss: Main Building Destroyed by Fire Thursday Noon," *Savannah Tribune,* January 11, 1913, 1; "Education Etchings," *Freeman,* March 8, 1913, 3; "J. O. Midnight," *Kansas City Advocate,* April 25, 1924, 1. The Board of Managers of the Freedmen's Aid Society evaluated

their schools and concluded that the denomination had too many universities. To be considered a college by the Freedmen's Aid Society a school had to have at least fifty students, six professors involved in college work, and an endowment of $200,000. Since Claflin did not meet the new requirements it lost its university status with the church.

133. Gore, p. 175; Department of the Interior, Bureau of Education, "Survey of Negro Colleges and Universities" (Washington, D.C.: GPO, 1929), pp. 683, 686.

134. *Private Negro Colleges and Schools of South Carolina: A Survey Report, Division of Surveys and Field Services* (Nashville, TN: George Peabody College for Teachers), 1947, p. 55; Charlestine Romelle Fairley, "A History of Claflin College, 1869–1987" (Ph.D. dissertation, University of South Carolina, 1990), 63; "A Rating Retained By Claflin College," *Chicago Defender*, February 9, 1952, p. 2.

135. Gore, p. 188.

136. Gore, pp. 199, 201; Winfred B. Moore, Jr., and Orville Vernon Burton, eds., *Toward the Meeting of the Water: Currents in the Civil Rights Movement of South Carolina During the Twentieth Century* (Columbia: University of South Carolina Press, 2008), p. 261.

137. Cecil Williams, *Freedom and Justice: Four Decades of the Civil Rights Struggle As Seen by a Black Photographer of the Deep South* (Macon, GA: Mercer University Press, 1995), pp. 143–144.

138. "Arrest 500 in Sit-Ins," *Chicago Daily Defender*, March 16, 1960, 1; "Like Wind Lashed Fire It Spreads," *Chicago Defender*, March 26, 1960, 1–2; Charles E. Cobb, Jr., *On the Road to Freedom: A Guided Tour of the Civil Rights Trail* (Chapel Hill, NC: Algonquin Books, 2008), pp. 145–146; Gore, pp. 214–215.; "NAACP Hires Town Sit-In Leaders," *Chicago Defender*, January 28, 1961, 4; "Miss. Riders Come From 13 States," *Chicago Defender*, June 10, 1961, 2; Raymond Arsenault, *Freedom Riders: 1961 and the Struggle for Racial Justice* (New York: Oxford University Press, 2006), p. 295.

139. Civil Rights Act (1964), http://www.ourdocuments.gov/doc.php?flash=true& doc=97&page=transcript; "Dr. King Sides With Students: Justice Department, Civic Groups Work for S.C. Peace," *Chicago Daily Defender*, February 15, 1968, 3; Fairley, p. 84.

140. "Tells Need For Support of Methodist Negro Colleges," *Chicago Daily Defender*, October 15, 1959, 10; "Receives $10,000 Grant," *Daily Defender*, December 29, 1959, 21; Fairley, pp. 84–85; Gore, pp. 219, 235, 240; "3 More Colleges Added To UNCF Membership," *Chicago Defender*, October 14, 1967, 4; Fairley, p. 88; "United Methodist Seek $2,000,000 Fund for 12 Negro Colleges," *Chicago Defender*, August 30, 1969, p. 24.

141. "Schools on List of Those Losing Loan Eligibility," *The New York Times*, July 29, 1982; Fairley, pp. 90, 122.

142. Fairley, pp. 100, 102; "7.1 Million in Grants Made To Small Colleges," *The New York Times*, December 16, 1984, sec. 1, Part 2, late edition; Claflin College received a $150,000 matching grant from the U.S. Department of Education to increase the size of their endowment; "Claflin University History," http://www.claflin.edu/AboutUs/Claflin-History.html. In 1996 Claflin College received a $1 million grant through the Historically Black Colleges and Universities Restoration and Preservation Act, designed to protect historic structures on HBCU campuses. In 1996 Claflin College also received a $249,114 grant to develop a strategic community plan on housing, and safety and support services for Orangeburg, South Carolina, residents. The funding was also used to start a small business center for local entrepreneurs.

143. "University of South Carolina, Claflin University to Partner on HIV/AIDS Cancer Initiative," *Diverse Issues in Higher Education* 22 (2005), p. 16; Herb Frazier, "South Carolina HBCU Launches Think Tank to Focus on Southern Black History, Culture and Policy," *Diverse Issues in Higher Education* 23:18 (2006), p. 37; "A Harvest of Good News on African-Americans in Higher Education," *The Journal of Blacks in Higher Education* 64 (Summer 2009), p 12; Wayne Washington, "Claflin Makes Science Strides," *The State*, March 22, 2010; Phil Sarata, "Haley Taps Tisdale for Transition Team," *Times and Democrat*, November 13, 2010.

144. Rachel Kranz, *African-American Business Leaders and Entrepreneurs: A To Z of African-Americans* (NewYork: Facts On File, 2004), p. 1; Carolyn O. Wilson Mbajekwe, *The Future of Historically Black Colleges and Universities: Ten Presidents Speak Out* (Jefferson, NC: McFarland, 2005), p. 191; Williams and Ashley, p. 328.

2

Private vs. Public:
The Politics of Access
with Opportunity

MEIGAN M. FIELDS AND
KOMANDURI S. MURTY

The issue of politics of access with opportunity as pertaining to historically black colleges and universities (HBCUs) is as old as the politics of race in the United States.[1] John Silvanus Wilson Jr., the executive director of the White House Initiative, identified and evaluated the three "great transformations" of HBCUs: up from slavery (1865–1915), up from poverty (1916–1969), and up from uncertainty (1970-present). Passing through these transformations over the past 150 years, HBCUs battled against many odds and provided access to higher education for a significant percentage of black Americans. However, monumental changes in the American social and political arena such as the 1964 Civil Rights Act, the *Adams* desegregation decision, and other federal regulations enforcing desegregation resulted in the gradual decline of black student enrollments at HBCUs. Currently, an overwhelming majority of black students (89.6 percent) attend predominantly white institutions. Both private and public HBCUs are forced to compete with community colleges, majority institutions, and other online to increase access and opportunity for students at all levels.[2]

The Private HBCUs

From 1865 to 1890, northern churches and missionary groups, American Missionary Association (AMA), as well as Baptists, Methodists, Presbyterians, Congregationalists, and the Freedmen's Bureau, helped found more than two hundred private black institutions in the south. Many included in their titles normal, college, and university, though they were largely elementary and secondary schools. These titles prophesied the eventual purpose the institutions would serve. Founded with haste and limited financial backing, many ceased to operate following 1900. Jenkins and Reisman contend that blacks played a minor role in establishing, financing, and administering these institutions, which were to become (in diminished numbers), "their schools." To the contrary, blacks played a major role in educating themselves with the aid of the AME, AMEZ, AME, black Baptist, and smaller black denominational colleges and schools.[3]

The private HBCUs, run and staffed by northern missionaries for black students, were different from other American colleges in both expectations and quality of students. Most were begun with the intention to teach former slaves to read and to train black clergymen. They became de facto teacher's colleges because of the small pool of clerical students and the great demand for black teachers. However, a number initiated college departments by or before 1872, including Atlanta, Fisk, Hampton, Howard, Leland, Shaw, and Wilberforce. Thirty-nine of the private HBCUs now in existence were established during the twenty-five year period following the Civil War.[4]

Howard University, named after General O.O. Howard, the commissioner of the Freedmen's Bureau, was started by the Freedmen's Bureau, and chartered by Congress in 1867 in Washington, D.C. Hampton University, originally named Hampton Normal and Agricultural Institute, was founded in 1868 by the AMA and the Freedmen's Bureau at Hampton, Virginia. Beginning with elementary and secondary programs (and stressing vocational education), it offered a bachelor's degree by 1922 and commenced graduate programs in 1956. Today it is recognized as one of the most influential schools in the history of black education. One of the first colleges to accept Native Americans and to invite African students, Hampton has world-renowned endowed chairs, supports a dance company focusing on black folklore, provides training programs in Africa, and offers a variety of publications and conferences on issues important to blacks. The Hampton library houses an outstanding collection of materials on black history. A private, coeducational, independent (controlled by a single governing body) institution, it currently combines liberal arts, teacher education, and vocational curriculum.[5] From a historical standpoint, some of the most important of the church schools founded in this period include Atlanta University (1865) in Atlanta, Georgia; Fisk University (1866) in Nashville, Tennessee; Talladega College (1867) in Talladega, Alabama; and Tougaloo Institute (1869) in Tougaloo, Mississippi. All four of these were established by the AMA. The Arkansas Agricultural, Mechanical, and Normal (AM&N) College began as a branch Normal School (two-year curriculum) in 1873 at Pine Bluff, Arkansas. Morehouse College in Atlanta, Georgia, was originally established in 1867 as the Augusta Institute in Augusta, Georgia. The American Baptist Home Mission Society initially supported Morehouse and was instrumental in founding Virginia Union University (1865) in Richmond, Virginia; Shaw University (1865) in Raleigh, North Carolina; and Benedict College (1870) in Columbia, South Carolina. The Methodist Episcopal church founded Rust College (1867) in Holly Springs, Mississippi; and Morgan State College (1866), now known as Morgan State University, in Baltimore, Maryland.[6] The financial support for these newly established schools came largely from three sources: (1) the AMA, (2) the Freedmen's Bureau, and (3) black church groups. The AMA, a Congregationalist-supported association, worked with the freedmen in all sorts of schools during and after Reconstruction. By 1870, it had provided financial support to 170 black colleges. The Freedmen's Bureau provided funds for a wide range of educational opportunities for blacks and poor whites. For five years, it attracted teachers from the north; cooperated with missionary and religious educational organizations; and assisted newly founded institutions, including Fisk, Berea, and Atlanta University.[7]

The black church groups included the African Methodist Episcopal Church and the African Methodist Episcopal Church Zion among others. For example, Franklin College (NC) Church of God In Christ, Kitrel College, Allen University, Daniel Payne College, Payne College (Cuthbert, Georgia, Edward Waters College, Wilberforce University, Campbell College, Central Park Normal and Industrial School, Western University, and Paul Quinn College were all founded by the AME Church. Livingstone College, Clinton Junior College, and Lomax-Hannon College were founded by the AMEZ Church. Miles College, Lane College, and

Mississippi Industrial College were founded by the CME Church. Friendship College was founded by black Baptists. These church-supported schools reflected the outlook of their Christian founders, and their overriding goal was a Christian education for all students. They did not consider females candidates for the clergy, but they were welcomed in all other fields of study. Seven or eight colleges were founded expressly for women, including Spelman Seminary in Atlanta. In addition to Christianity, these nineteenth-century colleges sought to convey to their students a sense of social concern and responsibility, and the sentiment of service to the less fortunate. Education was a tool for the building of a better world. One can see, through a reading of current HBCU catalogs, that these values and aspirations still exist. Black consciousness and identity have been emphasized since the civil rights movement beginning in the 1960s. For example, Adam Clayton Powell, Jr., the New York politician, said during his baccalaureate address at Howard University on May 29, 1966: "To demand these God-given rights is to seek black power."[8]

The Public HBCUs

Sixteen of the historically black public colleges now in existence were established during the years 1866 to 1890. Only one of these, Cheney State College (1837) in Pennsylvania, was created prior to the Civil War. All but two public HBCUs originally were listed as normal or industrial schools and none initially conferred baccalaureate degrees. Seventeen public black colleges, now in existence, were established under the second Morrill Act of 1890, which paved the way for the development of legally separated black and white public colleges in border and southern states. During the period from 1890 to 1899, one black public college was either planned or founded per year in each of the seventeen southern and border states. These public colleges were unequal and did not offer four-year college programs. The legacy of the industrial, mechanical and agricultural education of blacks in the South stems from this period, and all of the schools established under the Morrill Act offered degrees later on.[9]

Originally, public HBCUs were created for two reasons: (1) to limit black education to vocational training and (2) to prevent blacks from attending white land-grant colleges. Following Reconstruction (after 1877), southern legislatures enacted a host of Jim Crow laws including those that excluded blacks from all the white educational institutions. Yet the region had received federal funds for designated white institutions since the passage of the first Morrill Act in 1862. In order to prevent continued discrimination against blacks in public higher education, the federal government enacted the second Morrill Act of 1890, mandating that all states had to either provide separate educational facilities for blacks or admit them to existing colleges. All southern and border states opted to establish "separate but equal" agricultural and industrial schools for blacks in order to get federal money for white land-grant colleges. These facilities were never equal, and consequently, public HBCUs continue their efforts to bridge the academic and financial gap gained by their white counterparts.[10]

Politics of Desegregation: Goals, Functions, and Academic Standards

Despite the HBCUs history of struggling to break blacks free from the lowest economic layers of social stratification , HBCUs have been under pressure to justify their continued existence since *Brown v. Board of Education.* Some black and white educators and policy makers maintain that the HBCU's mission, to provide higher education for blacks who, by law and/or custom, were barred from attending white private and public colleges and universities prior to 1954, had been accomplished. Some claim that prior to the late 1960s, separate sets of standards were developed for black colleges and white colleges, but that these differential standards no longer exist. Black schools are being evaluated now on the same criteria as other colleges and universities. Therefore, in a society that is striving for racial integration, the further duplication of physical facilities, academic programs, and services within a racially segregated, two-tiered, higher education system is financially, philosophically and pedagogically counterproductive. Still others call HBCUs anachronisms because only slightly over 10 percent of black college-bound students currently attend them. Today, close to 90 percent of college-bound blacks go to integrated schools where they comprise only 11.9 percent of the total number of students.[11]

Several critics, including David Reisman and Christopher Jenks, define HBCUs as diploma-mill service centers for those who could not get into college anywhere else because of low Scholastic Aptitude Test

(SAT) scores. They claim that most HBCUs provide an intellectual disservice to students due to insufficient financial resources, underpaid and incompetent teachers, a dearth of research scholars, and a semiliterate student culture. Some contend, explicitly or implicitly, that black students must be educated in white colleges if they are to compete in an integrated society. Prominent social theorist Thomas Sowell argues that many black schools have stakes in maintaining mediocrity; that it is difficult for them to retain good faculty; and that bright students do not develop intellectually on HBCU campuses. According to Sowell, no HBCU ranks with a decent white state university. Jencks and Reisman describe both private and public black colleges, with the exception of the "Black Ivy League" schools— Fisk University, Morehouse College, Spelman College, Dillard University, Howard University, Hampton University, and Tuskegee University — as fourth-rank schools at the tail end of academia. These critics, among others, have denounced the administrative leadership in black colleges as an in-group of mis-managers who are only interested in protecting their turf but not in maintaining academic standards.[12]

Although there seems to be a general agreement about the usefulness of HBCUs in the past, they are now viewed by many whites and some blacks as ineffective, dispensable institutions that do not meet the academic levels of white institutions. In a 1980 poll of its subscribers, *Black Enterprise* reported that 82 percent of the respondents thought HBCUs were serving a purpose that could not be met by other colleges but that only half of this percentage hoped that their children would attend a black college. Many blacks, although expressing admiration for HBCUs, prefer white institutions for themselves and their children.[13]

Emphasis on Ethnic Education

Eddie Morris noted from his survey of 50 black colleges a "brain drain" of bright students and faculty from HBCUs since legal integration in 1954, owing generally to the pressures of federal government, which supposedly has resulted in an isolated, barren bleak campus cultural life.[14] Furthermore, Andrew Hacke, in his article on "Trans-National America," chronicled how some critics denigrate the education of black students by black educators in black schools. For example, these critics claim, that HBCU curricula places too much emphasis on African-

American cultural values and political education and not enough emphasis on educational skills and competency. Some black and white writers
among these critics claim that a new universal culture is developing, and
that Americans of all races are short on the skills that this culture
expects.— This lack of skills is true across all demographics whether one
is testing for mathematics, reading, or geography. Therefore, they advocate that black students "act white" in order to obtain and cultivate the
educational skills necessary for competition in this universal culture.
The implication is that this competency is best acquired in white schools.
In a similar vein, some writers seek to diffuse the issue of any special
ethnic and cultural education for blacks by blacks. They proclaim the
development of a non-ethnic society in the United States where ethnic
and racial origins are increasingly irrelevant. This may be the case for
whites but it is patently unrealistic for blacks.[15]

Reduction in Degrees Awarded

Until 1954, the traditional black institutions of higher education
trained the majority of professionals, educators, and leaders in the black
community. The total number of baccalaureate and higher degrees
awarded by HBCUs increased from 13,000 degrees in 1954 to 32,000
degrees in 1974, then declined to 30,836 degrees by 2002. There has been
a gradual decline in the number of degrees awarded by HBCUs at
the baccalaureate level since 1974 and the post-baccalaureate level since
1977. Predominantly white institutions granted an estimated 78 percent
of all baccalaureate degrees earned by black students during 2001. The
current trend suggests that the proportion of black students matriculat-
ing at and graduating from white institutions will probably steadily
increase.[16]

Table 1 shows that a total of 40,411 degrees were awarded in 2001–
2002 by all HBCUs. Of them, over 70 percent were awarded by public
HBCUs and nearly 30 percent by private HBCUs. Public HBCUs
awarded more degrees than their private counterparts at every level
except the "first professional." Public HBCUs accounted for 95 percent
of associate degrees, 66 percent of bachelor's, 86 percent of master's, 56
percent of doctorates, and only 37 percent of first professionals. Bachelor's degrees constituted a higher proportion of degrees conferred by
both private HBCUs (82 percent) and public HBCUs (67 percent).[17]

Table 2.1: Number of Degrees Awarded by
Public and Private HBCUs, 2001–02

Degree	Public		Private		Total	Percent Public
	Number	Percent	Number	Percent		
Associate's	3,265	11.4%	171	1.4%	3,436	95.0%
Bachelor's	19,101	66.8%	9,745	82.4%	28,846	66.2%
Master's	5,477	19.2%	861	7.3%	6,338	86.4%
Doctoral	204	0.7%	160	1.4%	364	56.0%
First Professional	531	1.9%	896	7.6%	1,427	37.2%
TOTAL	28,578	100.0%	11,833	100.0%	40,411	70.7%

Source: Compiled from Provasnik, S., and L. L. Shafer. *Historically Black Colleges and Universities, 1976 to 2001 (NCES 2004–062).* U.S. Department of Education, National Center for Education Statistics, Tables A27-A29, pp. 48–50, Washington, D.C.: Government Printing Office, 2004.

Response to the Critics

HBCU advocates are aware of the caustic criticisms and even concede to a few. They maintain, however, that the shortcomings of black colleges are the results of the social order in which the higher education of blacks has been historically constricted (by the white power structure) in order to render black institutions nothing more than second- and third-class imitations of white counterparts. HBCUs, they argue, despite their modest beginning and discriminatory problems, served black students with considerable effectiveness in that they have upgraded curriculum offerings and quality over the years, while maintaining a commitment to individual student development. Some HBCUs, they note have attained high academic status.[18]

Advocates during the civil rights movement of the 1960s were enmeshed in the problem of how to preserve HBCU identity on the one hand, while attempting to achieve integrated education on the other. By 1974, however, most black educators and black community members were convinced that the HBCUs should survive, be strengthened and made more competitive, and not be merged with white institutions of higher learning. Furthermore, they wished to maintain control over what they perceived to be "their own institutions," regardless of the racial composition of the student body. They contend that HBCUs provide assets for black students that are unavailable and unattainable in white institutions provide an accepting environment with emotional support; serve as repositories for the black heritage; foster ethnic pride and self esteem; enhance opportunities for the development of leadership roles;

furnish healthy social relationships; offer programs designed to meet the unique needs of black students and the black community; and, educate many black students with learning deficiencies. Thus, the proponents explicate advantages and the need for the continued existence of HBCUs within interrelated and overlapping topical categories.[19]

Continued Segregation of Public Elementary and High School and the Role of HBCUs

Despite numerous desegregation efforts following the **Brown** *decision,* predominantly black public elementary and high schools continued to have, for the most part, white faculties and white administrations. The need for more black teachers as role models at the public school and college level and for HBCUs to graduate many of these role models remained important. In 2007–08, however, fewer than five percent of black U.S. undergraduates were majoring in education. Additionally, education became the basis to perpetuate hypersegregation, as real estate agents began using school racial composition as a way of attracting potential white home buyers to invest in segregated neighborhoods surrounding inner-city. Jonathan Kazol observed that the percentage of black children attending integrated public schools reached its lowest level since 1968. For example, by the academic year 2000–01, Chicago public school enrollments comprised of 87 percent black or Hispanic and less than 10 percent were white. Similarly, black or Hispanic constituted 94 percent in Washington, D.C.; 82 percent in St. Louis; 78 percent in Philadelphia and Cleveland; 84 percent in Los Angeles; 95 percent in Detroit; 88 percent in Baltimore; and nearly 75 percent in New York.[20] Kozol reasons why these discrepancies are not widely known:

> There is, indeed, a seemingly agreed-upon convention in much of the media today not even to use an accurate descriptor such as "racial segregation" in a narrative description of a segregated school. Linguistic sweeteners, semantic somersaults, and surrogate vocabularies are repeatedly employed. Schools in which as few as three or four percent of students may be white or Southeast Asian or Middle Eastern origin, for instance — and where every other child in the building is black or Hispanic — are referred to, in a commonly misleading usage, as "diverse." Visitors to schools like these discover quickly the eviscerated meaning of the word, which is no longer a descriptor but a euphemism of a plainer word that has apparently become unspeakable.[21]

Furthermore, the academic tracking by school officials is a major obstacle in achieving democratic and equitable balance among schools. For example, Kozol recalled from his visits to many urban schools, including Fremont High School in Los Angeles, that students were tracked into vocational programs and classes intended to teach life skills, or programs aimed at preparing students for jobs in retail and service industry. In some instance, school counselors place high school female students in sewing and cosmetology classes. Kozol argues, understandably, that these classes are of no help when come to prepare student to compete with Advanced Placement (AP) and college tracked students.[22]

Segregation in charter schools is evidently an emerging new trend. In their recent report entitled *Choice Without Equity: Charter School Segregation and the Need for Civil Rights Standards,* Frankenberg et al. analyzed charter schools in 40 states, the District of Columbia and several dozen metropolitan areas in the nation. This study revealed extensive patterns of charter school segregation by continuously stratifying students by race, class and possibly language. Specifically the study noted that: (1) while the charter school enrollment presently accounts for nearly 2.5 percent of all public schools, they attract a higher percentage of black students than traditional public schools; (2) while segregation for blacks among all public schools has been increasing for nearly two decades, black students in charter schools are far more likely than their traditional public school counter parts to be educated in segregated settings; (3) fifty-three percent of black charter school students attend these intensely segregated minority schools; (4) one-half of Latino charter school students attend racially isolated minority schools; (5) patterns in the West and in a few areas in the South, the two most racially diverse regions of the country, suggest that charters serve as havens for white flight from public schools; (6) Midwestern programs show high concentrations of black students; and, (7) approximately one in four charter schools does not report data on low-income students. Thus, a generation after the *Brown* decision, the school segregation continues. The chief reasons for continued segregation in the public school system are residential segregation, tracking, and the failure of public school busing. Students usually go to school in the areas where they live.[23]

In sum, one can see the continuation of racism, discrimination, and segregation in the public school system; the failure of blacks to compete successfully with white students in integrated schools; and, the necessity of remedial courses for many college-bound black high school students. Therefore, HBCUs remain essential to the education of blacks in the United States for both symbolic and practical reasons.[24]

Goals, Central Mission, and Needs

HBCUs are united in a mission to meet the educational and emotional needs of black students. These goals, as described in black college catalogs, stress the preparation for student leadership and service roles in the black community. Some black students are not emotionally prepared to succeed in predominantly white colleges and many require the conditional admission and remedial course offerings that are provided by HBCUs; but, are not usually available in white schools. Scholars further argue that HBCUs are still necessary because, they educate many students who have weaker academic backgrounds, who are mostly first-generation college-bound, and who are economically disadvantaged and/or experience racial discrimination. For example, Justin Pope of the Associated Press has recently claimed that Elizabeth City State University, a public HBCU in North Carolina, "tries to identify who's struggling and throw every possible resource their way. The best professors teach introductory and developmental courses. There are mandatory sessions to help students correctly apply for federal financial aid. When students drop out, the university calls them to find out what went wrong and tries to persuade them to return." Ronald Walters, a longtime professor of political science at Howard University and the University of Maryland, lists six specific goals for HBCUs: (1) to maintain the black historical and cultural tradition (and cultural influences emanating from the black community) by preserving that tradition and acting as a repository of material records and by encouraging scholarly endeavors of faculty as they teach about and research the black condition; (2) to provide key leadership in the black community because college administrators, scholars, and students have an important social role to play in community affairs (the HBCU functions as a model social organization and contributes to the resources needed for the expansion of black community activities); (3) to provide an economic function in the black community (HBCUs often have the largest institutional budget within the black community which including the acquisition of funds, the distribution of these funds to workers and their families and to small businesses, and the investment of these funds in economic institutions); (4) to provide black role models in the black community who can interpret the way in which social, political, or economic dynamics at the general societal level impact black people; (5) to produce graduates with special competencies to deal with the issues between the minority and majority population groups; and, (6) to produce black agents for specialized research, training, and information dissemination when dealing with black and other minority communities.[25]

Some advocates of HBCUs claim that white colleges have not met the multilayered educational needs of the black population. Out of 5,242 doctoral degrees awarded nationally in the biological and biomedical sciences in 2003–2004, only 163 were earned by blacks. In Fall 2007, only five percent of all faculty members in the nation's degree-granting institutions and administrative offices were black. In 2004, only five percent of the students receiving Ph.D.s and only seven percent of the students receiving first professional degrees were black. More blacks are currently graduating from high schools than ever before, but they are still fewer in proportion than the percentage of whites who are enrolling in college. When compared to other minority groups, the numbers tend to fall slightly short as well. For example, the proportion of blacks among American students enrolled in college increased from nine percent in 1976 to thirteen percent in 2004, whereas the corresponding increases are from one to six percent for Asians and Pacific Islanders, and from four to eleven percent for Hispanics. White Ivy League schools, despite their claims to increase diversity among student populations, continue to show low enrollments of black students.[26]

Many claim that the HBCUs can best uplift the unprepared students while simultaneously stimulate the competent students. Black students frequently find white universities to be places where white students and faculty see them as "special admits" or beneficiaries of affirmative action. Moreover, black student adjustment at these institutions proves to be difficult and usually necessitates extreme assimilation, and in severe cases, the abandonment of cultural roots. The selection and admission policies at many white universities result in the recruitment of black middle-class students. This situation may further widen the chasm between the black middle and lower classes. In addition, some claim that optimizing the talents of bright black students is not as high on the list of priorities in white colleges as it is in black colleges. Many HBCUs have developed honors programs for talented students. Black students at HBCUs experience a greater degree of personal interaction with their professors and sustain personal relationships beyond the classroom including counseling sessions, faculty sponsored school activities, and student organizations than those on predominantly white college campuses. They are also oriented toward success more frequently on black campuses than on white campuses. A comparative study of black student attitudes on a black campus and those on a predominantly white campus, found that twice as many black students on the black campus as on the white campus felt that their school prepared them for mainstream America. This study also found that black students on the black campus experienced greater warmth and empathy in a viable student-teacher relationship and less racism than did their counterparts on white campus.[27]

Success Patterns

Several studies noted the successful history of HBCUs in enrolling, retaining, and graduating black students and thereby indirectly creating a substantial portion of the black middle-class leadership. Deskins observed that the attrition rates for black students on white campuses are five to eight times higher than those for white students on the same campus. Davis et al. also noted that seventy percent of African-Americans at predominantly white institutions (PWI) did not complete their baccalaureate education as compared to the twenty percent that failed to do so at HBCUs during the 1990s. Love and Costen et al. attributed the problem of retention and graduation of PWIs to campus climate, racial stereotypes, and faculty relations with African American students. The American Council on Education acknowledged that despite the tremendous 25 percent enrollment increase of black students to 17.8 million students between 1996 and 2006, African Americans and Hispanics (between 18 and 24 years of age with a high school diploma) continue to trail whites in their percentages of college attendance. While college participation rates went up from 31 percent in 1988 to 45 percent in 2007 for whites, they only increased from 22 percent to 33 percent for African Americans. Gender wise, the college participation rates for men and women increased by 7 and 15 percentage points respectively during this period.[28]

In the 1990s, the focus shifted to the underrepresentation of minorities in the disciplines of science, technology, engineering and mathematics (STEM), especially at the graduate level. Although many colleges and universities maintained that qualified minority students were impossible to find, the statistics showed that nearly 23,000 baccalaureate degrees were conferred annually in the United States upon African American, American Indian, Hispanic and Pacific Islander students in STEM fields. A report compiled by the Urban Institute also indicated that 51 percent of STEM graduates during 1992 and 1997 were from minority groups and these students earned a GPA of 3.25 or above. Dr. Claude Braithwaite, Louis Stokes Alliance for Minority Participation (LSAMP) project administrator, inferred that the promising potential of relatively lucrative employment upon completing a baccalaureate degree, combined with the fear of incurring additional educational debt and with the unfamiliarity with the graduate school process, might have dissuaded many of these minority STEM graduates from enrolling in graduate or terminal degree programs. To fill the gap, the Bridge to Doctorate (BD) initiative was established in 2003 as conceptualized by Dr. James Hicks, LSAMP director at the National Science Foundation (NSF), to operate under the Directorate of Education and Human Resource through the Division of Human Resource Development. Beginning in the fall of 2003, the initial cohort of BD participants received twelve-month stipends of $27,000 and $10,000 for tuition. In the fall of 2004, the second cohort saw increased stipends of $30,000 and tuition payments of $10,000. This effort gave not only a jump-start to bridge the racial gap in STEM fields but also extra muscle to LSAMP. For example the NSF noticed that in 1991 minority enrollment in STEM fields were 35,670 students, by 2003 STEM minority enrollment reached more than 205,000 students. In 2004–2005, 24,642 LSAMP students earned bachelor degrees. By 2006, nearly 250 students from underrepresented groups— a cohort of ten STEM graduates each year at each of the thirteen sites at participating institutions, including one HBCU (Jackson State University)— entered graduate degree programs through the BD initiative.[29]

DEGREES AWARDED

Black schools still grant high proportions of the baccalaureate and graduate degrees earned by black students. Although HBCUs constitute only three percent of all degree granting institutions, approximately 19 percent of the undergraduate degrees received by blacks in the United States in 2004 were conferred by HBCUs (24,464 of a total of 131,241 were received by blacks); 10 percent of the masters degrees (5,034 of 50,657); 9 percent of the doctorates (257 of 2,900); 17 percent of first professional degrees (1,014 of 5,930); and 12 percent of all degrees

(32,752 of a total of 271,911). While these numbers are impressive, when compared to 1976–1977, there were proportionately fewer blacks earning bachelor's degrees at HBCUs in 2003–2004 (35 percent vs. 19 percent). Although the number of bachelor's degrees earned by blacks at HBCUs increased from 20,800 to 24,464 during this period, the number of blacks earning degrees at other types of institutions rose at a faster rate.[30]

Eighty-five HBCUs (40 public and 45 private) confer bachelor's degrees. In 2001–2002, they conferred 28,846 bachelor's degrees, 25,122 (87 percent) to blacks, 2,278 (8 percent) to whites, and 1,446 (5 percent) to others (including 827 to nonresident aliens). Numerically, bachelor's degrees in business and management (6,213) were followed by education (2,401), social sciences (2,656), biological sciences (1,982), health professions (1,936), psychology (1,868), computer science (1,565), protective services (1,368), and communications (1,276). Of the 25,122 bachelor's degrees awarded to black students, 8,623 (34 percent) were awarded to males and 16,499 (66 percent) to females.[31]

Although the number of bachelor's degrees by discipline was not provided in the American Council on Education's 2009 supplement report, it did indicate that over 1.6 million bachelor's degrees were awarded nationally during academic year 2005–2006. Of those degrees, 140,771 (8.8 percent) were awarded to African Americans, an increase of 53.2 percent from the 91,915 degrees awarded in 1995–1996. African American males received 47,477 (3.0 percent) and their female counterparts received the remaining 93,294 (5.8 percent) degrees. Complying with historical trends, African American males continue to trail behind females, with corresponding growth rates of 3.0 percent and 5.8 percent during the decade of 1996–2006. Hispanics outnumbered Asian Americans receiving bachelor's degrees (113,026 vs. 104,824), and among both groups women outnumbered men.[32]

Forty-five HBCUs (36 public and 9 private) confer master's degrees. In 2001–2002, they conferred 6,338 master's degrees, 4,461 (70 percent) to blacks, 1,358 (21 percent) to whites, and 519 (8 percent) to others (including 264 nonresident aliens). Numerically, master's degrees in education (2,646) were followed by public affairs and services (723), business and management (651), health professions (561), psychology (362), computer and information technology (262), social sciences/history (173), engineering (122), and protective services (120). Of the 4,461 master's degrees awarded to blacks, 26 percent were awarded to males and 74 percent to females.[33]

In the year, 2005–2006 a total of 607,550 master's degrees were awarded nationally. Of these, 55,746 (9.2 percent) were awarded to African Americans. African American males received 15,736 (2.6 percent) and the remaining 40,010 (6.6 percent) were claimed by African American women. During the decade of 1996–2006, the number of master's degrees awarded to African Americans increased by an impressive 107.2 percent, but for males, this increase was only 86.6 percent, while the corresponding increase for women was 116.6 percent. Foreign students received as many as 69,065 master's degrees (11.4 percent), an increase of 39.6 percent since 1994. Asian American women and Hispanic women competed for master's degrees at almost the same rate in 2005–2006, having received 17,746 and 20,148 degrees, respectively. However, the trend between 1995–1996 and 2005–2006 shows a considerable increase among Hispanic women compared to Asian American women (i.e., a 90.7 percent increase for Asian American women and a 130.9 percent for Hispanic women).[34]

Nineteen HBCUs (twelve public and seven private) confer doctorates. In 2001–02, they conferred 364 doctorates, 256 of them (70 percent) to blacks, 61 (17 percent) to whites, 47 (13 percent) to others (including 34 degrees to nonresident aliens). Numerically, education doctorates (157) were followed by theology (38), psychology (30), biological sciences (24), social sciences/history (24), physical sciences/technology (18), public administration/public services (18), communications (16), engineering (15), area/ethnic studies (7), agricultural/natural resources (6), health professions (6), and mathematics (5). Of the 256 black doctorates, 108 (42 percent) were awarded to males and 148 (58 percent) to females. The underrepresentation of blacks and other minorities among doctorates remains an issue in American higher education. During the decade of 1975–1984, only 612 Ph.D.s were awarded to blacks in life, health, and medical sciences nationwide, while the total doctoral degrees awarded in this period exceeded 60,000.[35] Mingle found that: (a) the African American, Hispanic, and Asian American populations are growing and, by 2025, are expected to constitute nearly 40 percent of the college age (18–24 years) population; (b) college participation rates among black college age youth peaked between 1974 and 1976, but declined thereafter; and (c) the number of black students in graduate school dropped 19.2 percent between 1977 and 1985. Between 1996 and 2006, African American doctoral degrees jumped from 1,794 to 3,460 (a 92.9 percent increase). Yet African Americans constitute only 5.7 percent of all 60,682 doctoral degrees awarded in 2005–2006. Of these, African American men were awarded 1,180 degrees and women 2,280 degrees, a ratio of about 1:2.[36]

Thirteen HBCUs (four public and nine private) confer first professional degrees (dentistry, medicine, pharmacy, veterinary medicine, law, and theology). In 2001–2002, they conferred 1,427 such degrees, 997 (70 percent) to blacks, 126 (9 percent) to whites, and 304 (21 percent) to others—including 106 to nonresident aliens, 97 to Asians and Pacific Islanders, and 87 to Hispanics. Law degrees (445) were followed by pharmacy (406), theology (217), medicine (212), dentistry (94), and veterinary medicine (53). Of the 997 first professional degrees awarded to blacks, 399 (40 percent) were awarded to males and 598 (60 percent) to females. When compared to other major fields, pharmacy appears to be in significant demand among HBCU students since 1989 (in which only nineteen pharmacy degrees were awarded).[37]

A total of 89,874 professional degrees were awarded in the year 2005–2006. Of these, 6,031 (6.7 percent) were awarded to African Americans. African American males received 2,195 (2.4 percent) and the remaining 3,836 (4.3 percent) were claimed by African American women. During the decade of 1996–2006, the number of professional degrees awarded to African Americans increased by an impressive 17 percent, but for African American males this increase was only 2.6 percent. Asian Americans received almost twice as many doctoral degrees as African Americans in 2006 (10,929), an increase of 51.1 percent since 1996.[38]

Post-Graduation Success

Thompson's survey on graduates of black college corroborates the continuing success of HBCUs in preparing blacks for effective participation in the American social system. In his three-year-study of more than 2,000 alumni of these institutions, he found that nearly 90 percent of his respondents were professionals in medicine, dentistry, teaching, or law. Eight percent held white-collar jobs, and 3 percent were blue-collar workers. Moreover, he found that the average income of the families headed by black college graduates was $32,000, over $10,000 above the average income of families headed by non-college graduates. Thompson further reported that 50 percent of the graduates surveyed earned a master's or doctoral degree. Approximately 10 percent of the alumni received their post-baccalaureate degrees from Ivy League Schools. This profile covers graduates of HBCUs from 1940 to 1982.

Finally, only six percent of the alumni reported that their high schools adequately prepared them for college.[39]

Recently, the college Board reported the median earnings for full-time workers in the 25 to 34 age group by race and education. According to this report, the median income of black females with a bachelor's degree is $41,000 — a $16,500 increase over the black female with a high school diploma, whose median earnings are $24,500. Similarly, the median income for black males with a bachelor's degree is about $42,500 or a $12,500 increase over the median income of black males with only a high school diploma at $30,000 per year.[40]

Social-Psychological Supports, Racial Integration, and Comfort Level

Research findings show that the general attitude on HBCU campuses, as epitomized by the faculty, administrators, and staff, is more understanding, more accepting and less prejudiced than that on white campuses. Black students in black colleges are less likely to report instances of interpersonal stress. There is an apparently high level of satisfaction and camaraderie among black students at black schools that is not as prevalent among black students on white campuses. Though the facilities (physical conditions, computers, library and research materials, and visual aids), financial resources, endowments, and range of academic programs are not on par with those found on white campuses, the atmosphere is more comforting. Conversely, particularly in southern schools, black students are frequently faced with alienation, stress, and, at times, outright hostility from white students and faculties. Contrary to common practice on white campuses where many students are taught by graduate students and junior faculty members, students in HBCUs are more frequently taught by designated full-time senior faculty members.[41]

Though private and public HBCU faculties and student bodies are integrated, a black culture prevails. Of the total faculty members employed in all HBCUs, approximately 55 percent are black, 40 percent are white, and 5 percent are composed of other minorities and foreign nationals. Among private black colleges, blacks constitute 63 percent of the faculty, while among public black colleges, they make up 51 percent. Ninety percent of the administrators in black private colleges are black, and 70 percent in black public institutions are black. In the 1987–1988 academic year, more than one-third (38 percent) of the faculty at black private colleges sponsored by the UNCF were non-black. This is an enviable racial balance when compared to the extreme under-representation of black faculty on white campuses. Among the nation's more than three thousand predominantly white colleges and universities, less than four percent of the faculty members are black. Even among those schools that have encouraged relatively large numbers of black students to enter, there has been no appreciable development of a significant cadre of black faculty members. Additionally, black colleges have always served as forums for visiting scholars, political figures, business leaders and artists, regardless of race, creed or religion. Many HBCUs are now actively recruiting Hispanics, Asians and students of all races from third world countries.[42]

The black public colleges began increasing their white enrollments in the mid–1970s due to the Supreme Court decision *Adams v. Richardson* (1969), which mandated that institutions supported by state funding maintain a racial balance. In any case, HBCU student bodies have been racially mixed since inception. Southern private HBCUs, do not generally actively recruit white students and, in the rare case that a president may launch a campaign for this purpose, it is perceived as intent-defeating and the effort is abandoned. When black institutions were founded in the late nineteenth century, their administrators and faculty were mainly white and the leadership did not begin to shift to blacks until the mid–twentieth century. HBCU faculties today remain fully integrated.[43]

In addition to closer professional relationship at HBCUs, opportunities are available for black students to experience leadership positions in student government, fraternities, sororities, and other extra-curricular organizations. Through this involvement, student-support networks may be developed thereby fostering self-confidence, the ability to lead and self-esteem. In contrast, on white campuses, black students find themselves on the periphery of campus life.[44]

Transitional Ease

The black college experience prepares students to enter and succeed in the real world beyond the black campus, which serves as a buffer zone between the segregated society they encounter through home and community and the mixed society that they must enter after college. Being nurtured as adolescents in a supportive environment, free of racial tension, eases the cultural shock of movement from the black to the white world. Certain features of black campus life — a participatory ethos, an inclusive environment, an expectation of success, and an incorporation of a rich historical tradition — contribute to this passage. For example, Morehouse graduates refer to themselves as "Morehouse Men." A Morehouse Man embodies all that is supposedly good, noble and strong in the African-American college male. Finally, those enrolled at HBCUs escape the campus conflict between black and white students that are frequently found on white campuses.[45]

Black Consciousness and Culture

HBCUs emphasize the development of black consciousness and identity, black history, racial pride, and ethnic traditions. They provide an African American culture and ambience that many students find essential to their social functioning and mental health. Frequently, whites and many middle-class blacks either are unaware of this black cultural necessity or ignore it.

This African American culture emerges from two primary sources: African cultural traits and linkages to a black heritage and, cultural traits developed as a result of racial segregation in the United States. The point is not made that all blacks share these cultural elements in a uniform communal fashion. As with other ethnic groups, there are individual differences among blacks. They exert personal choices, face a variety of social situations, and belong to different social classes. One could distinguish the isolated young and poor or the professional black elite from other blacks. The point is made, however, that the foregoing set of elements composes what may be regarded as essential parts of a black ethos in the United States, that is, they are adhered to, more or less, by most American blacks.[46]

The literature about black students attending white schools documents campus problems involving interpersonal relationships, personal identity, and black consciousness. Establishing a meaningful personal identity, cultivating personal relationships, and gaining social acceptance are difficult for black students on white campuses. One could argue that these adjustment problems comprise the price that has to be paid for racial integration. The price is dear, particularly for those who find adjustment on white campuses difficult, and in any event, racial integration may be a dream only for some and undesired by others.[47]

Personal Choice

Blacks, like whites, desire and merit options in selecting institutions of higher learning. HBCU advocates should not be required to engage in dialogue about the legitimacy of racial self-segregation. Just as different white groups have such schools as Notre Dame, Harvard, Bob Jones University, Wellesley, Brandeis, Brigham Young, and so forth, blacks have HBCUs. Choice is a cherished feature of the American educational system. Moreover, in any case, HBCUs do not exclude white students or harm white society in any way. HBCUs do not comprise a monolithic educational enterprise. They have varied since inception, and still differ widely in curriculum, educational facilities, size, funding sources, administrative control and function, geographical location, quality, financial status, and prestige. Thus, they serve the needs of a wide range of students. Though there is a so-called Black Ivy League, the supporters of black higher education have usually assumed a more egalitarian stance than have their white counterparts.

Many choose an HBCU because of its physical proximity to their homes, and still others opt for an HBCU for financial reasons. The chances of receiving funds for specialized programs, federal aid, or philanthropic help of some kind may be greater at a particular HBCU than they are elsewhere. Many require a school with an open admissions policy and/or one offering a remedial program. Some desire, or are pressured to go where their parents went. Some feel an HBCU will enable them to build friendship networks necessary for future work and residence in the black community.[48]

Differences Between Black Student Populations on Black and White Campuses

HBCU proponents do not maintain that all black students should attend HBCUs; but, they point out that comparisons between black students on black and white campuses indicate the necessity of HBCUs for many black students. Despite social, economic, and educational disadvantages, however, black college students have the same education and professional aspirations as other students.[49]

Black students on HBCU campuses share backgrounds and opportunities that differ from those of their peers (black and white) on white campuses. They lag behind in terms of family socioeconomic status;

high school grades; university faculty, facilities, available academic majors, and opportunities for advanced study. They also tend to have lower standardized test scores and weaker high school backgrounds than do their peers on white campuses. When the psychological development of black students on black and white campuses is compared, however, students on black campuses excel. Black students at HBCUs possessed more positive self-image, stronger racial pride, and higher aspirations than did those on white campuses. Research studies by several scholars report that when HBCU students are compared to black students on white campuses, the former perform academically better, have a greater social involvement, and possess higher occupational aspirations.[50]

HBCU proponents are aware of the academic barriers faced by black students on white campuses. Black students at HBCUs do not phase admission requirements that rely on culturally and economically biased standardized tests, faculties that are dominated by white middle-class males, and high tuition rates, along with inadequate financial aid programs, dog-eat-dog competition, and denial of cultural pluralism.[51]

Synopsis

Though the debate continues about the viability of HBCUs, those that are stronger (in terms of educational programs, accreditation, and size of student body) are likely to continue for the foreseeable future. Several interactive aspects support this forecast: (1) many black educators and black community members want them; (2) many HBCUs have achieved known success, particularly with first-generation college students; (3) many HBCUs have and continue to educate considerable number of low-income and less privileged students, a segment that continues to exist under current social and economic conditions; and, (4) the black community needs HBCU-trained leaders and professionals to motivate youth guarding themselves against negative social forces.

Hodgkinson emphasizes the need for HBCUs in order to bring larger numbers of blacks into the nation's mainstream. Perhaps the role of HBCUs is more clearly understood through Astin's dual process framework of student-college matching. The first component of the framework is the applicant's prerogative in deciding which college he wants to attend. The second component invokes the school's influence in who it decides to admit based on the image the school wishes to portray and the standards to which it is committed. In this regard, HBCUs are capable of dominating a unique niche. To strengthen their position in American higher education, HBCUs should undertake marketability efforts to attract the 21st century applicant by: (a) Re-examining the curriculum to ensure optimal responsiveness to student interests and societal needs; (b) establishing an outcomes-based program of continuous improvement focusing on retention and graduation; (c) attracting and retaining exceptional faculty members who induce students to reach their full potential; (d) strengthening the infrastructure with regard to technology and facilities; (e) utilizing alumni power in both fund-raising and in the recruitment of talented students; and (f) developing partnerships with private and public agencies where students co-op internship and other employment opportunities.[52]

Finally, as Harper et al. indicated, "Consistent attacks on affirmative action; funding inequities for public institutions that annually offer college opportunity to more than a quarter million African American students; the implementation of policy initiatives that distract HBCUs from their original missions; and infrequent policy analyses will continually manufacture insufficient access and equity barriers for those who could ultimately benefit from college participation. While it is important to acknowledge and honor historical advances, contemporary times call for new policy efforts to solve persistent problems."[53]

Notes

1. For the purpose of understanding the politics of access with opportunity to private vs. public black colleges, we rely broadly on William H. Watkins' framework of "The White Architects of Black Education: Ideology and Power in America." As Watkins noted, the black education has been the struggle between the ideologies of both white and black architects. The ideology of white architects centered around philanthropic idealism, New South ideology, Social Darwinism, Protestant beliefs, and liberal capitalist thought. On the other hand, black architects envisioned a reconstructed nation in which education was the basic right and schools afforded to the laborer as much knowledge as their former masters enjoyed. In the end, the colonial education in the South as funded, created, and refined by the white architects and the educational agenda of blacks in the South conflicted and the black architects were defeated. The consequences of such a defeat continue to impact the black colleges even today in terms of massive budget cuts, crumbling buildings, overcrowded classroom, and a curriculum that measures success by standardized tests. Black colleges continue to face constrained finances and funding shortages, forcing them increase student tuitions, making harder to compete with predominantly white institutions for student enrollments, and causing difficulties to maintain national averages in terms of graduation and retention rates, and in some cases like Morris Brown College, losing accreditations and closing doors.

2. John Silvanus Wilson, Jr., "America's Historically Black Colleges and Universities

and the Third Transformation," *The Presidency* (Winter 2010), pp. 16–17; and U.S. Department of Education, National Center for Education Statistics, 2007–08 Integrated Postsecondary Education Data System (IPEDS), Spring 2008, Table 24.4. This percentage refers to fall 2007 statistics.

3. Christopher Jencks and David Reisman, *The Academic Revolution* (New York: Doubleday Anchor, 1968).

4. W.E.B. DuBois and A.C. Dill, *The College Bred Negro American* (Atlanta: Atlanta University Press, 1910).

5. Sharron A. Sharpe, "Hampton Institute," in Charles R. Wilson and William Ferris, ed., *Encyclopedia of Southern Culture* (Chapel Hill: University of North Carolina Press, 1989), pp. 288–89.

6. Augustus W. Law and V. Clift, *Encyclopedia of Black America* (New York: McGraw Hill, 1981), pp. 338–51.

7. Rufus K. Goodenow, "Black Education," in Wilson and Ferris, pp. 151–53.

8. F. R. Shapiro, ed. *The Yale Book of Quotations* (New Haven, CT: Yale University Press, 2006), p.629.

9. Law and Clift, *Encyclopedia of Black Americans*, pp. 338–51; James E. Blackwell, *Mainstreaming Outsiders: The Production of Black Professionals* (New York: General Hall, 1981).

10. Jane Browning and John B. Williams, "History and Goals of Black Institutions of Higher Learning," in Charles V. Willie and Ronald R. Edmonds, ed., *Black Colleges in America: Challenge, Development, and Survival* (New York: Teachers College Press, 1978), pp. 68–93; and Paul S. Baker, "Federal-State Relations," in Wilson and Ferris, pp. 249–50.

11. Mikyung Ryu, *Twenty-third Status Report: Minorities in Higher Education, 2009 Supplement* (Washington, D.C.: American Council on Education, 2009), p. 7; and Jacqueline Fleming, "Stress and Satisfaction in College Years of Black Students," *Journal of Negro Education* 50, no.3 (1981), pp. 307–18; and William B. Harvey and Lea E. Williams, "History of Black Colleges: Models for Increasing Minority Representation," *Education and Urban Society* 21, no.3 (1989), pp. 328–40.

12. Mack Jones, "The Responsibility of the Black College to the Black Community: Then and Now," *Daedalus* 100 (1971): pp. 732–34; and Sherman J. Jones and George B. Weathersby, "Financing the Black College in America," in Willie and Edmonds, pp. 313–27; Earl J. McGrath, *The Predominantly Negro Colleges in Transition* (New York: Teachers College Press, 1965); Thomas Sowell, *Black Education: Myths and Tragedies* (New York: McKay, 1972); James Junod, "Are Black Colleges Necessary?" *Atlanta Magazine* 27 no.6 (1987): pp. 78–119; and Andrew Hacker, "Trans-National America," *New York Review of Books* 37, no.18 (1990): pp. 19–24.

13. Herman R. Branson, "The Hazards in Black Higher Education: Program and Commitment Needs," *Journal of Negro Education* 56, no.2 (1987): 129–36.

14. E. W. Morris, "The Contemporary Negro College and the Brain Drain," *Journal of Negro Education* 41, no.4 (1972): 309–319.

15. Hacker, "Trans-National America"; and D.R. Alba, *Ethnic Identity: The Transformation of White America* (New Haven, CT: Yale University Press, 1989).

16. American Council on Education, *Minorities in Higher Education* (Washington, D.C.: American Council on Education, 1988); Stephen Provasnik and Linda L. Shafer, *Historically Black Colleges and Universities, 1976 to 2001* (Washington, D.C.: Government Printing Office, U.S. Department of Education, National Center for Education Statistics, 2004), pp. 33–38; U.S. Department of Education, "The Traditionally Black Institutions of Higher Education: Their Development and Status, 1860 to 1982," in *Historical Report* (Washington, D.C.: National Center for Education Statistics, 1985).

17. First professional degrees are the first entry level professional degrees linked to such areas of practice as medicine, dentistry, law, architecture, pharmacy, social work, religious ministry, engineering, accounting, education, forestry, etc. A first professional degree is generally required by law to practice the profession without limitation. On the

other hand, an advanced professional degree provides further training in a specialized area of a chosen profession.

18. Jacqueline Fleming, *Blacks in College: A Comparative Study of Students' Success in Black and in White Institutions* (San Francisco: Jossey-Bass, 1984); and Henry Bullock, *A History of Negro Education in the South, from 1619 to thePresent* (New York: Praeger, 1970).

19. Donald H. Smith, *Admission and Attrition Problems of Black Students at Seven Predominantly White Universities* (Washington, D.C.: National Advisory Committee on Black Higher Education and Black Colleges and Universities, 1981); Andrew C. Billingsley, "Building Strong Faculties in Black Colleges," *Journal of Negro Education* 51 no. 1 (1982), pp. 4–15; Kofi Lomotey, ed., *Going to School: The African-American Experience* (New York: State University of New York Press, 1989); Walter R. Allen, "Black Student, White Campus: Structural, Interpersonal and Psychological Correlates of Success," *Journal of Negro Education* 54 no. 2 (1985), pp. 28–29, 135–47; National Commission on Testing and Public Policy, *From Gate Keeper to Gateway: Transforming Testing in America* (Boston: Boston College, 1989).

20. Sarah Karnasiewicz "Apartheid America: Jonathan Kozol Rails Against a Public School System That, 50 Years After Brown v. Board of Education, Is Still Deeply and Shamefully Segregated," http://dir.salon.com/story/mwt/feature/2005/09/22/kozol/index 2.html; and Institute on Race and Poverty, *Examining the Relationship between Housing, Education, and Persistent_Segregation: Final Report* (Minneapolis: University of Minnesota, 2007).

21. Institute on Race and Poverty, p.21

22. Ibid, p. 303.

23. A. Hacker, "Trans-National America"; *New Work Review of Books* 37, no. 18 (1990); and E. Frankenberg, G. Siegel-Hawley, and G. Wang, *Choice Without Equity: Charter School Segregation and the Need for Civil Rights Standards* (Los Angeles: Civil Rights Project, 2010).

24. William B. Harvey and Lea E. Williams, "History of Black Colleges: Models for Increasing Minority Representation," *Education and Urban Society* 21, no.3 (1989): pp. 328–40.

25. Ronald Walters, "A Cultural Strategy for the Survival of Historically Black Colleges and Universities," paper presented at the annual conference of the National Council for Black Studies, Atlanta, Georgia, March 1991; Walter R. Allen, Joseph O. Jewell, Kimberly A. Griffin and De'Sha S. Wolf, "Historically Black Colleges and Universities: Honoring the Past, Engaging the Present, Touching the Future," *Journal of Negro Education* 76, no.3 (2007), pp. 263–280; Justin Pope, "Graduation Rates Dismal at Most U.S. Black Colleges," Associated Press, March 29, 2009.

26. U.S. Department of Education, National Center for Education Statistics, Digest of Education Statistics, 2005, (NCES 2006–030), p. 464; U.S. Department of Education, National Center for Education Statistics, "Employees in Postsecondary Institutions, Fall 2007" (Washington, D.C.: December 2008), p. 8.

27. Willa M. Hemmons, "From the Halls of Hough and Halstedt: A Comparison of Black Students on Predominantly White and Predominantly Black Campuses," *Journal of Black Studies*, 12 (1982), 383–402; and Andrew C. Billingsley, "Building Strong Faculties in Black Colleges."

28. Alberto F. Cabrera, Amaury Nora, Patrick T. Terenzini, Ernest Pascarella, and Linda S. Hagedorn. "Campus Racial Climate and the Adjustment of Students to College: A Comparison Between White Students and African American Students," *The Journal of Higher Education* 70, no.2 (1999), pp. 134–160; Mitzi Davis, Yvonne Dias-Bowie, Katherine Greenberg, Gary Klukken, Howard R. Pollio, Sandra P. Thomas, "A Fly in the Buttermilk: Descriptions of University Life by Successful Black Undergraduate Students at a Predominantly White Southeastern University," *The Journal of Higher Education*, 75, no. 4 (2004), pp. 420–445; Donald R. Deskins, "Winners and Losers: A Regional Assessment of Minority Enrollment and Earned Degrees in U.S. Colleges and Universities, 1974–84," in Walter

R. Allen, Edgar G. Epp, and Nesha Z. Haniff, ed., *Colleges in Black and White*, Albany: State University of New York Press, 1991, pp. 17–39; Derrick Love, "Revitalizing Retention Efforts for African-American College Students at Predominantly White Institutions," *Proceedings of the Allied Academies* 15, no.2 (2008): 117–122; and Wanda M. Costen, Steven N. Waller, and Angela J. Wozencroft, "Does Race Matter? Understanding the Role of Social Connectedness in Student Retention in Hospitality Programs," *International CHRIE Conference-Refereed Track* Paper 7 (July 28, 2010); and Brent Mallinckrodt and William E. Sedlacek, "Student Retention and the Use of Campus Facilities by Race," *NASPA Journal* 49, no. 4 (2009), pp. 566–572.

29. Xiaojie Li, "Characteristics of Minority-Serving Institutions and Minority Undergraduates Enrolled in These Institutions," National Center for Education Statistics, U.S. Department of Education NCES 2008–156 (Washington, D.C.: Government Printing Office, 2007).

30. U.S. Department of Education, National Center for Education Statistics, Digest of Education Statistics, 2005, (NCES 2006–030), 384.

31. Stephen Provasnik and Linda L. Shafer, *Historically Black Colleges and Universities, 1976 to 2001* (Washington, D.C.: Government Printing Office, 2004), pp. 34.

32. Mikyung Ryu, *Twenty-Third Status Report: Minorities in Higher Education, 2009 Supplement* (Washington, D.C.: American Council on Education, 2009).

33. Provasnik and Shafer, p. 35.

34. Ryu.

35. J. H. Wyche and H. T. Frierson, Jr., "Minorities at Majority Institutions," *Policy Forum* 31 (1990): pp. 989–991.

36. Ibid.; and James R. Mingle, *Trends in Higher Education Participation and Success: Focus on Minorities, Education Commission of the States* (Denver, CO: State Higher Education Executive Officers, 1987).

37. Provasnik and Shafer, p. 37.

38. Ryu.

39. D.C. Thompson, *A Black Elite: A Profile of Graduates of UNCF Colleges* (Westport, CT: Greenwood, 1986).

40. "Education Pays 2010," http://trends.collegeboard.org/education_pays, accessed on December 19, 2010.

41. Walter R. Allen, "Black Student, White Campus: Structural, Interpersonal and Psychological Correlates of Success," *Journal of Negro Education* 54 no. 2 (1985).

42. Andrew C. Billingsley, "Building Strong Faculties in Black Colleges"; B.B. Dupre, "Problems Regarding the Survival of Future Black Teachers in Education," *Journal of Negro Education* 55 (1986), pp. 58–63; and Harvey and Williams, "History of Black Colleges: Models for Increasing Minority Representation."

43. Harvey and Williams, "History of Black Colleges: Models for Increasing Minority Representation."

44. Sidney J. Barthelemy, "The Role of Black Colleges in Nurturing Leadership," in Antoine Garibaldi ed., *Black Colleges and Universities* (New York: Praeger, 1984), pp. 14–25.

45. Ibid.

46. Ibid.

47. J.T. Gibbs, "Patterns of Adaptation Among Black Students at a Predominantly White University," *American Journal of Orthopsychiatry* 44 (1974), pp. 728–40; and K. Davis and J. Swartz, *Increasing Black Students in Predominantly White North Carolina Colleges and Universities* (New York: College Entrance Examination Board, 1972); and Walter R. Allen, "Black Student, White Campus: Structural, Interpersonal and Psychological Correlates of Success"; and Costen, Waller, and A. J. Wozencroft, "Does Race Matter?"

48. Temple Jolly, "Why Choose An HBCU?" [Goldsboro, NC] *News Argus*, October 24, 2009.

49. Walter R. Allen, Edgar G. Epp, and Nesha Z. Haniff, eds., *College in Black and White: African-American Students in Predominantly White and in Historically Black Public Universities* (Albany: State University of New York Press, 1991).

50. Walter R. Allen, "The Color of Success: African-American College Student Outcomes at Predominantly White and Historically Black Public Colleges and Universities," *Harvard Educational Review* 62 no. 1 (1992): pp. 26–43; Gail E. Thomas, *Black College Students and Factors Influencing Their Major Field Choice* (Atlanta: Southern Education Foundation, 1984), pp. 389–99; Patricia Gurin and Edgar G. Epps, *Black Consciousness, Identity and Achievement: A Study of Students in Historically Black Colleges* (New York: Wiley, 1975).

51. Gurin and Epps.

52. Charlie Nelms, "HBCU Reconstruction," *The Presidency* 13, no. 1 (2010): 14–19; Harold Hogkinson, *All One System* (Washington D.C.: Institute for Educational Leadership, 1985).

53. Shaun R. Harper, Lori D. Paton, and Ontario S. Wooden, "Access and Equity for African American Students in Higher Education: A Critical Historical Analysis of Policy Efforts," *The Journal of Higher Education,* vol. 80, no.4 (July/August 2009), 389–414.

3

Survival Management Becomes Academic Autocracy

KOMANDURI S. MURTY AND JULIUS SCIPIO

[At Tuskegee]... in my mind's eye I see the bronze statue of the college Founder, the cold Father symbol, his hands outstretched in the breathtaking gesture of lifting a veil that flutters in hard metallic folds about the face of a kneeling slave, and I am standing puzzled, unable to decide whether the veil is really being lifted, or lowered more firmly into place; whether I am witnessing a revelation or more efficient blinding.

— Ralph Ellison[1]

An autocratic president stands between the faculty and the trustees of a college as the executive head of the institution with great power and broad discretion. He is the confidential adviser of the board in all matters of internal affairs of the college and his advice is seldom ignored. The board places in his hands the right of employing and discharging teachers at will, and often without an assigned cause. Even in the matters where faculty are assigned certain powers, the president keeps authority not only to veto, but to reverse their decisions, and when that happens his decision is final. Although such cases have a provision for appeal to the trustees, it is quite common for the trustees to support the president's decision. It may appear, from the outset, that the president's opinion is the college policy; but, in reality, his opinion mirrors the will of trustees because his existence and continuity depends on them. In other words, should the trustees doubt his loyalty and obedience he would be terminated. For example, E.L. Blackshear of Prairie View College in Texas and Thomas DeSaille Tucker of Florida Colored Normal School were fired when they stepped outside the boundaries that the boards set for them.[2]

On the other hand, Laurence C. Jones continued in his position as head of Piney Woods School in Mississippi for sixty years by carefully heeding the will of his white friends, seeking their advice and frequently sanctioning, and staying away from politics. In such situations, college faculty is neither in a position of asserting themselves or commanding their president's respect. Deprived of real authority, the faculty stand powerless before the president, who, in turn, stands powerless before the trustees in times of conflict. In essence, the president's views of college policy are modeled after the trustees, who control him rather than those he is hired to serve. He finds it necessary to discredit the views of faculty, no matter how crucial they may be for academic standards, when they are not aligned with the expectations of the trustees in order to stay in their good graces. The autocratic president is also a fanatic on the subject of "efficiency," which, to him, means mere "activity," not fruitful one but mindless activity of a kitten chasing its tail, a mere "paper exercise" without any purpose-driven or goal-orientation. This ideal he copies from his trustees as a way of pleasing them and uses it for advertising purposes, while omitting intellectual labor. The college president, in this situation, acts as a tyrant directing a body of experts and his very ignorance makes it unsafe to place the power of official life and death in his hands. The following example of Dr. Lewis K. McMillan, a professor of history at South Carolina State College, illustrates this scenario.[3]

A noted expert of the day in the history of the reconstructed South and distinguished history professor at South Carolina State College, McMillan earned his A.B. from Howard, B.Div. from Yale, and Ph.D. from the University of Bonn, Germany. In 1952 he self-published *Negro Education in the State of South Carolina*. In this work, he examined nine private colleges (five junior colleges and four senior colleges) and one public college in light of their grounds and buildings, purposes, and historical significance; and, found that although the conditions were typical of many Southern states, they were worse in South Carolina than in most. He charged college administrators with the fostering paternalism, and despotism, while proclaiming that the colleges were "failures" and "cut off from the currents of American educational and cultural life." That was the time that no African American had a real voice in the administration of the college. Its board of trustees consisted of six men, all white, representing businessmen and professionals of the Orangeburg region. Though the board was a powerful entity, the routine decisions were left to the president of the college. Benner C. Turner was the president at the time, whom the board selected in 1950 after satisfactorily answering two questions: (1) Do you believe in, and will you support, the Southern philosophy of race and education in administering the affairs of this institution? and, (2) Are you a member of the National Association for the Advancement of Colored People?[4]

On February 3, 1953, when Turner learned about McMillan's forthcoming book he confronted him and reminded him of the policy of (his) administration to "forbid any member of the staff to vilify the college or any sister institution in the State" and warned that he would be brought before the board of trustees for action, should his book prove to be of such character. Three months later, when the book was published McMillan learned from a college janitor that he was dismissed. The next day he received a letter from the president that terminated his employment. Neither the department chair nor dean had been informed of the dismissal of McMillan. When he sought to appeal to the board, the secretary of the board said, "Write your letter to the president. If he sees fit, he will turn it over to us." When he tried to appeal to the Southern Association of Colleges and Secondary Schools, it turned him down, saying the Association "does not have the time or the staff to investigate cases of individual misunderstanding between professors and administrations." In addition, the presidents of other black colleges were warned that he was a "troublemaker" and discouraged them from hiring him. In sum, it was a matter of scholarship, academic freedom, and struggle for justice to McMillan; and to the president Turner, it was a matter of survival strategy. Perhaps it did not come as a complete shock to McMillan because in an earlier work he saw the black college president as "an ignorant autocrat" who "stands a surer chance of keeping his job to the extent that he is hostile to the best interests of his own people" because "he is chosen by boards which are not in the least governed by the wishes of the faculty, the students, the parents, or the public at large."[5] Referring to the black college president's ordeal of "activity" to please his board, McMillan said:

> As regards the school administrators, like Tuskegee, their primary aid is to make a favorable impression. The noble purpose of creating fine, independent, original individual is not on the

college's program. For what do low-brow, cringing slaves know of independence and creativeness anyway! Long hours are spent in training the choir. Of course the music appreciation of the student group is neglected. The choir is not meant for them. Its business is to make friends for the school. When trustees and white friends visit the campus in goodly numbers the school closes down. The most beautiful girls are sent posthaste to the dining hall "for whites" and the president actually becomes head-waiter.[6]

Such an expectation on the part of board members from presidents is also affirmed by a Louisiana president who told Horace Mann Bond that they "ask you to do things and it's right that you should go do it. They give you your job. The other night I was got up at 2 o'clock in the morning doctoring on one of the school board member's horses." The presidents are also expected to apprise the board of what was going on inside the black community.[7]

The Impact of Private Philanthropy and Industrial Education on Academic Autocracy

Anchored in the nineteenth and early twentieth century theses of "scientific" racism, social Darwinism, and the eugenics movement, whites found ample justification for the hierarchical order of races, in which the naturally inferior blacks "must always occupy a socially subservient position." Industrial education, therefore, was seen as an appropriate method of educating blacks not only as a progressive reform, but also as a way to fill the void in southern agriculture created by black emancipation.[8] The white founder of Hampton Institute, General Samuel Chapman Armstrong (1839–1893), submitted the following vision statement to the Missionary Society in 1868:

> The thing to be done ... is clear: to train selected Negro youths who shall go out and teach and lead their people ... to teach respect for labor; to replace stupid drudgery with skilled hands; and in this way to build up an industrial system for the sake, not only of self-support and intelligent labor, but also for the sake of character.[9]

Founded in April 1868 with 15 students and two American Missionary Association appointed staff members (one teacher and one matron), Hampton doubled its student population in a month. Armstrong envisioned Hampton as a manual labor school that would provide (a) teachers for a mostly illiterate, alienated, and displaced black population; (b) training in building character, moral stance, and practicing religion in order to civilize the childlike and impetuous blacks. According to Anderson, the manual labor component was part of Armstrong's "self-help" ideology through which the normal school graduates were believed to possess appropriate values and character to teach the children of the South's black laboring class.[10] When Hampton opened for its first fall term, Armstrong wrote:

> This is no easy machine to run wisely, rightly. The darkies are so full of human nature and have to be most carefully watched over. They are apt to be possessed with strange notions. To simply control them is one thing, but to educate, to draw them out, to develop the germ of good possibilities into firm fruition, requires the utmost care. Eternal vigilance will be the price of success.[11]

Engaging students in manual labor in the mornings and studies in the afternoons and evenings, the Hampton model proved itself profitable to agricultural operations. For example, in the first year of the school, Armstrong cleared $900 for its pea crop; and another $2,000 for vegetables—all raised and harvested in spring of 1878 by students. Hampton did not offer bachelor's degrees; no standard four-year unified curriculum was adopted; and, did not offer any trade certificates until 1895, twenty-seven years after its founding. Hampton students came with a shaky elementary education and a condition for admission was the "intention to remain through the whole course and become a teacher." In Armstrong's view, industrial education served the purpose of accommodating blacks in the *new South*, where the "ignorant and degraded colored masses" had no use for Latin, Greek, or the higher mathematics. All that the teachers needed was a course in practical English and some comprehension of the needs of race and a genuine missionary spirit.[12]

For each annual commencement, Armstrong invited dignitaries including politicians, clergymen, journalists, and philanthropists from everywhere so that he could show off the school, its curriculum, and its graduates. Typically, these visiting guests toured the campus in the morning and quizzed students on what they learned. They listened to choral renditions of the Negro spirituals during noon meal and, during the celebration, Armstrong displayed his finished product (graduates) to impress white supporters and extol the Hampton ability in "cleaning up" black people and making them polite and useful: all to justify and attract additional funding.[13] Charles Brace, a guest at the 1875 commencement remarked:

> The girls looked like respectable working-girls, and the boys much as young country teachers would anywhere. All had remarkably good heads, and many showed large frontal development of the brain; some few were so white that at the North no one would have dreamed of their being of the negro race.[14]

Thus, no one could (or should) appear snobbish or threatening to the existing social order or their own subservient position in the South. Watkins asserted that Armstrong's 20 years of writings on politics, race, and education in *The Southern Workman*, a school newspaper that he founded in 1872, supported "black subservience and a sociopolitical inequality that characterized the next 100 years." Armstrong understood that both southern moderates and northern industrialists wanted social order without disturbing traditional race relations; that is, blacks should have been midway between slavery and freedom as semi-citizens with semi-freedom, which required a change, but, not too much of one, while at the same time, the northern industrial working class labor and wage system should remain unthreatened by peonage.[15] Armstrong himself wrote about southern class structure thus:

> In the old regime in the South there were three classes, whose fortunes have somewhat changed. The aristocracy or gentry being generally bankrupt, and without adaptation to the new order of things, are struggling against a tide of troubles. But some this class have met the change with wisdom and energy, and by making the best of things are improving their fortunes and have become rallying points of new efforts and hopes. The poor whites and the Negroes were the other two classes.[16]

Although Armstrong believed that blacks had intellectual capacity to learn, he did not think they required book knowledge. Instead, he thought they required the knowledge that would aid them out of the "ruts of barbarism." He identified the necessary tools as the knowledge of industry, self-restraint, and decency. Because blacks could not improve themselves, Armstrong believed in the spirit of the missionary, i.e., the teacher becoming the major agent in the development of civilization. That's what the Hampton model was expected to do: train black teachers.[17]

"The negro teacher is the hope of his race; he is looked up to; his influence for good or evil is vast; when well-fitted for his work he has not been found wanting. What the colored race needs most, and needs now, is teachers of the right sort, as well as preachers fitted for the pulpit by some stern discipline. Let us make the teachers and we will make the people."[18] Inspired by the Hampton ideal, Booker T. Washington, a Hampton student, became Armstrong's protégé; and, as a result, not only replicated the industrial education at Tuskegee but also became an enthusiastic advocate for it for several decades as a black leader. LeMelle and LeMelle, characterizing him as the "Wizard from Tuskegee," summarized his Atlanta Exposition speech in the following lines:

As President of Hampton Institute, Samuel C. Armstrong believed that it was the responsibility of the white race to rule over the weaker dark-skinned races until they were appropriately civilized. The primary means through which white civilization could be instilled in African Americans was by the moral power of labor and manual industry. As a result, during Armstrong's tenure at Hampton Institute, the main emphasis of training was on labor and industry (courtesy Williams College Archives and Special Collections, Williamstown, Mass., USA).

In the address Washington proclaimed his doctrine of economic development and growth for the black American, the acceptance of black disenfranchisement, the conciliation of the white South. It was a call for black America to give up the Reconstruction emphasis on rights for an emphasis on duties — a call from demands for integration to humble acquiescence and self-betterment. It was a statement of the philosophy of "Cast down your bucket where you are" as opposed to that of "Let your reach exceed your grasp.[19]

Thomas Jesse Jones, who worked at Hampton from 1902 to 1909, also aligned with Booker T. Washington in supporting industrial education for blacks. He argued that the relative poverty of blacks and their highly emotional nature made industrial education even more necessary for them than for whites. Jones joined the Phelps Stokes Foundation in 1912, where he spent the next 32 years as its educational director and "became an influential white architect of Negro education." During Jones' term, Phelps Stokes was able to influence philanthropic foundations shaping black education, such as the Rockefeller, Jeannes, and Slater foundations among others. Jones also worked with various missionary associations that cooperated with the corporate philanthropists. He knew that funding black schools was a way to influence black education, thereby maintaining the racial subservience of the status quo. Both Jones and Phelps Stokes emphasized that industrial education was the answer for progressive social change and that foundations could successfully motivate oppressed people to accept their ideologies. For example, Jones, in his book: *The Four Essentials of Education,* included "training for social civic responsibilities; health; recreational and aesthetic participation; and practical and occupational efficiency." To Jones, the central objective of the curriculum should focus on "consciousness of community"; that is, educa-

Booker T. Washington, founder of Tuskegee Institute and student of Samuel Chapman Armstrong. During his career as leader of Tuskegee Institute Washington was one of the leading proponents of industrial education (Library of Congress Prints and Photographs Division, LC-USZ62-128954).

tion for civic responsibility, the common good, and the essentials of group life — all of which served a civilizing mission by molding and developing character. Thus, all these essentials were within the realm of the Hampton model of industrial education, gradualism, and incrementalism.[20]

As Anderson noted, by 1915, the missionary societies established more than 30 colleges which enrolled over 60 percent of the college-level black students. Of them, Talladega, Atlanta University, Clark, Spelman, Morehouse, and Fisk are the more commonly known. Interestingly, missionary societies exercised ownership of these schools, but financial support came from the corporate philanthropies including the Slater Fund, Rosenwald Fund, Jeannes Foundation, Peabody Education Fund, Carnegie Corporation, and others. The influence of these foundations grew along with their power and wealth. By World War I the industrial philanthropies had supplanted missionary societies as the leading influence in black education. This adaptation and accommodation dominated education, the curriculum, and social policy for decades.[21]

Immune from the threat of elections, philanthropic agencies like Rockefeller and Phelps Stokes wielded government-like power. They were private entities making sweeping educational and public policy and they were accountable only to themselves. Further, since they could finance and administer projects completely, their actions had the effect of law. No twentieth-century quasi-government or nongovernment organization has enjoyed such influence thus far.

The Impact of White Southern Mores on Academic Autocracy

As pointed out by Anderson and Moss, the atmosphere of deteriorating race relations in the early twentieth century largely contributed to the intense opposition of southern whites even to the mildest program reform, because such reforms were viewed as attempts to elevate blacks at the expense of southern whites. To these southern white opponents, the promoters of black schools were "training the negroes to the vain hope of social equality with whites," and by doing so blacks would be of "less material advantage to them." Thus, the fear of southern white opposition played an important role in the structuring of northern philanthropy for the South.[22]

Some white and black observers felt that black schools were less effective, often pointing to black control as the basic problem. For example, B. C. Caldwell, white field officer of two influential philanthropic agencies, documented his belief in his reports that black schools run by white churches were superior because they had the "advantage in buildings, equipment, sanitation, refinement of surroundings, quality of teaching, and wholesomeness of living conditions." On the other hand, black controlled schools were "marked by detachment, isolation, frequently carried to the point of open hostility toward contact with white people, and a more or less skeptical attitude toward public schools controlled by white officials." Yet, grudgingly conceding to them, Caldwell admitted that schools run by the black churches had "close, direct relations with great body of negro population," which attracted "the sturdiest students to their classes."[23]

In the midst of these southern mores, many black colleges could not find much use for academic freedom or controversy. They preferred to hire only safe and congenial instructors rather than controversial ones and, if they did hire someone by mistake who did not "fit in" or who "did not understand the local situation," he was easily eliminated. In return, most of the Northern white colleges were reluctant to hire black administrators and faculty, leaving no safety net for blacks. If they lost their jobs as professors, the best available alternative in those days was a poorly paid federal civil service job in the Post Office or in similar establishments. Jenkins and Riesman observed the prevailing situation for blacks and whites as:

> So Negroes had to be cautious, for the consequences of a false move looked (and often were) disastrous. Understandably, Negroes living under such pressures were extremely resentful of the relative freedom of their more mobile white colleagues, and were bitter when such men criticized the ways in which Negroes kept the peace with local whites. The whites in turn could often feel that the career sacrifices they were making and the difficulties for their own families were not appreciated or understood by Negroes, for whom a professorship, even at a Negro college was one of the best positions a Negro could hope for.[24]

Black colleges provided a comparably free and more comfortable environment for educated blacks. For example, black critics of racial segregation could express their views on black college campuses like Tougaloo College, Fisk, Howard, and Atlanta universities. Integrated professional meetings were also held at Atlanta University, despite restrictions for such meetings on the local white campuses of Georgia Tech and Georgia State University. Similar situations prevailed in other places, where both black and white colleges were located in the same area. In other words, black campuses were sealed off from white world to keep whites from noticing their activities, as a strategy on the part of presidents to protect their faculty and students. It became necessary for black college presidents, more than their white counterparts, to rely on the "weapons of the weak: guile, charm, oratory, and seeming compliance" in order to maintain their connections with cosmopolitan whites and creating some breathing space in the black community.[25]

The Impact of Southern Communities and White Civic Leaders on HBCU Academic Autocracy

The intolerance of southern communities and white civic leaders toward black education can be illustrated by the history of Barber-Scotia College. Barber Memorial College of Anniston, Alabama, was established to educate African-American women. From the school's establishment, many in Alabama resented the college because it offered black women a way to escape backbreaking labor in the cotton fields, thus further reducing a fragile labor base. Twice between 1880 and 1910 the main building burned under suspicious circumstances. Each time the Northern Presbyterian Church quickly rebuilt the school. However, in the years before the second fire, campus leaders of Barber Memorial College, in an attempt to keep from upsetting members of the community, restricted certain majors and also ruled with an iron fist, stifling any efforts by the faculty that might be seen as unsettling to the white Anniston community.[26]

In 1929, after a fire devastated Barber a third time, church leaders sought to merge with Scotia Seminary, which also offered industrial, preparatory, and seminary education to colored girls (because such education was deemed necessary as those qualities were thought to be desirable for the highest type of mother and teacher). Scotia, chartered by Rev. Luke Dorland in 1870 in Concord, North Carolina, survived its own threats from angry southern whites who forced Dorland to seek refuge on more than one occasion in the loft of a barn.[27]

At any rate, at Scotia, college leaders severely limited student freedoms. Under the presidency of Dr. A.W. Verner, students were not allowed to write more than two letters (usually to families) and none of them were allowed to be addressed to boyfriends. All letters were to remain unsealed so that they could be read before mailing. All incoming packages and some letters were opened. If any student was caught in violation of the letter policy they were disciplined with demerits or by a loss of privileges. Day students had to get special permission to go to upper flights of dorms to visit classmates who lived at the college.[28]

Scotia also suffered from a poor financial base in terms of its ability to grow. To reduce costs students milked cows, fed hogs and chickens, performed janitorial tasks, and cooked and worked on the grounds. Even so, financial problems continued to plague the institution until 1929 when the burning of Alabama's Barber Memorial College allowed the School to receive the finances it needed to survive. For Scotia the prospect of the merger was made more appealing by the fact that Barber College's endowment was rumored to be more than $250,000. The amount actually received after the merger was less than $30,000. Despite this disappointment, Scotia continued to grow. In 1932, the name was changed to Barber-Scotia College. Fifteen years later the college awarded its first Bachelor's degree.[29]

Burke Industrial School in Charleston, South Carolina, presents another example. Burke was built on a dump in 1910, designed to maintain white supremacy and black subordination, the curriculum was based on the Hampton/Tuskegee model, and well into the twentieth century, the authorities believed that the school's purpose was to prepare students for jobs that were available "under present conditions." As young blacks were pushed out of the labor force in 1930s, School Superintendent A. B. Rhett created new courses "to supply cooks, maids, and delivery boys." Educational authorities in Charleston continued to control the outer reality of schooling at Burke until 1940s. There was not much sympathy or support for the idea of giving black students the opportunity to get a full education because of the prevailing attitude that black students had no need for intellectual development.[30]

The Black Quest for Civil Rights on Academic Autocracy

Miles Wolff, in his book entitled *Lunch at the 5 & 10*, chronicled how four college students launched a peaceful but successful protest against prevailing social order of white supremacy (and the local Jim Crow policies) through sit-in demonstrations at a North Carolina Woolworth's lunch counter.[31] On February 1, 1960, four African-American freshmen enrolled at the North Carolina Agricultural and Technical College (Franklin McCain, Ezell Blair Jr., Joseph McNeil and David Richmond), who were refused service at the Greensboro Woolworth's, sat down on stools that had, until that moment, been occupied exclusively by white customers, and refused to get up and leave. By the next day, February 2, the students were joined by several other students from North Carolina A&T. Nonviolent demonstrations cropped up outside the store, while other protesters had a turn at the counter. Sit-ins erupted in other North Carolina cities and segregationist states. There are ten black colleges within the radius of ninety miles of Greensboro, and about one hundred in the South. The students in other colleges and small universities, especially black schools, felt their problems were similar.[32]

That A&T was the epicenter of this protest surprised many. Dr. Ferdinand D. Bluford, president from 1925 to 1955, was known to be highly autocratic. He carefully selected his faculty and did not accept any of their dissent; threatened to fire them should they choose to join and/or participate in the NAACP; and, told them "you will make it here if you didn't move too fast or protest too much." He performed acts in public to please whites as a necessary strategy to increase funding chances for his school, but had a habit of returning nearly one-half of the budget at the end of each year to remain in the good books of the state legislature. His office was commonly known as "Uncle Tom's Cabin." Following the *Brown* decision, he served on the 19-member Special Advisory Committee of Governor Hodges (who vowed to continue segregation) as one of the only three black members and voted along with white members to pass the Pupil Assignment Act for removing state control over education and returning it to local school boards—a brilliant strategy the anti-desegregation whites came up with to facilitate an escape mechanism to protect the state from being sued by the NAACP and others for not adhering to the federal desegregation policy. In 1955, he sent a strong apology to Governor Hodges for the embarrassment caused by the student body when he mispronounced "negro" at the inaugural speech. Obviously, he would not have tolerated the sit-ins. Even under the administration of Bluford's successor, Dr. Warmoth T. Gibbs, speakers like Martin Luther King Jr. and Thurgood Marshall were denied an opportunity to speak at A&T in the late fifties because they were viewed as too controversial, a tradition that had continued since President Dudley (1896–1925). However, Gibbs made no attempt to stop the students as he saw nothing in the college rules "that said the students could not do something of this sort on their own free time." Although he made it clear that he had not given his consent, he explained his position thus: "the students feel deeply and sincerely that they have important basic interests at stake in the situation. They feel these matters so strongly that threats of arrest or intimidation do not seem to deter them. Consequently, this feeling must be understood in dealing with them in order to maintain their cooperation."[33]

In contrast, Southern University's Felton Grandison Clark acted decisively to destroy student protests. "Remote and dictatorial," Clark "treated Southern as his personal fiefdom, hiring and firing at will." When confronted with black student protests he threatened students with expulsion and suspension. However, this failed to stop student protests. Yet, when Clark expelled eighteen leaders, administrators at the school feared the backlash would spark a walkout of the institution's four thousand students. The *Louisiana Weekly* denounced Clark for his failure to support the students and carrying out the dictates of the board of education; and, opined that he should have resigned.[34]

However, Clark was not alone. Many frightened public black college presidents and administrators tried their best to discourage or suppress student activism. They harassed and intimidated student activists and when the activists did not cave in to the pressure, the presidents suspended or even expelled the protesters from their campuses. Moreover, the New Orleans chapter of Congress of Racial Equality (CORE) started having internal problems in February 1962, which resulted in the expulsion of fifteen members, most of whom were whites; and, the withdrawal of many more.[35] This, in turn, prefigured interracial tensions instead of racial integration. Fairclough noted:

> After the purge, and partly because of it, the New Orleans chapter lost much of its dynamism. Dominated by Oretha Castle and a small circle of friends, it failed to grow and expand, becoming simply one of several organizations operating within a broad coalition. The chapter's prestige further declined when, in the summer of 1963, it ended its boycott of Canal Street, leaving the NAACP Youth Council to picket alone when the white merchants reneged on their promises of fair employment.[36]

Private black institutions suffered likewise. Joy Ann Williamson described the events at Tougaloo College in Mississippi during the Civil

Rights movement. Nine Tougaloo students started a sit-in at the Jackson Municipal Library in March 1961. The ensuing arrests and media coverage inspired Mississippi African Americans; and therefore, the North Jackson NAACP Youth Council, West Jackson NAACP Youth Council, Tougaloo NAACP youth branch, and others alike protested discrimination and demanded justice. Jackson activists launched another effective boycott of white stores and conducted sit-ins in the following year. In 1961–1962, police arrested over 600 participants and infuriated white Mississippians. As in other places, local police and state agencies did not hesitate to bodily harm, jail or kill activists to take control of the situation. Reverend Dr. Adam D. Beittel, a white president of the college, whom the civil rights activists considered to be the friend of the cause, ended up resigning in September 1964 as the result of suspected conspiracy against him by the Board of Trustees, Brown University, the Ford Foundation, and the Mississippi Sovereignty Commission. Some viewed the financially strapped college seeking its revival through a Ford Foundation funded partnership with Brown University as putting Tougaloo in a vulnerable situation, while others doubted that the Sovereignty Commission's admonition to keep politics off the academic campuses could have precipitated Dr. Beittel's resignation. For example, on February 17, 1964, Lieutenant Governor Carroll Gartin called for an investigation of the college's role in demonstrations and civil rights activities. He reportedly accused the college of providing haven for quacks, quirks, political agitators, and possibly some communists. Gartin also accused the college of completely neglecting its charter by substituting civil disobedience instruction for the curriculum it was authorized to have. Tougaloo's involvement in civil rights activities worsened its relationship with the state; its financial status was further weakened, leaving it to the mercy of philanthropic agencies; and, institutional integrity was lost. The internal and external pressures collided and destabilized the college in 1964.[37]

The Long-Term Utilization of Outdated Management Styles by HBCUs on Academic Autocracy

While both white and black colleges appeared to be similar in terms of committing to the Anglo-Saxon tradition in the beginning, white colleges moved away from the "culture of theology." However, black colleges, which were founded, financed, and administered early on by whites and their churches, continued in that tradition. In fact, in an effort to reassert their equality with white colleges, black colleges were fervently opposed to harboring any habits and values that strayed from the standards set for them earlier by white leaders. LeMelle and LeMelle viewed it as a misguided socialization function because: (1) the relationship between black and white communities is not one of interdependence but one of a dominant majority and dependent minority: a colonial-type relationship; (2) the socialization function of education is to establish the legitimacy of dominant majority (white) values, ideals, and interests, thereby denigrating those of dependent black minority; and, (3) because the black minority has been thwarted in the pursuit of those values, ideals, and interests for such a long time, it was socialized to accept, and did accept the values, ideals, and interests of the majority resulting in the dysfunction to the real needs and interests of the black community.[38] Johnson also thought the basic characteristics of black colleges evolved as a result of adaptation to an often hostile "supersystem"—a conditioning as well as a survival process. He observed:

> Regardless of the kind of black college ... private, state, church-related or not — it is readily apparent that the basic operating decisions of the institution were in the hands of the president. Although there was, and remains, a wide spectrum of presidential behavior—from the modern Bledsoe model at Mississippi Vocational College to the enlightened approaches of some of the younger presidents— the fact remains that the ultimate locus of authority on campus is the presidency.[39]

Thus, although black administrators replaced many of the white presidents and boards in subsequent years, the authoritarian atmosphere which they inherited continued with intervening trustees, domineering but frightened presidents, who tyrannized their faculty. This tyranny was a tendency of the persecuted to identify with their persecutors and take their place at a later time, a process that prevailed in white academic history earlier. LeMelle and LeMelle called it *Presidentialism,* the tendency to relegate arbitrary and absolute decision-making power to the office of the president. This tutelary system of college administration was "imposed from without or considered to be expedient by presidents fearful of incurring white displeasure in any way."[40] Besides this as a survival strategy, the authoritarianism continued beyond its time due to inherent paternalism. In Johnson's words:

> The paternalistic president, like most whites, assumed that the black faculty members, even if capable of making sound educational and administrative decisions, were not responsible enough to execute them without close presidential supervision. Thus, such presidents would spend valuable time investigating the minute details of task execution — even menial activities which one might well have expected custodial and maintenance staffs to execute without such prestigious oversight.[41]

Excessive jealousy and competition among faculty and staff for presidential favor were also seen as a significant contributing factors to presidential control or presidentialism. While faculty, at least collectively, might have influence over academic programs, they received neither significant intrinsic satisfaction from their work (relating to achievement, advancement, recognition and status) nor extrinsic satisfaction from their work environment (relating to pay, security, and policy). On the extrinsic side, working conditions are poor; salaries are far below national average; secretarial and other support services tend to be bad or nonexistent; and the bureaucracy might be unbelievably rigid, and hence frustrating. Presidentialism, of course, tends to be dominant because a president's overarching influence is based on his "authority to hire and fire, to reward and finish, to determine budgetary priorities, and to influence the basic value structure and orientation of the school."[42]

The Survival Strategy

The two-pronged response pattern to white power, i.e., caution (accommodation) and activism (challenge), was most commonly prevalent for most of the 1900s. In order to survive it was necessary for black leaders (and black people in general) to live up to the expectations of those who provided funding and paid their wages. "Many children were taught early to bow and scrape before white folk, lest they endanger themselves and, later, their families," as Chafe wrote. Many black leaders sought for advancement of black community within the existing white power structure. However, there was simultaneously a counter force applied by activists who constantly insisted on the necessity of equality and dignity. To these, black advancement would never come without directly challenging white dominance and oppressiveness.[43]

Subscribing to the first strategy, some black leaders like Booker T.

Washington adopted the ideology of accommodation, which many viewed as an attempt to please the opposition "rather than to resolve the conflict." LeMelle and LeMelle described this ideology further in following lines:

> In the conflict of black-white relations, the ideology of accommodation is the belief that the black American best serves his own interests in an unprotesting acceptance of the role assigned to him in the white community. In terms of changing that role to a more meaningful one, the burden of proof lies with the black man who must demonstrate that he is "worthy" of being given a position more responsible than the one assigned to him.... Obviously, the final arbiter of the black community's capacity for progress is the white community.[44]

The above description is consistent with that of Booker T. Washington below:

> The Negro in the South has it within his power, if he properly utilizes the forces at hand, to make of himself such a valuable factor in the life of the South that he will not have to seek privileges, they will be freely conferred upon him.[45]

In 1916, when Robert Russa Moton was selected to succeed Washington because the board viewed him as "safe, sane, and conservative," he faithfully affirmed the wisdom of the Tuskegee's founder in terms of harmonious cooperation with whites in his inaugural address, "not by arrogant self-seeking, not by bluff, sham, or bombast, not by fault-finding, not by shirking at difficulty, or shirking from duty, not by the cherishing of prejudice against white man ... ignorance, shiftlessness, disease, insufficiency, and crime are entirely too prevalent among our people."[46]

To them and those who embraced their ideology (often referred to as Washingtonians) the accommodationist strategy is safe, provides skillful racial diplomacy, fends off the threat that disfranchisement and open challenges to white supremacy might cause by grossly reducing or eliminating the economic support needed for the survival of black public schools. Their advocacy of industrial education also helped to gain the economic support of northern philanthropists and southern white tax payers. For example, at Tennessee State Agricultural and Industrial Normal School, founded in 1909, college leaders regained the confidence of their white trustees, who suspected the college might be slipping away from its original purpose, when the school's long-serving president William Jasper Hale called upon the assembled students to stand up if they took agriculture and the entire student body got up on its feet. In

Georgia, Rev. Joseph W. Holley sought the support of local whites to the Albany Bible and Manual Training Institute (established in 1903) by promising them to graduate "well-trained domestic servants and efficient farm laborers."[47]

However, opponents criticized many black college presidents for being white man's "biggest Negro" in their leadership style. In 1920s student rebellions began challenging the authority of traditionally autocratic college presidents, and in 1930s black intellectuals confronted southern college presidents as practitioners of a bankrupt strategy. In 1940s and 1950s, despite the apparent tendency of movement of white and black schools in South toward equalization and the Supreme Court ruling on *Brown v. Board of Education*, blacks remained politically powerless and suffered systematic discrimination. Even in 1960s, despite the national visibility of and support for student sit-ins and other forms of defiance on several college campuses, some college presidents like Ferdinand Bluford (North Carolina Agricultural and Technological College), Samuel Proctor (Agricultural and Technological College, Virginia Union), Leland Cozart (Barber-Scotia College), Lionel Newsome (Johnson C. Smith and Central State Colleges), and James Cheek (Shaw University) relied on their traditional autocratic leadership strategies and attempted to stifle student protests in a number of ways: suspension, dismissal of faculty, withholding of resources, etc. Some college presidents, like Warmoth T. Gibbs, adopted an avoidance strategy by passing on the responsibility of handling such protests to their deans and faculty so that if there was any trouble the deans and faculty were the ones to be blamed, and not the presidents.[48]

Yet, the activists continued their demands for reconciliation through equal rights and status for the black man in American society. Organizations like the National Association for the Advancement of Colored People (NAACP) and the Urban League supported this point of view. In the end, neither of the ideologies could create the miracle they were hoping for, and traditional black higher education has generally produced "a cadre of black Americans psychologically unprepared to take on the leadership role normally expected of and assumed by the better educated and trained in any community. As a result, the black community as a whole has been cheated and so has American society in general."[49] Nevertheless, the survival strategy of black colleges remained a necessary function, despite disagreements over ideologies by the leaders and supporters of HBCUs. Johnson said:

> When we talk about resources, however, we must look at the black college to the supersystem: those institutions and persons who control the resources these colleges need to continue to exist. For the black colleges are in the main penurious, and their well-being depends largely on their ability to demonstrate to the potential benefactors in the supersystem —for example, the national foundations, federal and state governments, nonprofit private corporations— that the schools are worthy of their support. Convincing these mostly white potential benefactors of the worthiness of these institutions is, as black college administrators know all too well, not always an easy task.[50]

Samuel Nabrit saw the problem with this trend:

> In fact, their (black colleges) greatest fault has been that they have been forced to imitate in order to be accredited and have not been encouraged to be innovative and independent. They are still assessed by a few foundations and agencies which pass on to the larger giving public their impressions of the colleges' worthiness according to standards set by others rather than those set by the colleges and communities they are intended to serve.[51]

These autocratic presidents, with respect to their ideologies, leadership philosophies, styles, and justifications may be classified into four types. First, the "Moronic" leader, who, ill-equipped to be an effective faculty member given his mediocre academic record, chooses the administrative career path. He serves as a token to white power or powerful boards and his whole purpose is to please them at all times and at all costs, not out of loyalty, but to protect his job. A strong believer in using power to his convenience, he remains shortsighted about the college's future. He fails to build strong academic programs, expand faculty development programs, or to do anything relating to substantive business matters. He is seldom respected by faculty, staff, or students, and is viewed by these groups as self-centered and traitorous. Ellison's characterization of Dr. Bledsoe in his novel *Invisible Man* may fall in this category. Dr. Bledsoe's philosophy of leadership, as he explained was to his student:

> I'se big and black and I say "Yes, suh" as loudly as any burrhead when it's convenient, but I'm still the king down here. I don't care how much it appears otherwise. Power doesn't have to show off. Power is confident, self-assuring, self-starting and self-stopping, self-warming and self-justifying. When you have it, you know it. Let the Negroes snicker and the crackers laugh! Those are the facts, son. The only ones I even pretend to please are the big white folk, and even those I control more than they control me. That is a power set-up, son, and I'm at the controls. You think about that. When you buck against me, you're bucking against power,

rich white folk's power, the nation's power — which means government power![52]

The second type of leader is the "Messiah." This president makes a concerted effort to "save the damned." He expresses feelings of superiority and assumes a paternalistic attitude toward his campus, faculty, and students. Well-educated and knowledgeable about the state of affairs in the community at large, he perceives his mission as "bringing in the sheep." The "Messiah" is not well received by his colleagues as he tends to foster mistrust and feelings of alienation and hostility. Leaders like President Benner C. Turner of South Carolina College belong to this category. President Turner tried to "save" Professor Lewis McMillan, while maintaining his superiority, "Now, Doctor, the policy of the administration-that is, of the president is to forbid any member of the staff to vilify the college or any sister institution in the State. If your book is of such a character, your case will be brought before the Trustee Board for action. Remember, now, Doctor McMillan, that you have a good job here at the college."

Turner made it clear to Lewis that he would be better off by burning the book and keeping his job than publishing it and losing the job, an honest attempt to save him.[53]

The "Marginal Leader" incorporates a conflict of two cultures into his function. Not overly concerned with his opponents' views, this educated leader tries to please both sides: powerful board on one side and the faculty and students on the other. Consequently, this leader assumes the dichotomous roles of community member and alien. As a member of the black community, he experiences cognitive dissonance from both of his worlds wherein he seeks social acceptability. A believer in appeasement, the "Marginal Leader's" function is to work towards an accommodation of two cultures. In this role, he perceives himself as providing a reality contact for each racial group and a communication bridge between them. Most of the early presidents like Booker T. Washington, Robert Moton, and their followers fall within this category.

Finally, the "Run-of-the-mill" type of leader believes in ruling like a tyrant. He is trained in that tradition, has developed a single-focused, "die-hard" authoritative personality, and convinced himself that imposing his will is the only way to "get things done." A "Run-of-the-mill" leader also thinks he "knows it all" and knows what is the best for the college he heads. For him to admit his faults or any wrongdoing is a major sin and for others to point out his mistakes is suicidal. He exercises his power without any regard to the ramifications, even when he witnesses the adverse results. Often these tyrannical leaders blame others for their shortcomings by accusing them of being "lazy, irresponsible, spendthrift, incompetent, visionless, clueless, etc." and, expects faculty to "shut up and put up," by proudly making examples of the victims of his power. He is viewed on campus as "the great cat roaming his domain unbeholden, unrestrained, unafraid, and unreal." If he is fired or receives a vote of "non confidence" at one college, he simply moves to another, but his leadership style does not change. He perfects the methods of forming his own "fiefdoms," and protects them at all costs. Though a false hero, he does achieve some fleeting success (especially when the campus leadership is in turmoil because of high turnover and a highly rebellious campus community), which he uses to justify his actions: i.e. a self-fulfilling prophecy. This leader is disliked and despised by his faculty and students, who breathe a sigh of relief when he leaves the institution. However, the destruction he leaves in his wake sets the institution back decades of growth (depending upon the term he headed the institution). Although President Felton Grandison Clark of Southern University in Louisiana was in this category, examples of this type of leader can be found from the times of establishment of academic institutions to the present.[54]

Notes

1. Ralph Ellison, *Invisible Man* (New York: Vintage, 1972), p. 36.

2. George R.Woolfolk, *Prairie View: A Study in Public Conscience, 1878–1946* (New York: Pageant, 1962), pp. 108–198; Gilbert L. Porter and Leedell W. Neyland, *History of the Florida State Teachers Association* (Washington, D.C.: National Education Association, 1977), pp. 43–46.

3. "Negro Historian Fired for Attack on South Carolina College System: McMillan Was Warned By President Turner Not to Print Book," *The Harvard Crimson* (June 17, 1954); and Alferdteen B. Harrison, *Piney Woods School: An Oral History* (Jackson: University Press of Mississippi 1982), pp. 109, 116.

4. "Negro Historian Fired for Attack on South Carolina College System: McMillan Was Warned By President Turner Not to Print Book," *The Harvard Crimson* (June 17, 1954).

5. Lewis K. McMillan, "Negro Higher Education as I Have Known It," *Journal of Negro Education*, 8 (January 1939), pp. 14–15, 18.

6. Ibid.

7. Horace Mann Bond and Julia W. Bond, *The Star Creek Papers: Washington Parish and the Lynching of Jerome Wilson* (Athens: University of Georgia Press, 1997), pp. 43–45.

8. William H. Watkins, *The White Architects of Black Education* (New York: Teachers College Press, 2001), pp. 24–40.

9. Ibid., pp. 47–48.

10. James D. Anderson, *The Education of Blacks in the South: 1860–1935* (Chapel Hill: University of North Carolina Press, 1988), p. 34.

11. Edith A. Talbot, *Samuel Chapman Armstrong: A Biographical Study* (New York: Doubleday, Page, 1904), 170–171.

12. Louis R. Harlan, *The Booker T. Washington Papers*, (Urbana: University of Illinois Press, 1972), p. 49; Edith A. Talbot, *Samuel Chapman Armstrong: A Biographical Study* (New York: Doubleday, Page, 1904), p. 169; and Anderson, *The Education of Blacks in the South*, p. 34.

13. Anderson, *The Education of Blacks in the South*, p. 34.

14. Louis R. Harlan, *The Booker T. Washington Papers*, p. 55.

15. Watkins, *The White Architects of Black Education*, pp. 52–53.

16. Samuel C. Armstrong, *The Southern Workman* (April 1876), p. 26, quoted in Watkins, *The White Architects of Black Education*, p. 53.

17. William H. Watkins, *The White Architects of Black Education*, pp. 52–53.

18. Samuel C. Armstrong, *The Southern Workman* (December 1877), p. 94, quoted in Watkins, *The White Architects of Black Education*, p. 59.

19. Tilden J. LeMelle and Wilbert J. Lemelle, *The Black College: A Strategy for Relevancy* (New York: Praeger, 1969, p. 46).

20. Watkins, *The White Architects of Black Education*, p. 110; Thomas Jesse Jones, *Four Essentials of Education* (New York: Scribner's, 1926), 9; and S.T. Correia, "For Their Own Good," (Ph.D. dissertation, University of Chicago, 1993), p. 272.

21. For example, American Missionary Association, Methodist Episcopal Freedman's Aid Society, Presbyterian Board of Missions for the Freedman, and American Baptist Home Mission Society.

22. Eric Anderson and Alfred A. Moss Jr., *Dangerous Donations: Northern Philanthropy and Southern Black Education, 1902–1930* (Columbia: University of Missouri Press, 1999), p. 7.

23. B. C. Caldwell, "Report to Conference of State Agents for Negro Rural Schools," Battery Park Hotel, Asheville, North Carolina, November 26–28, 1921, in General Education Board Papers, Box 28, Folder 1998, Rockefeller Archive Center, Pocantico Hills, New York, quoted in Anderson and Moss, *Dangerous Donations*, p.19.

24. Christopher Jenkins and David Riesman, *The Academic Revolution* (New York: Doubleday, 1968), p. 420.

25. Ibid., pp. 420–421.

26. Ibid.

27. James E. Lyons, "In the Beginning Faith: Oral History of Barber-Scotia College," unpublished paper, Barber-Scotia College, 1976, p. 2.

28. Ibid., 30–31.

29. Vann Newkirk, "Barber-Scotia College: A Case for Faith-Based Education," paper presented to the Barber-Scotia Board of Trustees, October 2005.

30. Scott Baker, "Education and Equality: African-American Teachers and the Civil Rights Movement, 1940–1963," in *Beauty is in the Details: A Global View of Persons of Color* (Scarborough, ME: National Association of African American Studies and Affiliates, 2010), pp. 1024–1040.

31. Miles Wolff, *Lunch at the 5 & 10* (Chicago: Elephant, 1970), p. 165

32. Ibid.

33. Ibid.; William H. Chafe, *Civilities and Civil Rights: Greensboro, North Carolina, and the Black Struggle for Freedom* (Oxford: Oxford University Press, 1980), pp. 21–23, 50, 61.

34. Adam Fairclough, *Race and Democracy: The Civil Rights Struggle in Louisiana, 1915–1972* (Athens, GA: University of Georgia Press, 1995), pp. 266, 270; J. Farmer, *Lay Bare the Heart: An Autobiography of the Civil Rights Movement* (New York: Arbor House, 1985), p. 193.

35. K. Tollett, "Southern Justice for Blacks," *Ebony* (1971), p. 60.

36. Fairclough, *Race and Democracy*, p. 296.

37. Joy Ann Williamson, "This Has Been Quite a Year for Heads Falling: Institutional Autonomy in the Civil Rights Era," *History of Education Quarterly 44* (2004), pp. 554–576.

38. Tilden J. LeMelle and Wilbert J. Lemelle, *The Black College: A Strategy for Relevancy* (New York: Frederick A. Praeger, 1969), 62. A few private black colleges such as Morris Brown in Atlanta, Wilberforce in Ohio, Shorter in Little Rock, Edward Waters College in Jacksonville, Paul Quinn College in Texas, Livingstone Colleges in North Carolina, and Allen University in South Carolina were controlled by all-black denominations.

39. Tobe Johnson, "The Black College as System," *Daedalus* 100 (1971), 800.

40. Tilden J. LeMelle and Wilbert J. Lemelle, *The Black College*, 85; and Christopher Jencks and David Riesman, *The Academic_Revolution* (New Brunswick, NJ: Doubleday, 1968), 425.

41. Tobe Johnson, "The Black College as System," p. 801.

42. Tobe Johnson, "The Black College as System," pp. 803–804, 810.

43. Chafe, *Civilities and Civil Rights,* p. 23.

44. LeMelle and Lemelle, *The Black College: A Strategy for Relevancy*, 46.

45. Booker T. Washington, *The Future of the American Negro* (Boston: Small, Maynard, 1902), p. 201.

46. Robert Russa Moton, *Finding a Way Out: An Autobiography* (Garden City, NY: Doubleday, Page, 1921), pp. 217–218.

47. Lester C. Lamon, "The Tennessee Agricultural and Industrial Normal School: Public Higher Education for Black Tennesseans," *Tennessee Historical Quarterly* 32 (Spring 1973), 42–58; Adam Fairclough, "'Being in the Field of Education and also Being a Negro Seems Tragic': Black Teachers in the Jim Crow South," *The Journal of American History* 87 (2000), pp. 65–91.

48. John M. Barry, *Rising Tide: The Great Mississippi Flood of 1927 and How It Changed America* (New York: Touchstone, 1997), p. 322.; and Wolff, pp. 34–35, 41, 55. President Warmoth T. Gibbs, when approached by students to let him know that they were staging a sit-down strike at Woolworth's, called Dean William H. Gamble, but gave him no specific instructions. Gamble said "let them sit," and saw nothing he could do as long as no law was broken. Gamble also said in an officially issued statement that his college "had no authority to restrict students' private activities of this kind." Gibbs left Gamble in complete charge for the entire period, because Gamble would have to take the blame in case of any trouble.

49. LeMelle and Lemelle, *The Black College: A Strategy for Relevancy*, pp. 59–60.

50. Johnson, "The Black College as System," p. 799.

51. Samuel Nabrit, "Reflection on the Future of Black Colleges," *Daedalus* 100, p. 671.

52. Ralph Ellison, *Invisible Man*, p. 118.

53. *The Harvard Crimson*, June 17, 1954 .

54. Donald E. Walker, "When the Tough Get Going, the Going Gets Tough: The Myth of the Muscle Administration," *American Society for Public Administration*, 36 (1976), p. 440.

II. Operational Challenges and Models for Improvement

4

Continuing the Fiefdom: A Matter of Governance and Management

Komanduri S. Murty

Leadership, despite its success in offering solutions to many organizational problems, appears to be problematic across higher education. Leaders in higher education have been subjected to considerable criticism for failing to exhibit effective skills and apply their knowledge of leadership and management to govern their institutions in an increasingly complex internal and external environment.[1]

Before discussing particulars about governance at HBCUs or other academic institutions, it is important to understand the concept of academic management and managerial and organizational techniques. Academic institutions are set up very much like governments. Some may be democratic, such as those in public institutions, with an elected head administrator and a tree that branches out with every administrator holding some power. Others may be oligarchies, such as those in many private, particularly Ivy League, institutions where wealthy call the shots. Many HBCUs however, have a different mode of governance. It is akin to a more medieval type of management: a fiefdom.[2]

A fiefdom refers to an area, organization or a sphere of activity that is controlled or dominated by a particular person or group. Deriving its roots from the medieval European feudalism, it may not be the only ancient practice that has survived through modern times, but it certainly is one of the most detrimental. Conventionally applied only to corporations, the "fiefdom syndrome" has actually been affecting and infiltrating the walls and offices of the academic arena as well. The next few pages will focus on how it has affected the progress of historically black colleges and universities.[3]

Since their inception in the early 1860s, HBCUs have faced many obstacles from blacks and whites alike. Early administrators like Booker T. Washington and other black officials performed a tricky and dangerous balancing game of keeping the ultimate white power-holders appeased. In this dance, to stand one's ground meant death; professional and literal. One had to be malleable, able to compromise and to believe completely in the goal of professional and social uplifting of black society as well as in the old age adage that "the end justifies the means." Where leaders like Washington were seen by many as "unwavering accommodationists" and men who not only obeyed, but approved of the laws of the Jim Crow South, the other side of the table shows they were doing everything in their power to keep the institution afloat so that it may survive the segregation and prejudice and be a beacon of hope and strength to the community.[4]

The problems that the HBCU founding fathers had to overcome lessened in severity as time wore on but did not become manageable until the end of the Civil Rights movement. From this we can deduce that, like the times, the administration methods had not changed much either. This authoritarian, paternal, sometimes inappropriate, system of "ruling the school" started out as survival strategy but quickly became a hindrance to progress. Once the threat of Jim Crow demised, the university was left with a legacy of archaic administration, with a dictatorial style leader.

By no means is authoritarian rule only an HBCU issue. In June 2009, at Florida Atlantic University there was a mass lay-off of faculty due to budget cuts. However, according to the faculty union, the layoffs that occurred violated union rules "mandating that non-tenured faculty members be the first to be eliminated and that any person who had worked at the university for more than three years should be given a year's notice." As explanation, the associate provost said, "the contract calls for one year's notice if practicable, where circumstance permit." The associate provost also said that notice was not practicable in this case. The terminated faculty are currently filing grievances and some are considering other legal action.[5]

The big kahunas in academia are controlled by a more subtle fiefdom: alumni. Schools like Harvard, Yale and Princeton are very generously supported by alumni contributions and therefore bend to the will of these past students. While the board of directors and president definitely have power, the alumni control much of what goes on in these schools.

Even though there are several other examples, not including the aforementioned ones, of fiefdoms in predominantly white institutions, it is important to underline the particular significance fiefdoms have on HBCUs. As has been reviewed, fiefdoms have a potentially fatal impact on an institution. There are only 104 Historically Black Colleges and Universities. They compose less than five percent of all higher education enrollment and yet still produce significant numbers of African-American professionals. If a few white colleges were to close it would not significantly affect the whole, it would even, arguably, strengthen the overall academic arena for white schools. However, HBCUs cannot afford this kind of amputation. Each black university or college loss is a threat to the livelihood of HBCUs on the whole. If these fiefdoms continue to exist and suck the life out of these institutions, there will be an overwhelmingly negative impact on the higher education for black Americans. HBCUs are vital to American higher education. They provide an element that other institutions cannot and thus produce many invaluable contributors to society. Many famous HBCU alumni like Thurgood Marshall, Toni Morrison, Ed Bradley, Alice Walker, Earl G. Graves, and Douglas Wilder attribute their successes to being educated in an environment with "outstanding professors, affordable price tags, academic reputation, top-notch research facilities, and diversity."[6]

The pressing problems faculty and students have with administration at HBCUs seem to follow a pattern: (problems with) following rules; using the proper chain of command; pay scales; and, lack of professional courtesy. During feudal times, lords of the fiefdoms were immune from laws that governed their subordinates. They were not subject to the same consequences even though their infractions resulted in much more significant consequences. This mentality has proliferated into current administrators' minds. The popular misconception is that they are above the law and rules of the institution. Subsequently, when administrative mistakes surface, HBCU leaders often retaliate with ugly behavior and immature schemes. The wellbeing and educational strength of the university takes a backseat to the whims of said administrators' fancy, whether that be in terms of power or pay. The result is the loss of accreditation of many universities to date, the insult of many professors and therefore the loss of their talents, and the diminishing morale and respect for the institutions that once were a source of pride for the community.

The fiefdom stems from the inclination of leaders or managers to become fixated on their own activities, their own careers, their own territory or turf to the detriment of those around them. They are determined to make decisions their own way, leading to runaway costs, increased bureaucracy and slow response times. Institutions infected with fiefdom syndrome tend to kill or stifle individual creativity, leading to the "freeze factor," allowing projects to be frozen or stuck in place, and competitors to reap the benefits. Commanders of fiefdoms control information, stifle creativity, and are unwilling to cope with change. It is as if power is in short supply, so everyone scrambles on the floor to get as much as he can. Then the begging question is, if all the supposed leaders' eyes are focused downward, who is looking ahead?

The key to better governance is organization. Max Weber, a German sociologist, provided a most comprehensive theory of organizational management. He concluded that the most efficient form of organization was the *bureaucracy* in which the overall work of an organization is divided into sets of specific tasks that are assigned to the individual units of the organization. Briefly, Weber's theory of bureaucratic organization included the following elements: (1) each unit of an organization should be assigned one particular type of work or set of closely related tasks, to be performed more or less continuously; (2) The units of the organization should be arranged into a hierarchy of offices, each having responsibility for a specific type of work and for the work of all its subordinate offices, and each office should have exactly the authority it needs to carry out these responsibilities; (3) Each person in an organization should be assigned to the office he/she is most competent to fill, and competence should be determined by objective means such as standardized tests or competition among applicants; (4) All of the relationships among the organizational units, and thus among the people who fill various offices, should be regulated by a formal, uniform, and consistent set of rules and policies; each office should have authority to set the rules and policies for its subordinate offices, subject to the authority of higher offices; (5) The exact procedures to be followed for the completion of every task should be determined in advance and established by the appropriate authorities; (6) All work should be reported by means of written documents, reviewed by supervising authorities as necessary, and kept in permanent files for future reference.[7]

Building on Weber's organizational management theory, psychologist Abraham Maslow published a theory of human motivation that explained all behaviors in terms of small set of universal human needs. According to Maslow, humans everywhere have physical needs like food, drink, shelter from the harsh environment, and psychological needs like a need for friendship, love, affection, and a sense of belonging, self-respect and fulfillment of personal gratification. These needs, though they exist in a hierarchical structure, must be satisfied in order for humans to be motivated to work.[8]

In all, the general theme of both these theorists have been to apply the knowledge gained from the behavioral sciences to improve the productivity of business or government enterprise and to increase the satisfaction of workers' physical and psychological needs. For example, Blake and Monton tried to integrate these theories into management and phrased it Grid Organizational Development. According to this integrated theory, every organization has two dominant concerns: the concern for production (meeting of organizational goals) and the concern for the welfare (both physical and psychological) for the organization's members and employees. This theory also acknowledges that organizations vary in the amount of attention that is paid to each of these concerns, which depends on their management style and skills.[9]

In the post-modern era, service oriented organizations developed different management styles. As the economy expands, the sophistication and level of services improve. New services are developed and provided. Some fifty years ago, Clark argued that as nations develop, there is a shift of the labor force from agriculture to manufacturing to services. This phenomenon is often described as transformation of economy from agrarian to industrial to a post-industrial society. The United States has developed into a post-industrial society where the standard of living is not defined by the quantity of goods and materials available but by the sophistication and quality of the services available. Today, more people in the U.S. are employed in the service sector.[10] However, this sector is hard to define. Haywood-Farmer and Nollet summarized service industry's definition dilemma as follows:

> Despite more than 25 years of study, scholars in the field of service management do not agree on what a service is. Indeed, instead of coming closer to a definition they seem to be less

certain ... the problem is, trying in a few words to describe 75 percent of the economic activity of developed nations. Is it any wonder that there are exceptions for all definitions?[11]

This post-modern service era has certain characteristics that make it different from the industrial and agrarian era. (1) Service system must interact with customers as they are a part of service delivery process. (2) Services are created and consumed simultaneously. (3) Service is a perishable commodity, which if not consumed at the time of its offering cannot be kept for later use. That is, unused service is lost forever because it cannot be stored. (4) Services are ideas and concepts that are not patentable and can be replicated. (5) The customer involvement in the service delivery process along with the intangible nature of services results in large variation of services from customer to customer. By all accounts academic institutions fall into the category of service industry. In recent years, universities have substantially increased their research activities and dramatically revised traditional ninteenth century definitions of university "service" to the community. Bolling et. al. explained: The prospect is for the society to look increasingly to the university for various kinds of assistance, thus perpetuating the current stress within the university over the priorities assigned to teaching, research and service.[12]

The Hierarchy

In colleges and universities, management abilities and academic insight are two critical requirements. Most academic institutions have become very big and complex organizations. The hierarchy in academic institutions is as follows: president, provost, dean, department chairs, and faculty. Let us describe these players from the bottom of hierarchy who are the most important players in academic institution.

Faculty

Faculty are the one of the most important constituencies in an academic field. They are the first line of offense and defense for the students. The challenges facing the faculty are many and multi-faceted: eroding self-esteem and eroding sense of security on behalf of students, relative and continuous decline of income, and a sense of slipping public respect. The purchasing power of today's faculty salary has shrunk significantly over the last fifteen years and have not kept up with market inflation. These challenges are complicated by the loss of excitement the faculty feel as the reality of their immobility becomes clear as time goes by. The loss of excitement is compounded by a sense of the reduced number of genuine students who are interested in study for its own sake. Taken together, these are very important factors. The shift of values regarding expectations of scholarly research and service to the institution creates further anxiety among faculty. Many institutions noted for teaching excellence are now finding ways to pressure faculty to do more research and publication. However, some faculty are ill-prepared to do research and some who are able to and interested in doing research are not provided the freedom, funds or tools. On the other hand, institutions noted for their excellence in research realize that funding and support for research projects are limited. Some research institutions are displaying more attention to the importance of teaching without providing sufficient assistance to the researchers.[13]

If one looks carefully into the history of this country, the most important figure in the university seems to be the faculty member rather than a dean or an administrator. He is an entrepreneur and a person who was the bridge between the foundation, the government department the corporation and the society. This was because of the notion that the best university is the least governed one. Traditionally, faculty and students are in fact members of a collectivity, members of a community, with a legal standing. They are not simply clients and employees; they are in some sense the "core" of the institution.

Department Chairs

Academic institutions succeed or fail due to what happens in individual departments because the academic department is central to a university's mission whether the department is focused on teaching or on research/scholarship. The department chair is the administrative and academic officer of the department and, as such, has the primary responsibility and authority for: (1) leadership in developing high quality academic programs which fulfill department, college, and university objectives; (2) leadership in the implementation of college/university policies and programs at the department level; (3) leadership in developing resource requests and an appropriate departmental budget; and (4) service on the college/school executive committee.[14]

The department chair is first a faculty member. He/she is primarily a teacher-scholar serving as a leader of his/her departmental colleagues. He/she is a role model for faculty responsibility. The department chair is responsible for providing mechanisms and processes for members' participation in discussion and decision making within the department. All members of the department should be informed of these mechanisms and processes. Regular meetings of the department should be held by the chair for purposes of communicating information, discussing issues, and making decisions on department matters.

The department chair is expected to communicate faculty perspectives and concerns to the administration and other segments of the community as appropriate. The department chair is the primary spokesperson for the faculty of the department. He/she will also convey administrative views and concerns to the faculty. A skillful negotiator and conflict manager, he/she will be better able to navigate and succeed as chair.[15]

In many institutions, chairpersons come to the position without preparation, work in relative isolation from other chairpersons and faculty, and serve with very little attention or reward for any accomplishments. Selection of department chairs is not easy. Too often, those who express interest in becoming chair are seen as too ambitious by colleagues while those who express no interest are then pressed into service, not surprisingly, such chairs show no enthusiasm for the job.

Deans

Deans administer individual schools as chairs do for individual departments. Deans report to the provost or vice-president of Academic Affairs Moreover, deans are in a better position to know the leadership challenges facing the institution as a whole than chairpersons. At the same time, the dean has an opportunity to create a shared spirit among the chairs. That is, they have to work on both sides of the leadership ladder. Thus deans have to be attentive to the needs of chairs, sensitive to their individual situations, provide support for on-going scholarly research, and continued teaching effectiveness.

In many institutions, Deans of Arts and Sciences have the most complex job because of the diverse disciplines involved, larger sizes of students and faculty, larger requirements of resources and physical plants, control over larger budget and budgetary items; and most importantly, the position require dealings with the many different personalities of faculty and chairs as well as student/parent-issues. Unfortunately, at many schools, the dean of arts and sciences does not have excessive funding because many departments (especially arts and humanities) do not receive contracts or grants. Gifts or grants to the university are much more likely to go to professional schools, such as the business school or the medical school. Therefore the deans of arts and sciences have two choices: increase the size of classes or hire more inexpensive teaching faculty. Because the first alternative receives much disapproval from faculty members, deans often resort to the second choice of hiring part-time/adjunct instructors.[16]

Provost

The candidate for provost is likely an on-campus dean, especially if the president is an outsider. As the chief academic officer, the provost is often called vice-president of academic affairs. He/she must deal with the concerns of deans of all schools and colleges of the institution. He/she manages the entire academic enterprise and functions academically closer to the president, trustees, legislators, and external community. In many institutions, the provost is recognized as the "number two" person behind the president in regards to scope, leadership, and authority.

The provost is heavily involved in rule-making and rule-enforcement in regards to the faculty. He/she is also responsible for determining the status of faculty regarding the granting of tenure and rank. Moreover, the provost's role in controlling academic matters is carefully crafted to avoid any damage, embarrassment, or legal action affecting the president.

Some academic institutions have other vice-presidents for student affairs, business affairs, and budget and finance. The various possibilities for vice-presidential positions depend on needs expressed by the university.[17]

President

The president is the leader and final authority on policies, procedures, and total functioning of the institution. He/she is in charge of fiscal, physical, educational and other institutional responsibilities. However, presidents depend on provosts to keep them sufficiently informed to maintain their credibility both on and off campus. So, a mutual trust, respect and reliance between the provost and president must exist. Presidents of academic institutions can be categorized amongst various types: dictatorial presidents providing authoritarian leadership; anxious and fearful types who are afraid of controversy; pre-retirement types presidents who have mentally retired long ago and so allow the institution to drift aimlessly; and, politician-type presidents who are interested in spinning the issues in their favor.[18]

A candidate for president often has the experience of being a president at another university or a provost either on or off-campus. The candidate should be knowledgeable about the finances of the university, be good at public relations, and must look the part. Presidential search committees often contain individual members with personal agendas, but final decisions are made by governing boards or board of trustees. Those who usually hire are looking for candidates who will be strong on campus but less so when meeting with the university board.

College/university presidents have existed in the United States since the founding of Harvard in 1636; and traditionally, this role has involved managing the day-to-day operation and controlling costs. Presidents today are often involved in virtually every component and process in the university. Kerr has described the multi-faceted roles of the president, who ideally expected to be a friend of the student; a colleague of the faculty; a good fellow with alumni; a sound administrator with trustees; a good speaker in the public; an astute bargainer with the foundations and federal agencies; a politician with state legislature; and a friend of industry, labor and agriculture; a persuasive diplomat with donors; a champion of education generally; and a supporter of the professions.[19] This is not to say that having one good president is the solution. On the contrary, it is also important that there is an inherent understanding between the board and the president. Stability is the key according to several former HBCU presidents. Former Virginia State University president Eddie Moore said that because VSU's board had such a high turn-over rate, his board did not have a clear understanding of the needs of the school. "We started what we call a 'Board Education Program' with all the information and news of what's going on campus." Former Stillman College president Cordell Wynn says that higher education is burdened with conflict but cites a strong board and president relationship and a clear goal for the university as the primary reason for his success. "There is more pressure on president today in higher education than ever before.... I had a Board of Trustees that was in sync with the goals for the school. We worked for Stillman College ... not any one person."[20]

Governance and Management of the American Universities

Governance and management of American universities include the following five areas: (a) trustees; (b) administrators; (c) faculty members; (d) students; and (e) general public, state and federal legislatures, and alumni organizations. A conference was held in late 1960s to discuss these and other matters of the governance of higher education and over 40 renowned and distinguished academicians around the nation had participated in discussion. The summary of their views are published in two parts by MIT Press.[21] Some of the salient features of these discussions, which are deemed to be relevant to current academia, are presented below:

Trustees and Administrators

The primary responsibility of the board of trustees is to keep the institution functional. The second responsibility is to provide guidance and policy to the administration. Governing Boards also must insure that the financial resources are available to enable the college/university to carry out its proposed programs. Trustees, as a way of their operation plan, should develop institutional objectives, intellectual and other goals derived from these objectives, and then develop strategies for pursuing the goals.

The trustee's task is almost always a part-time and usually unremunerated one. Most trustees are drawn from either successful business ventures or in some cases come from the bar. Very rarely they are drawn from scholarship or the arts, which are more usually the main concern of the university's curriculum. However, the selection of trustees should go beyond businessmen and corporate lawyers to include various segments of the university community such as students, faculty, and certain members of the communities around the university.

It is important to have an informed board of trustees; and a sensitive, informed, and determined administration. Absentee and/or passive trusteeship constitutes an ethical problem and amounts to what is called absentee landlord, where the faculty might be regarded as tellers at a bank. Because the term "governance" involves not only keeping things going but also makes institutions relevant to the needs and problems of the times, the role of trustees becomes vital. Therefore, trustees need to be picked correctly, educated, and be assigned significant tasks to do.

Trustees combined with administrators put pressures on faculties. If severe pressures develop to force faculties to change their ways, especially in directions that deviate from the primary concentration on teaching and knowledge, then the large scale unionization of the academic profession may evolve. The application of the business model to a university is a flawed approach where the board of trustees is akin to the board of directors of a corporation; administrators are like executives; and faculty are like production-line workers in a factory; and students are like the fabricated product.[22]

The university/college in the post-war America had a substantial shift in the disciplinary composition of the status, order and numbers in the faculty. In the 1920s, the professors of languages, literature, and history would have been the people who were heads of faculty committees of any of the great universities. Now the natural and social scientists carry the heavy weight. Social scientists, in particular, started getting involved in cities' problems as a field work. This was not only society pushing functions on the university, but also the university accepting these extra functions that the faculty actually enjoyed. This way, the faculty became a bridge between the university and the government and other corporations. Thus the university/college started becoming a place, where people live near one another without necessarily becoming conformists, without necessarily becoming "small-towners." The university/college provided a sense of attachment and made one feel that he/she was leading his/her life in a meaningful way.[23]

In the Western culture, a faculty is seen as a model who embodies something; he/she is not just an abstract person who is satisfactory in terms of his learning or style, but as a person who has mastered a body of thought. He/she is seen as a person who had lived a satisfactory life in his/her way. The old word "magister" or "master" carries with it an important concept — one that has mastered something. The teacher, master, does not have only a state of consciousness, but has a consciousness of something — that something being consciousness of an intellectual tradition with all its emotional content.[24]

The idea that the teacher/faculty is a professional, idealistic role model puts a tremendous burden on the teacher at the university. At the same time, in the totality of the academic institution the faculty do not have administrative control. In fact, they are being monetarily, socially, psychologically, and politically controlled by the administrators and the board of trustees.

Models of Governance:

The literature on college and university governance reveals three possible models, despite the fact that each college and university tends to have its own unique approach to management and governance. First is the top-down or **corporate administrative model.** This model allows college presidents or university leaders to make all of the important decisions with little input from faculty or staff. The appeal of the corporate administrative model is one of speed and efficiency. This model, however, does have its obvious shortcomings. Faculty become disenfranchised with this system that devalues their input; decisions are increasingly made by administrators without clear information about the everyday workings of the institution, and a crippling "us versus them" mentality can take hold. Many HBCUs, like some other colleges, constantly complain of minimal or lack of communication from administrators to faculty and students. The American Association of University Professors noted in its recent report that many faculty members who were laid off due to the economic downturn at Clark Atlanta University were not even informed as to who was going to be effected, what criteria would be used for layoffs, or when to expect said layoffs. Sadly, it all took place in the middle of Spring 2009 and caused unprecedented disruption. The AAUP report (January 2010, 4) observed that:

> On Thursday, February 5 [2009] the administration sent out a broadcast e-mail message to the faculty instructing all faculty members to report to campus the next day. At the same time, announcements were circulated classes were canceled for Friday and the following Monday.
> On Friday, February 6, some sixty fulltime members of the Clark Atlanta faculty — twenty of them formally holding tenure, others with long years of service, and most of them (perhaps as many as 75 percent) in the School of Arts and Sciences— received identical letters signed by the director of human resources, that were delivered in many cases by their dean, notifying them that their positions at the university had "been eliminated and [their] employment ... ended effective today." According to the letter, the elimination ... is part of a University-wide reduction in the work

force designed to reduce costs and gain operational efficiencies. The University president was quoted in the Atlanta press as having reiterated that the University is in a financial posture that remains strong"but stating that "the layoffs were necessitated by an 'enrollment emergency' exacerbated by current economic conditions"[25]

Thus, this model becomes dysfunctional and allows the administration to form its fiefdom.

Second is the **collective bargaining model** which was found in situations of growing antagonism between faculty and administration and a sense among faculty that they have no security or clear channels for negotiation. In this situation, the faculty comes to see unionization as empowerment. The vote of no confidence is a powerful tool for faculty to show their dissatisfaction in administration in this governing type. Unfortunately, this, too, often results in an "us" and "them" environment, when faculty and administrators are no longer free to address each others as peers or fellow stakeholders in the institution. In these models, faculty input is often channeled through only a few individuals and representative faculty senates can further lose their influence. On the other hand, administration finds it justifiable to conceal any controversial decisions and/or information from faculty, only to further widen the gap between them and the faculty at a later time; i.e., when these actions are deliberately discovered or uncovered. Therefore, in a dysfunctional state, this model is also subject to give rise to fiefdom.

Another model is the **shared governance model** which implies interdependence and assumes faculty members and administrators are peers who share common academic values. Although many institutions incline to prefer this model, in a strict sense, it is too ideological to have an absolute shared governance model. For example, not all faculty agree on everything, not all administrators agree on everything (but they yield to the president's choice), and, sometimes, it is hard to know the degree of agreement on any side (i.e., faculty or administration) because not every individual member expresses his/her opinion openly. Sometimes the confidential nature of matters warrant restrictions on the amount of sharing and qualified audience. Therefore, in practicality, the shared governance is a matter of relativity to other models. In order for it to be effective, it is necessary to have general commitment on the part of the faculty, staff, and administration to work together to strengthen and enhance the university through communication and appropriately shared responsibility.

One other model that is not widely discussed in the literature is the **external factor model**, whereby an individual, group or an organization that is not an integral part of the college or university influences its governance and leadership. This factor can be viewed as the king-maker model or remote-control model. Here the fiefdom remains as an outer element but invisibly pervades at every key position in the college or university. For example, Adair asserts that AME colleges:

> have been and are totally controlled by the all black AME church organization ... by the whimsical interference of the (most powerful) Bishops ... in the management of these institutions. Powerful Bishops who often lack expertise in either education or its management are typically controlling the board of these colleges, along with other ministers.[26]

For example, Morris Brown College, founded by the AME Church in 1881, was headed by clergymen in the form of principals and presidents through the 1990s. As a result, Morris Brown College had difficulty in attracting financial support and finally lost accreditation in 2002. To cite another example, a recent news article (dated January 8, 2010) highlights the audit findings of financial mismanagement and questionable leadership at Edward Walters College in Jacksonville, Florida:

> An "environment of no accountability" exists at Edward Waters College from the top down that has allowed unexplained payments to the former President and his wife, produced graduation rates of less than 20 percent and created a climate of fear and distrust for faculty, according to an internal audit of the college's operations. The private report, obtained by the Times-Union, places much of the blame on the Board of Trustees and (the institution's former president), who, despite his resignation in February, still receives more than $15,000 a month in salary and benefits.[27]

Edward Waters College does not have effective governance. In other words, the EWC's Board of Trustees and the senior administrators at the college have failed in their stewardship and fiduciary responsibilities, said the report prepared by auditor Marty Khan, acting director of internal auditing at the University of North Florida who volunteered his services to Edward Waters. His sweeping 63-page audit unveiled a series of critical findings such as no-bid contracts awarded to college trustees and politically connected consultants and the hiring of faculty and staff with criminal backgrounds and questionable academic credentials. The news article further disclosed that:

> Edward Waters arranged for the audit following a plagiarism
> scandal that briefly cost the school its accreditation. The Southern
> Association of Colleges and Schools said Edward Waters leaders
> lacked integrity and didn't exercise oversight and control of
> the application for reaccreditation, a process that occurs every
> 10 years. The private, historically black college won back its
> accreditation for at least one year after filing a federal lawsuit,
> but administrators must clean up the problems or risk further
> punishment.... The audit also included a faculty survey. The sur-
> vey results and calls and e-mails from faculty members led Khan
> to conclude the school suffered from "a climate of malaise."[28]

Incidentally, Edward Waters College is also an institution established by AME in 1883. To help these institutions, Adair suggested, that
bishops should engage themselves in fund-raising events—an activity
in which they were possessed a great deal of experience. Perhaps it is
even more critical now than ever before. A faculty not deeply and com-
munally involved in governance, whether through its own disinterest or
through active devaluation by others, will cease to have an interest in
their university. If this happens, there will be a real danger that the qualities that make a university the unique and special institution that it is
will be lost. Then, the fiefdom returns to its core.

Faculty Governance

The involvement of faculty in decision making process is very
important in academia because faculty represent the moral and intellectual guides of the academic enterprise. If one considers any major university initiative such as increasing faculty diversity, enhancing the
quality of education, or developing new professional degree programs,
the ability to effectively involve faculty will likely determine the quality
of outcomes. Yet, there is always a blatant undermining of faculty in
shared governance at HBCUs. In 2002, James T. Minor, an assistant professor at Michigan State University, conducted a national study of governance at four-year colleges and universities on a sample of 27 HBCUs.
The following year the survey was conducted on the remaining 61 four-
year HBCUs. The findings of combined data from these two surveys
about the faculty involvement in governance at HBCUs are as follows:
HBCU faculty have significant authority over academic matters such as
undergraduate curriculum (73 percent) and policies related to tenure
and promotion (60 percent). But they have significantly less influence

over non-academic matters such as athletics, setting of budget priorities, and selection of president. These patterns are relatively common across most HBCUs.[29]

Ivory Paul Phillips, professor of social science education at Jackson State University, disagreed with Minor's finding that HBCU faculty has significant authority on policies related to tenure and promotion, and listed the critical areas where the shared governance in HBCUs is grossly lacking: (a) faculty representation on policy and decision making bodies, (b) searches and hiring of academic personnel, (c) faculty grievances, (d) promotion, tenure, and post-tenure hearings and procedures, (e) evaluations of peers and administrators, (f) salary determination and other budgetary matters, (g) program development, review and revision, (h) development and revision of faculty handbooks, (i) access to information needed for decision making, and (j) status of the faculty senate as a decision and policy making unit.[30]

John Lachs, a professor of philosophy at Vanderbilt University, noted that shared governance is actually a myth, even among some predominantly white institutions of higher education. He observes the "growing disempowerment" of faculty members, as a result the poor economic health of states. These financial downturns led to sharp reductions in level of funding allocated by states to higher education. It has also led to an increased distance of governing boards from campus processes. Carefully choreographed, board meetings have become more of display of administrator achievement than academic advancement. As trustees and other governing members are not intimately involved with campus affairs, they evade their duties of inquiry and defer the majority of governance to the administrators. So long as these administrators are able to hide serious problems and maintain an unruffled campus scene, they stay in power and potentially deep-rooted issues affected institutional efficiency are pushed to the wayside.[31]

Administrators: Real Governors of Academic Institution

HBCUs were started by either religious groups or the federal government through the reconstruction legislation and the Morrill Act. For years this historical context continued to influence American black higher education. In the mid 1770s, George Washington argued that educating slaves would create a troublesome society with disturbed social environment. In the early 1900s, Booker T. Washington emphasized vocational training for blacks rather than liberal education. Thus higher education was not a natural societal expectation in America when it came to educating young African-Americans. The consequences of this process led to the development of segregated colleges. Such institutions were given meager funding and administrators of these institutions forced institutional leaders to follow dictates of community leaders and trustees of the board. Today, although many of the old patterns have disappeared, the oppressive manner in which many HBCUs are run has not.[32]

Phillips articulates the chronic recycling of incompetent administrators that debilitates the executive wing of many HBCUs. He cites numerous cases where presidents who received sanctions for unethical or illicit behavior yet are retained for extended periods by boards of trustees and, if and when they leave, are still hired for same or similar positions in other black colleges.[33]

Governing Boards

Perhaps the most important management body in an academic institution is the Board of Trustees. Whether appointed, elected, or selected from wealthy and influential community leaders, the members of the board have their own private and/or public agenda as trustees. There are always going to be in-groups and out-groups among the trustees. However, on surface, they are supposed to be working as a group for the welfare of the institution. It is the job of the Board of Trustees to devote sufficient time and effort to help institutions flourish and become flexible, innovative, and cost-effective. In principle, the success of an academic institution is usually the result of its Board of Trustees' leadership and governance.

Addressing the issue of strengthening HBCU governance for the 21st century, Phyllis Palmiero, director of the Institute for Effective Governance in Washington, D.C., remarked:

> Most presidents have a vision of where the institution can go and ... are familiar with academic programs and buildings. So, why even worry about a strong board? Lay trusties, after all, often have had little or no experience with higher education; they have little familiarity with special protocols that govern the campus, insufficient grasp of academic freedom, faculty governance, etc.

> When they get involved they can micro manage and interfere ... it is important for trustees to find ways of better connecting the dots between the promise and the practice of effective oversight.... A strong board allows the president the creative room to balance board and faculty ... [it] provides the feedback and reality check that a president needs.... Board members should work with the president to define the mission of the institution, to establish a niche, and pursue strategic and development plans.... Together, the president and board can make the tough decisions to achieve their common vision for the institution and to ensure that the very important mission and success of the HBCUs will continue.[34]

Phyllis Palmiero suggested following five recommendations for effective functioning of HBCU boards:

1. Identify the university's goals and objectives.
2. Allocate resources accordingly.
3. Develop merits for measuring the achievement of those objectives.
4. Ensure accountability.
5. And, do all of these in an inclusive way that reduces distrust among affected constituencies.[35]

In her concluding remarks, she observed that a trustee's job is not easy. Many underestimate the time commitment and research required to be an effective trustee. The bottom line is, trusteeship is hard work requiring dedication of time and effort. So, what is a trustee to do? How should a board of trustees govern an academic institution? The problem is that the existing culture of an academic institution's trusteeship promotes the status quo, discourages actively informed trustees, and must be a part of parties, dinners and social functions that administrators put forth for them. In reality, trustees have a responsibility to make decisions that serve the community and promote responsible policies for the welfare of all the members of the academic institution.

Dr. Drew Miller, a regent at University of Nebraska, has developed guidelines for the effective and responsible governance of academic institution by their board of trustees. These guidelines call for the training of trustee boards and the submission of major spending and policy decisions for cost-benefit analysis. This is, as he claims, is fairly simple but rarely done at board meetings. What happens is, that since the administrators have resources to do analysis and they do not like trustees to micromanage, the normal practice for trustees is to engage no cost-benefit analysis, listen and nod as administrators speak and vote "yes" to their policies and decisions. Trustees should be bold enough to periodically vote "no" at meetings, and prevent some good-for-the-school-but-bad-for-the-public proposals from making it to the board for a vote, should they want to do the job properly.[36]

In addition to this objective, Miller recommends: (a) the hiring of a paid board secretary who would be responsible to the board and not to the university or college administrators; (b) development of real committees and meaningful committee meetings that tackle issues; (c) thorough investigation of budget details and policies; (d) the development of good outcome measures and key performance indicators for the college/university to promote better accountability; (e) systematic review of administrative costs and work on efforts to undertake cost-cutting (Reducing administrative cost is a continuous improvement effort that will often involve personnel reductions, and reduce administrative layers, which may help redirect the savings to education); (f) development of a prioritization process along with strong and specific criteria that will lead to growth in the most important courses and programs funded by cuts in programs that are not essential for core education or the state's economy; (g) establishment of an issues/requests tracking system, so when information is requested or action is agreed to by the board, the request actually gets done; (h) challenge superficial analysis that is often designed to market programs to boards which do not present an honest assessment of pros and cons (The board should reject sloppy and deceitful work and insist that the administration come back at the next meeting with realistic and honest appraisals and information that cover all costs and benefits of the proposal); and (i) frequently question college administrators, who often focus on the narrower interests of the college/university rather than the broader public interest. Responsible trustees should refrain themselves from spending more time attending athletic events, parties, and dinners with administrators and, instead, should focus on researching and questioning as a continuous practice.

Notes

1. Estela M. Bensimon, Anna Neumann, and Robert Birnbaum, *Making Sense of Administrative Leadership: The "L" Word in Higher Education* (Washington, D.C.: George Washington University, 1989); Lee G. Bolman and Terrence E. Deal, "Reframing Leadership: The Effects of Leaders' Images of Leadership," in Kenneth E. Clark, ed., *Impact on leadership* (Greensboro, NC: Center for Creative Leadership, 1992), pp. 269–280; M.S Green, "Not for Cowards or Wimps: Leadership in the Post-Heroic Age," *Educational Record* 61, no. 3 (1994), pp. 55–60.

2. Mary L. Tucker, Bernard M. Bass, and Larry G. Daniel, "Transformational Leadership's Impact on Higher Education Satisfaction, Effectiveness and Extra Effort," in Kenneth Clark, ed., *Impact on leadership* (Greensboro, NC: Center for Creative Leadership, 1992), pp. 170–175.

3. Robert J. Herbold, *The Fiefdom Syndrome: The Turf Battles That Undermine Careers and Companies — And How to Overcome Them* (New York: Doubleday, 2004).

4. Kenrick I. Grandison, "Negotiated Space: The Black College Campus as a Cultural Record of Postbellum America," *American Quarterly* 51, no.3 (1999), pp. 529–579.

5. "Union Protests Layoffs of 5 Tenured Professors as Florida Atlantic U. Slashes Its Budget," *Chronicle of Higher* Education, June 9, 2009.

6. Lyneka Little, "HBCUs are Still Vital to American Education," http://www.thegrio.com/2009/09/separate-but-equal-the-hbcu.php.

7. Ibid.

8. Abraham H. Maslow, "A Theory of Human Motivation," *Psychological Review*, 50, no. 4 (1943), pp. 370–396.

9. Abraham H. Maslow, *Eupsychian Management* (Chicago: Richard D. Irwin and Dorsey Press, 1965); and R. R. Blake and J. S. Monton, *The New Managerial Grid* (Phoenix, AZ: Gulf, 1978).

10. Colin Clark, *The Conditions of Economic Progress* (New York: Macmillan, 1957).

11. John Haywood-Farmer and Jean Nollet, *Service Plus* (Quebec, Canada: Morin, 1991).

12. Landrum R. Bolling, et al., "The Governance of the Universities II," *Daedalus*, 98, no. 4. (1969), pp. 1092–1154; and Jennifer M. Allen and Rajeev S. Sawhney, *Administration and Management in Criminal Justice: A Service Quality Approach* (Thousand Oaks, CA: Sage, 2009).

13. Kathryn Masterson, "Economy Slows College's Ability to Hire and (Maybe) Retire Too," *Chronicle of Higher Education* (Washington, D.C., July 25, 2010); John B. Jones, "Faculty Governance in Difficult Times," *Chronicle of Higher Education* (Washington, D.C., November 19, 2009); Ben Gose, "Goodbye to Those Overpaid Professors In Their Cushy Jobs," *Chronicle of Higher Education*, July 25, 2010; Libby Sander, "Faculty Member Discuss What Role They Play in Governing Athletics," *Chronicle of Higher Education*, October 16, 2007; "Fostering Effective Faculty Governance," *Chronicle of Higher Education*, April 4, 1990; Peter Schmidt, "Governance of Alabama Universities Under Attack," *Chronicle of Higher Education*, April 5, 2002; and Jill Laster, "One-Third of Faculty Members See Dip in Their Salaries," *Chronicle of Higher Education*, March 8, 2010.

14. James B. Carroll and Mimi Wolverton, "Who Becomes a Chair?" *New Directions for Higher Education,* 126 (2004), pp. 3–10.

15. Walter H. Gmelch, "The Department Chair's Balancing Act," *New Directions for Higher Education,* 126 (2004), pp. 69–84.

16. Mimi Wolverton and Walter Gmelch, *College Deans Leading From Within* (Westport CT: Greenwood, 2002); and Jeffrey L. Buller, *The Essential Academic Dean: A Practical Guide To College Leadership* (San Francisco, CA: John Wiley, 2007).

17. Buller.

18. Elwood B. Ehrle and Bennett, *J.B. Managing the Academic Enterprise* (New York: Macmillan, 1988).

19. Clark Kerr, *The Uses of the University* (Cambridge, MA: Harvard University Press, 2001).

20. Linda L. Meggett, "The HBCU Presidential Pressure Cooker: Historically Black Colleges and Universities," *Diverse Issues in Higher Education*, June 21, 2007.

21. Landrum R. Bolling, "The Governance of the Universities II," *Daedalus*, 98, no. 4. (1969), pp. 1092–1154.

22. Richard Chait, et. al., *The Effective Board of Trustees* (Westport, CT: Oryx, 1993); Mary Beth Marklein, "College Trustees Feel Unprepared," *USA Today*, May 7, 2007.

23. Kellie Bartlett, "The Changing Role of Faculty in Academe," *Chronicle of Higher*

Education, November 26, 2003; and Elwood B. Ehrle and J.B. Bennett, *Managing the Academic Enterprise.*

24. Kellie Bartlett, "The Changing Role of Faculty in Academe," *Chronicle of Higher Education,* November 26, 2003.

25. "Academic Freedom and Tenure: Clark Atlanta University," http://www.aaup.org/AAUP/programs/academicfreedom/investrep/2010/clarkatlanta.htm.

26. Alvis V. Adair, *Desegregation: The Illusion of Black Progress* (Lanham, MD: University Press of America, 1984).

27. "Audit Harsh on Waters College: Internal Report Finds Evidence of Mismanagement Under Former President, Who's Still Being Paid," http://www.redorbit.com/modules/news/tools.php?tool=print&id=233465.

28. "Audit Harsh on Waters College.

29. James T. Minor, "The Danger of Deference: A Case of Polite Governance," *Teachers College Record* 107, no. 1 (January 2005): 137–156; and James T. Minor, "Dilemma of Decision-Making in Historically Black Colleges and Universities: Defining the Context," *Journal of Negro Education* 73, no. 1 (2004), 40–52.

30. Ivory Paul Phillips, "Shared Governance on Black College Campuses," *Academe* 88, no.4 (July–August 2002).

31. John Lachs, "Shared Governance is a Myth," *The Chronicle of Higher Education,* February 6, 2011.

32. Ivory Paul Phillips, "Shared Governance on Black College Campuses."

33. Ibid.

34. Phyllis Palmiero, Strengthening HBCU Governance for the 21st Century. https://www.goacta.org/publications/downloads/PalmieroTougalooRemarks11-1-06.pdf.

35. Ibid.

36. Drew Miller, "What Trustees Must Do, After A.U," *Inside Higher Education* (2006).

5

Compliance and Accreditation: Pressures and Challenges

KOMANDURI S. MURTY AND JULIUS SCIPIO

Compliance with a set of standards as prescribed by an accrediting agency, regional and/or professional, is a requirement for membership. For example, the recent compliance criteria as prescribed by the Southern Association of Colleges and Universities (SACS) are posted on its website. These criteria include compliance with each of the following: the principle of integrity, core requirements, comprehensive standards, and federal requirements. Although accreditation began as a voluntary process it has now become a necessary and inevitable *qualification* that all colleges and universities must maintain to receive federal financial aid.

Institutional Accreditation: An Overview

Toward the end of the ninteenth century, federal government, philanthropy, foreign countries, professional organizations and the academic institutions themselves felt the need for devising some mechanism to identify the better colleges and universities, primarily because of the existence of large number of institutions that varied in "quality and content." Therefore, in 1885 organizers established the nation's first regional accrediting body, the New England Association of Colleges and Secondary Schools. Shortly after this milestone, the Middle States, North Central, and Southern Associations emerged. In the years since colleges across the nation formed other regional accrediting bodies such as the Northwest Association in 1917, and the Western Association in 1962. They also formed a handful of specialized national accrediting bodies as well as nearly a dozen discipline-specific accrediting agencies.[1]

In the South, the first accrediting agency was started in 1895. The Southern Association of Colleges and Schools (SACS) is a non-profit, voluntary, non-governmental association and serves eleven Southern states— Alabama, Florida, Georgia, Kentucky, Louisiana, Mississippi, North Carolina, South Carolina, Tennessee, Texas, and Virginia — as well as Latin America and other geographical areas. SACS was developed by a band of Vanderbilt University faculty members who called upon esteemed faculty from the other top Southern Universities to pursue three main goals: (1) to organize Southern schools and colleges for cooperation and mutual assistance, (2) to elevate the standard of scholarship and to effect uniformity of entrance requirements and (3) to develop preparatory schools to enhance college preparedness. Other initial members of the association included University of North Carolina, University of the South, University of Mississippi, Washington Lee University and Duke University.[2]

In brief, the history of accrediting is as follows: (a) it was initially established voluntarily, not by government order; (b) the process began from two sources simultaneously, by professions from without and by institutions from within higher education; and, (c) accrediting was done for both types of organizations and was the outgrowth of genuine and sincere efforts to solve serious academic problems and issues of the times.[3]

Early Reactions from Educators

However, the involvement of several organizations (both academic and professional) in accrediting left educators unhappy. Chief among the educators' complaints were: (1) There are too many accrediting agencies: in some instances, there were as many as six agencies seeking to set standards and to accredit the same specialized segment of higher education (2) Professional accrediting agencies were concerned with only one particular segment of an institution, and not the institution as a whole; as a result, it was not uncommon to see as many as a dozen groups arriving on the campus of a complex institution on a dozen different occasions, each making demands for special consideration with little regard for the objectives or stability of the institution as a whole; (3) Professional accrediting agencies exhibited too much control over individual colleges because most of the professional accrediting agencies managed to back their demands with state licensing laws, grants of money, blacklisting, discriminatory hiring practices, and other inducements, including prejudicial treatment of alumni; (4) Division of authority and responsibility was tearing the administration apart and threatening the very existence of institutions because institutional matters such as curricula, staff, facilities, hiring practices, faculty code, grading systems, and textbooks, were dictated by arbitrary application of fixed national standards to institutions serving different constituencies. (5) Institutions were suffering from a flood of questionnaires and other reporting forms. Some large universities could afford to keep a staff member occupied full time collecting, arranging, and rearranging data for accrediting agencies; but, it was taking toll on small and medium size institutions. Much of the requested material bore little demonstrable relationship to the real quality of education provided by the faculty of an institution. In essence, accrediting turned out to be a police function; an inspection rather than a consultation. It became a mechanical process of checking to see that all institutions maintain an arbitrary set of minimum standards rather than a constructive process of helping all institutions to improve beyond their current level of achievement. (6) Institutions placed increasing emphasis on specialization and standardization in the scientific world, and made increasing demands for larger portions of curriculum time to be devoted to professional-technical training. In turn, strong national accrediting organizations supported these demands and neglected general or liberal education which forced colleges into offering specific courses and sequences. Thus, the flanks of general education became vulnerable to attack by professional studies hungry for more curriculum space. The clash of these interests resulted in imbalance between the two. (7) Accrediting costs too much. Although several agencies make no direct charges to institutions for their services; the procedures demanded by the accrediting agencies make the cost that is involved in collecting, compiling and processing data and preparing required reports burdensome.[4] While it is arguable that the costs may be warranted given that the a large portion of tuition revenues come from federal financial aid, legalists do not agree that state tax dollars or private donations should be used to support national agencies over which the contributing institutions have no control and in the budgeting of whose funds they often have no voice.[5]

National Commission on Accrediting and Subsequent Organizations

In 1949, the National Commission on Accrediting was established because: "Institutions of higher education found themselves beset with many new, and sometimes questionable, organizations seeking to accredit specialized programs on their campuses. The administrative officers of these institutions concluded that something had to be done, otherwise, their institutions would be pulled and tugged in a hundred different directions by these accrediting organizations with their varied and different standards and procedures." The Commission had seven constituent associations in its membership, namely: Association of American Colleges, Association of American Universities, Association of Land-Grant Colleges and Universities, Association of Urban Universities, National Association of State Universities, Association of Teacher Education Institutions, and American Association of Junior Colleges. Each of these associations elected six members to sit on the executive body of the Commission; and, replaced two of those six representatives each year as part of a rotating membership plan.[6]

The Commission's goal was to bring together all parties concerned and coordinate the efforts of developing policies and procedures in everyone's best interest. Recognizing the need for administrative control, but not wanting centralization under a federal agency, the Commission turned to the six voluntary Regional Accrediting Associations. As a result, the strategic accrediting plan emerged. Under this plan, each institution was to be evaluated as a whole institution, but each party was also to receive the benefits of traditional "segmental" evaluation (for example, experts in legal education would evaluate the law school experts in medical education would assess the medical school). That is, the evaluators, representing the various professional agencies, would act as a team studying each part program in its relation to other parts and in the perspective of the entire institution: a unified effort. Under the direction of the Regional Associations, there was no duplication of effort in evaluation and institution-wide policies, procedures, and objectives were given proper due. Professional agencies started issuing their own lists and the Regional Associations began publishing their lists of institutions approved on an institution-wide basis.[7]

In 1974, the National Commission on Accrediting and the Federation of Regional Accrediting Commissions of Higher Education (FRACHE; an association of regional accreditors) merged to form the Council on Postsecondary Accreditation (COPA), which had the purpose of promoting and ensuring the quality of accreditation. COPA dissolved in 1993 because of irreconcilable tensions among the different types of accreditation agencies that comprised its membership. As a result, the remaining members formed the Council for Recognition of Postsecondary Accreditation (CORPA). Three years later, in 1996, COPRA evolved into the Council for Higher Education Accreditation (CHEA), which functions for the purposes of providing national advocacy for self-regulation of academic quality through accreditation and providing scrutiny and certification of the quality of higher education accrediting organizations, including regional, faith-based, private career, and programmatic accrediting organizations. Presently, CHEA has around 3,000 academic member institutions and recognizes about 60 accrediting agencies.[8]

Accreditation and HBCUs

In 1917, there were 625 private black institutions (academies or trade schools), in which 1,588 students were doing some college level work, but none of them were accredited by a regional or national association. In 1929, SACS agreed to appoint a Committee on the Approval of Negro Schools. This committee, chaired by Henry Highsmith from the North Carolina Department of Education, was responsible for conducting site visits to black institutions; reviewing supporting documentation; and, making recommendations. Highsmith's Committee invited eighty-five black institutions to submit applications and request inspections, but only sixty were able to complete the application process. Of these, the committee selected only nine for review. SACS produced its first approved listing for black institutions in 1930, which showed that Fisk

University was the only one that satisfied all accreditation standards. However, the agency included six other HBCUs in the listing for demonstrating general quality that was sufficient to run a graduate program.[9]

In 1957 (i.e., three years after the *Brown* case), SACS required 59 black institutions, whose eligibility to apply for full membership with the Commission was already determined, to undergo a re-evaluation, and approved only 18 of them for membership. Some scholars, such as Drewery and Doermann (2001) saw two possible explanations for such action: one, discriminatory behavior on the part of SACS against black institutions by subjecting them to double screening; or, two, SACS might have self-corrected its initial wrong-doing by re-evaluating them. However, there might be another possibility. SACS might have approved 59 schools with the notion of publishing them separately (as before), but because the *Brown* case ruling had just come into practice and restricted SACS from publishing a separate list. As a result, SACS chose to reevaluate the HBCUs on the same criteria and scale they used for predominantly white schools. Using this barometer SACS approved only one-third of the HBCUs that they initially planned to certify. Should this conjecture hold true, it was probably a signal to black institutions in the South that they were better off without desegregation for want of their ability to demonstrate academic and institutional strength on par with predominantly white institutions. Critics of desegregation efforts may find comfort with such an interpretation on the grounds of declined enrollments of African American students in later periods.[10]

Today, seventy-five of the 103 HBCUs are under SACS jurisdiction because of their location in the southern region and bordering states. Over the years, SACS has gained reputation for paying disproportionate attention to HBCUs and sanctioning them. For example, Donahoo and Lee observed that 25 percent of all sanctions made by SACS between 1996 and 2005 were against black institutions, although they constitute only 13 percent of the member institutions. Jones observed that between June 1996 and June 2002, SACS placed 188 institutions on *warning* or *probation*, of which 25 were HBCUs and 21 of those 25 were private institutions. Thus, SACS sanctioned 21 of the 45 private HBCUs operating within their system during this period (an indicator of a higher vulnerability of private HBCUs). Moreover, since 1989, nearly one-half of the twenty institutions that lost SACS accreditation were historically black. Table 5.1 shows the current state of HBCUs and their accreditation status.[11]

Table 5.1: HBCUs by Current Accreditation Status

Institution	Accrediting Body	Public Sanction	Initial Accred.	Last Reaffirm.	Next Reaffirm.	Control	Level	Degrees
Alabama A&M University, AL	SACS	None	1963	2004	2014	Public	V	A B M ES D
Alabama State University, AL	SACS	None	1966	2001	2010	Public	V	A B M ES D
Albany State University, GA	SACS	None	1951	2008	2018	Public	IV	B M ES
Alcorn State University, MS	SACS	None	1948	2011	2021	Public	IV	A B M ES D
Allen University, SC	SACS	None	1992	2007	2017	Private	II	B
American Baptist College, TN	ABHE	None	1971	2003	2013	Private	II	A,B
Arkansas Baptist College, AR	NCACS	None	1947	2006	2010	Private	II	B
Atlanta Metro	SACS	None	1976	2001	2012	Public	II	A
Barber-Scotia College, NC	*Lost accreditation in 2004 (SACS)*							
Benedict College, SC	SACS	Probation	1946	2011	2021	Private	II	B
Bennett College, NC	SACS	None	1935	2011	2021	Private	II	B
Bethune-Cookman College, FL	SACS	None	1947	2011	2021	Private	III	B M
Bishop State College, AL	SACS	None	1992	2005	2015	Public	I	A
Bluefield State College, WV	NCACS	None	1949	2003	2013	Private	II	A B
Bowie State University, MD	MSCHE	None	1961	2006	2016	Public	III	B M
Central State University, OH	NCACS	None	1949	2002	2012	Public	III	B M
Cheyney University, PA	MSCHE	None	1951	2006	2016	Public	III	B M
Claflin University, SC	SACS	None	1947	2011	2021	Private	III	B M
Clark Atlanta University, GA	SACS	None	1990	2006	2016	Private	VI	B M ES D
Clinton Junior College, SC	TRACS	None	2003	2008	2018	Private	I	A
Coahoma Comm. College, MS	SACS	None	1975	2011	2021	Public	I	A
Concordia College, AL	SACS	Probation	1983	1999	2019	Private	II	A B
Coppin State Univ., MD	MSCHE	None	1962	2008	2018	Public	III	B M
Delaware State University, DE	MCSHE	None	1945	2007	2017	Public	III	B M
Denmark Tech. College, SC	SACS	None	1979	2005	2015	Public	I	A
Dillard University, LA	SACS	None	1938	2010	2020	Private	II	B
Edward Waters College, FL	SACS	Warning	1979	2006	2015	Private	II	B
Elizabeth City State Univ., NC	SACS	None	1947	2011	2021	Public	III	B M
Fayetteville State Univ., NC	SACS	None	1947	2011	2021	Public	V	A B M D
Fisk University, TN	SACS	Probation	1930	1999	2009	Private	III	B M
Florida A&M University, FL	SACS	None	1935	2001	2019	Public	VI	B M D
Florida Memorial College, FL	SACS	None	1951	2002	2012	Private	III	B M
Fort Valley State College, GA	SACS	Warning	1951	2010	2020	Public	III	A B M
Grambling St. University, VA	SACS	None	1949	2010	2020	Public	V	A B M ES D
Hampton University, VA	SACS	None	1932	2008	2018	Private	VI	B M D
Harris-Stowe St. Univ., MO	NCACS	None	1924	2010	2021	Public	II	B
Hinds Comm. Coll., Utica Campus; MS	SACS	None	1928	2007	2017	Public	I	A
Houston-Tillotson Univ., TX	SACS	None	1943	2010	2020	Private	II	B
Howard University; DC	MSCHE	None	1921	2004	2014	Private	VI	B M ES D
Interdenominational Theological Center; GA	SACS	Warning	1984	2001	2011	Private	V	M D
Jackson State University, MS	SACS	None	1948	2011	2021	Public	VI	B M ES D
Jarvis Christian College, TX	SACS	Warning	1967	2003	2014	Private	II	A B
Johnson C. Smith Univ., NC	SACS	None	1933	2007	2017	Private	II	B
Kentucky State University, KY	SACS	None	1939	1999	2009	Public	III	A B M
Knoxville College, TN	*Lost accreditation in 1997(SACS)*							
Lane College, TN	SACS	None	1949	2002	2013	Private,	II	B

Table 5.1: HBCUs by Current Accreditation Status (*cont.*)

Institution	Accrediting Body	Public Sanction	Initial Accred.	Last Reaffirm.	Next Reaffirm.	Control	Level	Degrees
Langston University, OK	NCACS	None	1948	2006	2016	Public	V	A B M D
Lawson State Comm. Coll., AL	SACS	None	2005	2010	2020	Public	I	A
Lemoyne-Owen College, TN	SACS	None	1939	2007	2013	Private	II	B
Lewis College of Business, MI	*Lost accreditation in 2007(NCACS)*							
Lincoln University, MO	NCACS	None	1926	2002	2012	Public	IV	A B M ES
Lincoln University, PA	MSCHE	Warning	1922	2008	2018	Public	II	B M
Livingstone College, NC	SACS	None	1944	2010	2020	Private,	II	B
Martin University, IN.	NCACS	None	1987	2008	2014	Private	II	B M
Mary Holmes College, MS	*Lost accreditation in 2002 (SACS Closed in 2005)*							
Meharry Medical College, TN	SACS	None	1972	2007	2017	Private,	V	M D
Miles College; AL	SACS	None	1969	2003	2013	Private	II	A B
Mississippi Valley State Univ.	SACS	None	1968	2002	2013	Public	III	B M
Morehouse College, GA	SACS	None	1932	2009	2019	Private,	II	B
Morehouse School of Medicine, GA	SACS	None	1986	2011	2021	Private	V	M D
Morgan State University, MD	MSCHE	None	1925	2008	2018	Public	V	B M D
Morris Brown College, GA	*Lost accreditation in 2002(SACS)*							
Morris College, SC	SACS	None	1978	2002	2012	Private	II	B
Norfolk State University, VA	SACS	None	1969	2008	2018	Public	V	A B M D
N.C. A&T State University	SACS	None	1936	2000	2010	Public	V	B M D
North Carolina Central Univ.	SACS	None	1938	2009	2019	Public	V	B M D
Oakwood University, AL	SACS	None	1958	2001	2012	Private,	III	A B M
Paine College, GA	SACS	None	1944	2011	2021	Private	II	B
Paul Quinn College, TX	TRACS	*Lost SACS accreditation in 2009.*						
		Currently accredited by TRACS						
Philander Smith College, AR	NCACS	None	1949	2006	2016	Private	II	B
Prairie View A&M Univ., TX	SACS	None	1934	2010	2020	Public	VI	B M D
Rust College, MS	SACS	None	1970	2004	2014	Private	II	A B
Saint Augustine's College, NC	SACS	None	1942	2011	2021	Private	II	B
Saint Paul's College, VA	SACS	Probation	1950	2000	2010	Private	II	B
Saint Phillip College, TX	SACS	None	1951	2006	2016	Public	I	A
Savannah State University, GA	SACS	Warning	1951	2001	2011	Public	III	B M
Selma University, AL	ABHE	None	2005	2009	2014	Private	III	A B M
Shaw University; NC	SACS	None	1943	2002	2012	Private	III	A B M
Shorter College, AR	*Lost Accreditation in 1998 (NCACS).*							
		Currently a candidate for TRACS membership						
Simmons College, KY	ABHE	Candidate	Gained initial candidacy in 2010. 1st scheduled review in 2014				II	A B
Soujorner Douglass College	MSCHE	Warning	1980	2006	2016	Private	II	B
South Carolina State Univ.	SACS	None	1941	2010	2020	Public	V	B M ES D
Southern Univ., Baton Rouge, LA	SACS	None	1938	2010	2020	Public	V	A B M ES D
Southern Univ., New Orleans, LA	SACS	None	1938	2010	2020	Public	V	A B M
Southern Univ., Shreveport, LA	SACS	Warning	1938	2010	2020	Public	V	A B M ES D
Southwestern Christian College, TX	SACS	Warning	1973	2010	2020	Private	II	A B
Spelman College; GA	SACS	None	1932	2011	2021	Private	II	B
Stillman College; AL	SACS	Warning	1953	2000	2010	Private	II	B

Table 5.1: HBCUs by Current Accreditation Status (*cont.*)

Institution	Accrediting Body	Public Sanction	Initial Accred.	Last Reaffirm.	Next Reaffirm.	Control	Level	Degrees
Talladega College; AL	SACS	None	1931	2009	2019	Private	II	B
Tennesse State University, TN	SACS	Warning	1946	2000	2010	Public	VI	A B M ES D
Texas College, TX	SACS	None	2001	2006	2016	Private	II	A B
Texas Southern University, TX	SACS	None	1948	2010	2020	Public	VI	B M D
Tougaloo College, MS	SACS	None	1953	2009	2019	Private	II	A B
Tuskegee University, AL	SACS	None	1933	2008	2018	Private	V	B M D
University of Arkansas-Pine Bluff	NCACS	None	1950	2006	2016	Public	III	A B M
Univ. of the District of Columbia	MSCHE	None	1970	2010	2014	Public	IV	A B M ES D
Univ. of Virginia at Lynchburg	TRACS	None	2005	2010	2020	Private	IV	A B M D
Virginia State University, VA	SACS	None	1933	2008	2018	Public	V	B M D
Virginia Union Univ., VA	SACS	None	1935	2010	2020	Private	V	B M D
Voorhees College, SC	SACS	None	1946	2003	2012	Private	II	A B
West Virginia St. Univ.	NCACS	None	1927	2005	2014	Public	II	B M
Wilberforce University, OH	SACS	Monitor.	1939	2001	2014	Private	III	B M
Wiley College, TX	SACS	None	1933	2003	2013	Private	II	A B
Winston-Salem State University, SC	SACS	None	1947	2010	2020	Public	III	B M
Xavier University, LA	SACS	None	1938	2010	2020	Private	V	B M D

Source: Websites of Regional Accreditation Associations, as accessed on December 25, 2010 and June 30, 2011

HBCUs Facing Accreditation Challenges and Pressures

Most HBCUs are likely to face reprimands and revocations of accreditation due to financial resources, institutional effectiveness and faculty qualifications (see Table 5.2). However, there are other compliance issues that HBCUs share with other institutions for which they can receive warnings, probations, and recommendations including but not limited to, qualified administrators, acceptable quality enhancement plans, campus infrastructure and resources, student enrollments, and even library holdings. Subscribing to these observations, Hawkins noted that a record number of HBCUs are embroiled in fiscal mismanagement or recently confronted serious financial problems, among them — Grambling State University, Texas College, Wilberforce University, Fisk University, and Central State University. More importantly the period witnessed nearly a dozen HBCUs lose accreditation or receive serious sanctions from accreditors due to financial concerns, institutional effectiveness and faculty qualification. Listed below are specific details from many of these cases.[12]

Table 5.2: Patterns of Non-compliance During 2005–2006

Rank Offsite, Onsite	Item	Brief Description	Percent Noncompliance Based on Off-site Reviews (n=156)	Percent Received Recommendation Based on On-site Reviews (n=75)
0, 1	2.12	QEP	n.a.	72%
3, 2	3.5.1	General education competencies	61%	42%
1, 3	3.7.1	Faculty Qualifications	88%	36%
4, 4	3.4.1	Programs approved by faculty/learning outcomes	58%	32%
2, 5	3.3.1	Institutional effectiveness	62%	27%
0, 6	2.12*	QEP — as Core Requirement (where applicable)	n.a.	16%
8, 7	2.5	Institutional Effectiveness	35%	11%
11, 8	3.7.2	Faculty-Evaluates Effectiveness	33%	8%
12, 8	3.8.3	Library/Learning Resources-Qualified Staff	30%	8%
20, 8	3.10.1	Financial Stability	23%	8%
9, 11	3.4.7	Consortia & Contractual Agreements	34%	6%
5, 12	2.11	Resources	55%	5%
6, 12	3.2.10	Evaluation of administrators	50%	5%

Source: Compiled from "Identifying and Exploring Issues of Compliance: An analysis of the external peer review process for institutions seeking reaffirmation of their accreditation during 2005–2006, A Report to the Executive Council Commission on Colleges Southern Association of Colleges and Schools," December 2006. Available at (*www.sacscoc.org/pdf/COC%20Research%20Project.pdf*).

Barber Scotia College (Concord, North Carolina; four-year Presbyterian institution): SACS rescinded accreditation in 2004 because of serious academic issues. Chief among the academic problems was the granting of degrees to twenty-eight students who had not met graduation requirements. With an enrollment of just fifty full-time students, the college scheduled an on-site visit from a team of represenatives from the Transnational Association of Christian Colleges. Unfortunately, in August 2011, the accrediting agency declined to offer membership due to the college's outstanding debt to the Department of Education. Currently, college officials are negotiating with the Department of Education to abate or postpone payment on the debt. If such an agreement is reached TRACS has promised to reconsider the college's application.[13]

Bennett College (Greensboro, North Carolina; four-year Methodist women's college): The college was placed on probation in 2002 for financial issues and then later removed from that status in 2004. The turnaround occurred after Johnnetta B. Cole, the institution's new president, began a successful campaign for support with former Sen. Robert Dole acting as the chair of the campaign. Regrettably, in June 2011, SACS placed Bennett College on probation for a second time, citing a lack of sufficient resources. Major factors contributing to this action were decisions by college leaders to construct several new buildings despite the fact that enrollment at the school had grown little since 1980. Another factor contributing to the outcome was a donor who defaulted on a pledge, causing the school to give extra dollars to students who had been promised financial aid. Said school president Julianne Malveaux after the action, "It came like a shot in the dark."[14] In December 2011, SACS removed the sanction from Bennett College.

Cheyney State University (Cheyney, Pennyslvania; four-year public institution): Cheyney received a warning from the Middle States Commission on Higher Education in November 2009. The state-run Cheyney has long struggled with financial woes and declining enrollment, and failed to meet three of the commission's fourteen standards. The three lacking standards are: (1) the development and implementation of a comprehensive institutional strategic plan that links long-range planning to decision-making and budgeting processes; (2) the development and implementation of a budget process and a long-term financial plan that are aligned with the institution's mission, goals, and strategic plan; and (3) the development and implementation of administrative and financial policies and procedures, in particular regarding financial aid, student accounts, and student registration, in a manner that ensures adherence to these policies. In June 2011 the Commission removed the sanction.[15]

Concordia College (Selma; Alabama; four-year institution affiliated with the Lutheran Church-Missouri Synod): On June 24, 2010, the college was denied reaffirmation and placed on probation for faculty and financial concerns. In December 2010, the Commission removed the sanction.[16]

Edward Waters College (Jacksonville, Florida; four-year institution affiliated with the African Methodist Episcopal Church): SACS initially rescinded accreditation in 2004 because the administration plagiarized large portions of a quality enhancement plan from Alabama A & M University and submitted it to SACS for its reaccreditation. In 2005, SACS reinstated accreditation as a result of the settlement of a lawsuit brought by the college against SACS. The institution recently obtained SACS reaffirmation, but was placed on warning again in December 2011 because the institution failed to demonstrate it had an adequate number of full-time faculty. The college also failed to assess the quality and effectiveness of its educational program. Although SACS granted the institution twelve months to correct these problems at the writing of this report the future of Edward Waters College is still very much in doubt.[17]

Fisk University (Nashville, Tennessee; four-year private institution): On December 6, 2010, SACS denied the institution's reaffirmation of accreditation and placed it on a six month warning for failing to comply with core requirements pertaining to financial resources and financial stability. In December 2011, the Commission placed Fisk University on probation.[18]

Fort Valley State University (Fort Valley, Georgia; four-year public institution): In December 2011 SACS placed the University on warning because the university failed to provide evidence that it: (1) employs faculty members qualified to accomplish its mission and goals, (2) exercises appropriate control over all its financial resources, and (3) is in compliance with its Title IV program responsibilities.[19]

Grambling State University (Grambling, Louisiana; four-year public institution): SACS originally placed the university on probation in 2001 because of the institution's disorganized financial records (the Louisiana State Auditor has been unable to audit the university since 1997). The state approved Grambling's records in 2002; however, SACS required a longer probation before reinstating accreditation, as it wanted the institution to demonstrate a longer track record of stability.[20]

Interdenominational Theological Center (Atlanta, Georgia; four year, church-related institution): SACS placed the College on warning in December 2011 because the institution failed to provide evidence that it engages in ongoing, integrated, and institution-wide research-based planning and evaluation processes. The Commission also maintained that the Interdenominational Theological Center, among other things, failed to identify expected outcomes of and show improvements in the areas of student learning and educational programs, administrative support services, research, and community service; employ qualified personnel in several areas; and exercise appropriate control over its financial resources. The Commission granted the College twelve months to fix the issues before reevaluating the institution in December 2012.[21]

Jarvis Christian College (Hawkins, Texas; four-year, church-related institution): SACS placed the College on warning in December 2011 because the institution failed to provide evidence that it has a sound financial base and a recent financial history demonstrating financial stability. Officials from SACS also maintained that Jarvis Christian College failed to submit timely audits for financial aid programs as required by federal and state regulations, nor did the institution identify expected outcomes and uses findings to improve educational programs. The Commission granted the College six months to fix the issues before conducting a follow-up evaluation in June 2012.[22]

Knoxville College (Knoxville, Tennessee; four-year, church-related institution): The college lost accreditation from SACS in 1996 because its debt reached $3.2 million and enrollment dropped by two-thirds, from 1,200 to 400 students. As a result of losing accreditation, the college reorganized itself as the first black college to join the six-member Work College Consortium — a group that includes Alice Lloyd College, Berea College, Blackburn College, the College of the Ozarks, Sterling College, and Warren Wilson College.[23]

LeMoyne Owen College (Memphis, Tennessee; four-year Church of Christ institution): SACS placed the college on a twelve month probation. In December, 2005, after it determined that LeMoyne Owen College needed to reduce its $6 million debt and further improve the qualifications of the business school's faculty. Enrollment dropped from 1,200 to 800 during this scandal. However in recent years, thanks to many financial contributions from the City of Memphis and United Negro College Fund among others, the situation at the college has stabilized. SACS reaffirmed accreditation in 2007.[24]

Lewis College of Business (Detroit, Michigan; two-year private institution): The North Central Association of Colleges and Schools (NCACS) concluded in early 2006 that the college did not comply with requests to provide information on its financial position and administrative procedures and placed it under "show case" status, the final step prior to loss of accreditation. Prior to this judgment, the accreditor determined that the board of directors was not involved in the college's affairs and the institution did not show a clear administrative structure. The institution ultimately lost accreditation in 2007, one of three HBCUs to lose accreditation under NCACS.[25]

Lincoln University (Lincoln University, Pennsylvania; four-year private institution): On June 23, 2011, the Middle States Commission on Higher Education placed Lincoln University on warning because the institution failed to demonstrate that it assesses student learning. In 2012 representatives from the Middle State Commission on Higher Education will reevaluate the College to determine in the sanction will be removed or continued.[26]

Mary Holmes College (West Point, Mississippi; two-year institution affiliated with the Presbyterian Church): The college lost accreditation in 2003 because of financial concerns and declining enrollment. In 2004 the Board of Trustees voted to pursue bankruptcy. Mary Holmes closed its doors in March 2005.[27]

Morris Brown College (Atlanta, Georgia; four-year institution affiliated with the African Methodist Episcopal Church): The college lost accreditation in 2002 after accumulating $23 million in debt and allegedly using federal allocations for student financial aid to pay overdue bills. College officials pledged to reapply for accreditation; but, as the institution's outstanding loans still totaled $27,000,000.00, the chances of regaining accreditation do not appear very high.[28]

Paul Quinn College (Dallas, Texas; four-year institution affiliated with the African Methodist Episcopal Church): SACS attempted to revoke the college's accreditation in 2009 for failure to demonstrate its ability to comply with the core requirements of financial strength and institutional effectiveness. Paul Quinn has filed suit against SACS; and, on August 27, 2009, the U.S. District Court for Northern Georgia issued a preliminary injunction that reinstated the accreditation of Paul Quinn College as a member on probation with the Commission on Colleges of the Southern Association of Colleges and Schools (SACS COC). The Order expired in 2010. Though the college tactfully gained the TRACS membership during the period of stay to ensure its eligibility for federal aid, its enrollment has plummeted to the current level of less than 150 full-time students.[29]

St. Paul's College (Lawrenceville, Virginia; four-year institution affiliated with the Protestant Episcopal Church): On June 24, 2010, the college was denied reaffirmation and placed on twelve months probation for finances, concerns questions about the competency of administrative/academic officers, and institutional effectiveness. In May 2011, in an effort to help ameliorate its financial condition and retain accreditation, the college's governing board voted to discontinue the college's athletics program. In part due to this effort, SACS voted to give the college a second twelve months of probation on June 22, 2011. However, the future of the college is still very much in doubt as fewer than 300 students were enrolled for the fall 2011 semester as of August 21, 2011.[30]

Savannah State University (Savannah, Georgia; four-year public institution): In December 2011, SACS placed the University on warning because the institution failed to provide evidence that it employs an adequate number of full-time faculty members to support the mission of the institution. The Commission granted the College six months to fix the issues before conducting a follow-up evaluation in June 2012.[31]

Selma University (Selma, Alabama; four-year institution affiliated with the Alabama State Missionary Baptist Convention): In 1996, Selma lost SACS accreditation because of a $10 million debt. Subsequently unaccredited, the university applied for and obtained new accreditation through the Association for Biblical Higher Education (ABHE) in 2002. This allowed the school to receive federal financial aid.[32]

Soujourner-Douglas College (Baltimore, Maryland; four-year private institution): In November 17, 2011, the Middle States Commission on Higher Education placed Sojourner Douglass College on warning because the institution failed to provide evidence that it had sufficient operational resources, and that it was in compliance with standards related to institutional assessment and the assessment of student learning. In November 2012, the Middle States Commission on Higher Education is scheduled to review the College's status again.[33]

Southwestern Christian College (Terrell, Texas; four-year Church of Christ): In December 2011 SACS placed the College on warning because the institution failed to demonstrate it has a published policy for evaluating, awarding, and accepting credit and that it places primary responsibility for the curriculum with its faculty.[34]

Stillman College (Tuscaloosa, Alabama): On December 6, 2010, SACS denied the institution's reaffirmation of accreditation and continued it on a year-long warning for failing to demonstrate compliance with core requirements pertaining to financial resources and financial stability. The maximum time that an institution may be on warning is two years. In December 2011, SACS voted to continue Stillman College on warning until June 2012.[35]

Talladega College (Talladega, Alabama; four-year Church of Christ institution): SACS placed the college on a twelve month probation in December 2005 for poor finances and institutional effectiveness. This marked the second sanction issued to the college between 2003 and 2005. At the time of the 2005 probation, enrollment fell to 303 students, health insurance for the staff was suspended, and the campus had millions of dollars in deferred maintenance. However, since those dark days the college's fortunes have improved allowing Talladega College officials to remove the sanctions and increase enrollment. As of October 2010, the college enrolls approximately 800 students.[36]

Tennessee State University (Nashville, Tennessee; four-year public institution): On December 6, 2010, SACS denied the institution's reaffirmation of accreditation and placed it on a twelve month warning for failing to demonstrate compliance with core requirements pertaining to institutional effectiveness. In December 2011 the Commission reaffirmed the University and removed it from warning.[37]

Accreditation and Small Traditionally White Colleges

HBCUs are not alone in facing the crisis of accreditation. Over the last decade, scores of TWIs have lost regional accreditation or faced accreditation problems. For these institutions, mainly small, private, church-related schools, conditions are identical to the ones facing black colleges: limited resources, problems with institutional effectiveness, and high administrative turnover leading to continuing problems with accreditors. Representative of this problem is Sue Bennett College, a smaller institution, located in London, Kentucky. Sue Bennett College's problems began in the 1980s when low enrollment led the college to admit men. However, this did little to help waning enrollment. In the years following this decision, the tuition-driven school tried a number of efforts to increase enrollment, even adding a football team. However, nothing worked. Finally, in 1996 SACS removed the college from its list of accredited schools. According to a report in the *Chronicle of Higher Education* no one was more surprised than Dr. James Cheek. On the very day that he agreed to become president, Check learned that the college had lost its accreditation for financial reasons. He then discovered that the college had a $2,000,000 deficit. Jack Early, the college's former vice president of development, commenting on the problem, acknowledged that raising $2,000,000 would be difficult since "people don't like to pump money into what they view as a sinking ship." Although the college filed a suit to regain its accreditation, the courts ruled in favor of SACS. Consequently, the college's Board of Trustees voted to close the college in 1997.[38] Other TWI losing accreditation over the last twenty years included: Upsala (1995), Southern Virginia (1996), East Coast (1999), Bradford (2000), Wood (2003), Hiwassee (2007), St. Andrew's (2008), and Dana Colleges (2010), as well as Lambuth University (2010).*

---

*East Coast, Bradford, Wood and Dana colleges closed their doors shortly after losing regional accreditation. In April 2011, the trustees of Lambuth University voted to close the University on June 30, 2011. Bill Seymour, Lambuth president, said the university is still in talks with interested higher-education institutions looking to acquire the campus. However, as of May 2011 no deal had been struck.

Consequences of Non-accreditation

The public heavily relies on accreditation to make their choices regarding where they want to send their children to obtain higher education upon graduating from high school. That is the reason for such a drastic decline in student enrollment following the loss of accreditation among the previously listed institutions. Unaccredited colleges cannot join funding agencies such as the UNCF. Employers, governmental as well as private, are less inclined to hire graduates of unaccredited schools. Accredited schools hesitate to accept transfer students or advanced-degree candidates from schools that have lost accreditation. Other institutions show reluctance to merge with those without accreditation for two reasons: fear of diluting their program quality and fear of adding financial burden to themselves. A case in point: when Morris Brown College in Atlanta lost its accreditation, none of the five neighboring black institutions in the Atlanta University Center considered a merge. State licensing boards may not permit graduates of unaccredited schools to practice a profession within the state. Schools lose their ability to attract donors and conduct fund-raising campaigns that are necessary to sustain their operating budgets.

Additionally, the federal government itself relies on a system of private accreditation in determining which college or university is eligible to participate in federal student aid programs. It is essential to meet three checkpoints in order to establish eligibility: federal certification of financial and administrative capability; state licensing or approval to operate in a state; and, accreditation by a recognized accrediting agency.[39] Enactment of the Higher Education Act of 1965 (HEA) increased the importance of accreditation in determining institutional eligibility for student aid. The 1992, 1998, and 2008 reauthorizations of the HEA made the federal government's recognition of accrediting agencies substantially more regulatory in nature. They did so by requiring institutions to address such subjects as institutional default rates, federal program compliance, student outcomes, and student complaints, as well as legislating a loan default rate threshold, beyond which an institution would no longer retain access to federal student loan programs. Thus it tightened the relationship between federal aid and accrediting agencies.[40] A slight allowance for legal recourse is available for institutions whose accreditation is withdrawn or denied to challenge the accrediting agency's decision for wrongfully disaccrediting them on a couple of grounds: one, that such decision of disaccreditation would irreparably harm the institution; and, two, that the agency did not follow its own rules in reaching the decision and utilized procedures that were inherently unfair to the school. However, these procedures are costly and the outcome is uncertain.[41]

Given that at least eighty percent of students who attend HBCUs depend on federal financial aid, the loss of accreditation can have a snowball effect. It could very well make it impossible for the institution to operate, compete, recover financially or programmatically: all resulting in the unthinkable happening, i.e., the permanent closing of the school's doors.

Moving Forward

Generally speaking, membership in an accrediting agency is not simply a matter of free choice for colleges and universities. Regional accreditation is preferred since it provides greater access to student aid. Recently, many schools, after failing to meet the standards of regional accreditors, turned to less prestigious national accrediting groups. For example, after losing SACS accreditation in 1996, Selma University in Alabama obtained accreditation with the ABHE. In 2009, Paul Quinn College in Texas filed a lawsuit against SACS when the agency tried to remove the college from membership. In the meantime, Paul Quinn gained membership in the Transnational Association of Christian Colleges and Schools (TRACS) to ensure its eligibility for federal aid, regardless of the lawsuit's outcome. In recent years, turning to other accrediting agencies to retain access to federal financial aid is becoming a new strategy for many small, independent, enrollment-driven HBCUs.[42]

Some of the difficulties expressed by black college administrators among other are the necessity to adjust to sudden changes in SACS policies that influence the future destinies of their institutions compounded by the issue of disclosing sensitive information without violating the confidentiality of those involved. To help HBCU leaders in this direction, the Southern Education Fund (SEF) established a three-year HBCU leadership program in 2004, with support from the Charles Stewart Mott and Andrew Mellon foundations. The initiative provided small grants from $10,000 to $20,000 for special projects to help institutions secure their accreditation status. For example, if one institution requires a certain software program while another needs a consultant to address financial issues and meet the financial stability measures SACS requires—all are products or tasks designed to help them move toward a reaffirmation review — those schools can apply for and secure SEF grants. The SEF also sponsors institutional leaders attendance at SACS conferences and educational programs along with hosting a special, day-long conference dedicated to issues faced by HBCUs, so that the administrators of these institutions can not only benefit from knowledge distributed, but also establish working relationships with the accreditors, thereby developing the familiarity and comfort necessary to ask questions pertinent to their preparation for certification of accreditation. Ideally, maintaining data bases and documentation on institutional standards and quality enhancement of academic programs shall become a matter of routine, so that preparation of accreditation will no longer be a monumental effort, starting from scratch every time the institution is up for reaffirmation. Following such a practice on regular basis can help to avoid last-minute procedural and data errors which can become a basis for official sanctions.[43]

As a recent effort in this direction, in May 2010, the United Negro College Fund received a $500,000 grant from the Walmart Foundation to expand its Institute for Capacity Building's Fiscal and Strategic Technical Assistance Program (FASTAP). This initiative focuses on the financial and administrative management of UNCF member institutions. Specifically, FASTAP works to assist member colleges "to prepare for accreditation visits by providing reaffirmation readiness reviews, financial support and comprehensive institutional assessments that focus on financial management, institutional effectiveness, institutional advancement and enrollment management."[44]

Further, it is also encouraging to see the appointment of the first black president to head the SACS's Commission on Colleges, Belle S. Wheelan in 2005. Wheelan is aware of the past tension between HBCUs and the Commission and is willing to increase communication with and provide educational programs for all institutions, including HBCUs. Wheelan has also favored the notion of hiring more African American employees to help the image of SACS and improve relations with its HBCU members.

It is important that HBCUs understand and take the necessary steps to meet compliance requirements. Otherwise, they might attempt arbitrary methods to gain the acceptance of less credible accreditation agencies which prove, in the end, to be a waste of time and money. For example, an experienced accreditation specialist for various HBCUs, in his role as consultant, made some of the following observations. Several years ago, a four-year private black college, after facing scrutiny from SACS, instead of hiring the proper administrators and staff who understood compliance, the college, boldly published an article in the local newspaper saying that it was implementing a dress code for students. It was the hope of many at the school that the dress code would impress SACS. However, none of the requirements for SACS state anything regarding student dress codes.[45]

At another HBCU facing serious sanctions, the president and the Board of Trustees refused to eliminate the football team despite the fact the college facing a deficit of more than $1,000,000 for two consecutive years. During this period, the college was so "cash-strapped" that it was forced to cancel a football game because it could not afford helmets. The school was also unable to participate in any home football or basketball games because it did not have enough money to grade the field to NCAA standards or repair the leaky gym roof of the basketball court. Still, despite consultants' advice to cancel the athletic program, the college administrators refused to do so. As a result, SACS placed the college on probation for *finances, faculty qualifications and institutional effectiveness*. The main reason identified for the college's unwillingness to comply with consultant recommendation was the requirement for all participating teams in its corresponding athletic league to field football teams. For that reason, the institution was willing to jeopardize the loss of regional accreditation.[46]

At another school, the president created a climate of fear. Anytime anyone did anything that president perceived as wrong, he fired them. Unfortunately most of the time *anything* the college's staff did was wrong in his eyes. Consequently, every year the president had an entirely new executive council. When faced with SACS problems the leadership was paralyzed and all of the senior administrators refused to write anything or prepared to make any moves to address the problem — knowing the ramifications of president's wrath. As a result, this college was placed on probation because the staff was afraid of the president. Ultimately, a bold consultant came forward to write the direly needed responses to the satisfaction of SACS.[47]

Ultimately, the majority of the work in maintaining or regaining accreditation falls on the shoulders of the HBCUs themselves. It is imperative that HBCU leadership hire the best administrators possible and empower them to do their best work. These leaders MUST hold the highest standards for themselves, their staff, and faculty and create working environments in which individuals develop a firm commitment to excellence. Excellence in the form of shared governance and responsibility. Also, as demonstrated by some administrators like President Cole at Spelman as well as Bennett Colleges, the HBCU presidents must know how to obtain funds (sometimes direly needed) for improving the financial health of their institutions.[48]

Dr. Leroy Davis, who has held several positions including SEF consultant, recommended the following helpful tips to HBCU presidents to improve their institution's chances of getting accreditation: (1) Study the principles of accreditation thoroughly and well; (2) Review your institution's most recent self-study; (3) Develop personal and institutional calendars; (4) Assign responsibility to key individuals; (5) Obtain all accreditation handbooks, manuals and other resources; (6) Attend all SACS COC meetings; (7) Conduct mock certification audits every 2–3 years; (8) Become actively engaged in SACS activities; (9) Keep your board informed on accreditation issues; (10) Review and understand the finance-related requirements; (11) Review and revise your institutional mission statement and strategic plan periodically; (12) Develop a strong institutional research capacity; (13) Review institutional files documenting faculty credentials annually; (14) Begin development of the quality enhancement plan (QEP) early; (15) Develop budget line items for accreditation planning; (16) Designate the institution's leadership team as soon as possible; (17) Set internal deadlines; (18) Identify and appoint the most competent person on your campus; (19) Work with your SACS COC representative; (20) Develop a good relationship with the SACS COC staff member; and (21) Emphasize to staff the need to demonstrate personal, professional and institutional integrity.[49]

In 1967, Reisman and Jencks conducted a study and came to a blanket conclusion about black colleges and universities, labeling them as "academic disaster areas." In response, President Benjamin Mays of Morehouse College found that two years before the aforementioned study, "there were 401 predominantly white colleges in the country too feeble in academic performance to be rated by any one of the six regional accrediting agencies, which places them below the weakest of the accredited Negro colleges." None of the issues and problems discussed in this book apply to HBCUs alone. On the contrary, as cited by Dr. Mays, there are more predominantly white colleges with these very issues. However, the concern herein lies with survival. Comprising three percent of the nation's institutions, HBCUs cannot afford to let these issues dominate. The detrimental effects these problems in management will have may very well eventually stamp the life out of HBCUs. Hence, it is essential that HBCU leaders take immediate action to correct these operational weaknesses. In addition, because HBCUs graduate approximately thirty percent of all African American students, it is obvious that this would be a tragedy indeed. As Lynn Huntley, president of the Southern Education Foundation Inc. (SEF), stated in 2004, "Many people look at the South that gave African Americans the short end of the stick. Now they think HBCUs are no longer needed because African Americans can go to white schools. But HBCUs remain a vital part of the nation because they are not the cause of problems."[50]

Notes

1. Amanda Asgill, "The Importance of Accreditation: Perceptions of Black and White College Presidents," *Journal of Negro Education* 45, no. 3 (1976), pp. 284–294.

2. Southern Association of Colleges and Schools. http://www.sacscasi.org/region/history/.

3. Ibid.

4. Fred O. Pinkham, "The Accreditation Problem," *Annals of the American Academy of Political and Social Science* 301 (1955), pp. 65–74.

5. William K. Selden, *Accreditation: A Struggle Over Standards in Higher Education* (New York: Harper and Brother, 1960).

6. Frank G. Dickey, "Recognizing and Monitoring Professional and Specialized Accrediting Associations," Proceedings of the Northwest Association of Secondary and Higher Schools Annual Meeting (Portland, OR: Northwest Association of Secondary and Higher Schools, 1973).

7. Ibid.

8. William K. Selden, *Accreditation*.

9. Melanie Carter, "From Jim Crow to Inclusion: An Historical Analysis of the Association of Colleges and Secondary Schools for Negroes, 1934–1965" (Ph.D. diss., Ohio State University, 1996); and St. Clair Drake, "The Black University in the American Social Order," *Daedalus* 100, no. 3 (1971), p. 846.

10. Melanie Carter, "From Jim Crow to Inclusion," (Ph.D. diss., Ohio State University, 1996).

11. Bronte D. Jones, "Restoring Accreditation in Two Private Texas Historically Black Colleges" (Ph.D. diss., University of Texas at Austin, 2005), 7; Saran Donahoo and W. Lee, "The Adversity of Diversity: Regional Associations and the Accreditation of Minority Serving Institutions" in Marybeth Gasman, Benjamin Baez, and Caroline Sotello Turner, ed., *Understanding Minority Institutions* (New York: State University of New York Press, 2008), pp. 292–310; American Association of University Professors, *Historically Black Colleges and Universities: Recent Trends* (Philadelphia: University of Pennsylvania, 2007); and Burton Bollag, "Trying Prevention Before Punishment," *Chronicle of Higher Education*, June 2, 2006, p. A21.

12. American Association of University Professors, *Historically Black Colleges and Universities: Recent Trends*; and Denise B. Hawkins "Doing More with Less: Despite Having Fewer Resources, HBCUs Have Outpaced Majority Institutions in Producing Black Professionals, but Experts Say Strong Leadership Will Be the Key to Their Long-Term Survival," *Black Issues in Higher Education* 21, no. 9 (2004): 44–52.

13. American Association of University Professors, *Historically Black Colleges and Universities: Recent Trends*; and interview with Vann R. Newkirk.

14. American Association of University Professors, *Historically Black Colleges and Universities: Recent Trends*; "Actions Taken by the SACSCOC Board of Trustees, June 23, 2011," http://sacscoc.org/2011%20June%20Actions%20and%20Disclosure%20 Statements/11cract%20june.pdf; and Yasmine Regester, "Malveaux Hopeful Bennett College Probation Will be Lifted," *Carolina Peacemeaker* (Greensboro, NC) July 7, 2011.

15. Middle States Commission on Higher Education, "Statement of Accreditation Status," http://www.msche.org/documents/SAS/125/Statement%20of%20Accreditation %20Status.htm.

16. Southern Association of Colleges and Schools Commission on Colleges, "Accreditation Actions and Disclosure Statements," http://www.sacscoc.org/accreditation Disclosure.asp.

17. American Association of University Professors, *Historically Black Colleges and Universities: Recent Trends.*

18. Southern Association of Colleges and Schools Commission on Colleges, "Accreditation Actions & Disclosure Statements," http://www.sacscoc.org/accreditationDisclosure.asp.

19. "Questions Regarding the Status of Fort Valley State University," http://sacscoc. org/2011%20December%20Actions%20and%20Disclosure%20Statements/Fort%20 Valley%20State%20University.pdf.; and "Actions Taken by SACSCOC Board of Trustees December 5, 2011," http://sacscoc.org/2011%20December%20Actions%20and%20Disclosure%20Statements/11cract%20december.pdf

20. Southern Association of Colleges and Schools Commission on Colleges, "Accreditation Actions & Disclosure Statements," http://www.sacscoc.org/accreditationDisclosure.asp.

21."Questions Regarding the Status of the Interdenominational Theological Center," http://sacscoc.org/2011%20 December%20Actions%20and%20Disclosure%20Statements/Interdenominational%20Theological%20Ctr.pdf.

22."Questions Regarding the Status of Jarvis Christian College," http://sacscoc.org/2011 %20December%20Actions%20and%20Disclosure%20Statements/Jarvis%20Christian %20College.pdf

23. Southern Association of Colleges and Schools Commission on Colleges, "Accreditation Actions & Disclosure Statements," http://www.sacscoc.org/accreditationDisclosure.asp.

24. Ibid.

25. Ibid.

26."Statement of Accreditation Status," https://www.msche.org/documents/sas/ 184/Statement%20of%20Accreditation%20Status.htm.

27. "Historic Mary Holmes College Closes After More Than a Century of Service," *Presbyterian Voice* 16, no. 2 (2005).

28. Vann Newkirk, " Barber-Scotia College: A Case for Faith-Based Education," paper presented to Barber-Scotia College Board of Trustees, October 2005.

29. 35. Southern Association of Colleges and Schools Commission on Colleges, "Accreditation Actions and Disclosure Statements," http://www.sacscoc.org/accreditationDisclosure.asp.

30. Ibid.

31."Questions about Savannah State University," http://sacscoc.org/2011%20 December%20Actions%20and%20Disclosure%20Statements/Savannah%20State%20 University.pdf.

32. Vann Newkirk, " Barber-Scotia College: A Case for Faith-Based Education," paper presented to Barber-Scotia College Board of Trustees, October 2005., 10.

33."Public Disclosure of Soujourner-Douglas College," http://www.msche.org/ institutions_sas_pds.asp?idInstitution=441.

34. "Questions Regarding the Status of Southwestern Christian College," http://sacscoc.

org/2011%20December%20Actions%20and%20Disclosure%20Statements/South western%20Christian%20College.pdf.

35. Southern Association of Colleges and Schools Commission on Colleges, "Accreditation Actions and Disclosure Statements," http://www.sacscoc.org/accreditationDisclosure.asp.

36. Ibid.

37. Ibid.

38. "Leaders of Sue Bennett College Say They Were Kept in the Dark on its Problems," *Chronicle of Higher Education*, September 19, 1997.

39. Maureen Casile and Alison Davis-Blake, "When Accreditation Standards Change: Factors Affecting Differential Responsiveness of Public and Private Organizations," *The Academy of Management Journal* 45, no. 1 (2002), pp. 180–195.

40. William E. Spriggs, "Major Trends Facing Historically Black Colleges and Universities," *Diverse Issues in Higher Education* 23 (2006); National Association for Equal Opportunity in Higher Education, *The State of America's Black Colleges: Expanding Access, Ensuring Success, Promoting Global Competitiveness*, (Silver Spring, MD: Beckham, 2008), pp. 1–6.

41. William A. Kaplin, "Judicial Review of Accreditation: The Parsons College Case," *The Journal of Higher Education* 40, no. 7 (1969), p. 543–554.

42. Katherine T. Phan, "ABHE Announces Newly Accredited Christian Colleges," *Christian Reporter*, February 26, 2009; "Federal Court Halts Move to Deny Paul Quinn College Accreditation," *Diverse Issues in Higher Education*, August 28, 2009; and "Paul Quinn College Gains New Accreditation," *Enis Daily News*, April 15, 2011.

43. Amanda Asgill, "The Importance of Accreditation: Perceptions of Black and White College Presidents," *Journal of Negro Education* 45, no. 3 (1976), pp. 284–294; and Maureen Casile and Alison Davis-Blake, "When Accreditation Standards Change: Factors Affecting Differential Responsiveness of Public and Private Organizations," *The Academy of Management Journal* 45, no. 1 (2002), pp. 180–195.

44. Joye Griffin, " The Walmart Foundation Grants $500,000 To UNCF For Institute For Capacity Building," UNCF News and Media, May 12, 2010.

45. Vann R. Newkirk, interview by author, Fort Valley, GA, 29 November 2010.

46. Ibid.

47. Ibid.

48. Marybeth Gasman, "Accreditation of Black Colleges: Future Success?" *Diverse Issues in Higher Education,* July 14, 2008.

49. Leroy Davis, Sr., *Still Striving: What HBCU Presidents Need to Know About SACS Accreditation* (Atlanta, GA: Southern Education Foundation, 2007).

50. Crystal L. Keels, "Investing in HBCU Leadership: Southern Education Foundation Creates Three-Year Initiative to Facelift HBCU Accreditation," *Black Issues in Higher Education*, September 9, 2004.

6

Going Global:
The International Focus

KOMANDURI S. MURTY

The world in which most adult Americans grew to maturity no longer exists. The Cold War is over. The domestic economy is global. The "melting pot" is boiling over. Our world is in flux. The approach of the 21st century foreshadows not simply a new millennium, but a completely new and different globe.... Super-power confrontation has been replaced by regional instability. Jobs lost at home reappear abroad. Industrial accidents spread pollution across borders. Public health problems vault oceans. Goods and services flow freely across borders and among great trading blocks. American graduates must compete with their peers from overseas. In truth, the line separating "foreign" from "domestic" is much harder to define today than it was yesterday, and much of our domestic success depends on events taking place elsewhere.[1]

The focus on international issues fits within the context of an increasingly globalized world described in the above quotation. Scholte defined globalization as the "spread of trans-planetary connections between people," which have both economic and social impacts. The economic impacts relate to globalization in international trade, foreign direct investment, and capital market flows. For example, the share of international trade in total output in developing countries grew from 33.8% to 48.9% between 1990 and 2001. On the other hand, the social impact can be understood from the diversity point of view, in that the

United States, a country of immigrants, is composed of various cultural and ethnic groups. This suggests a compelling need for American institutions and citizens to develop fluency in foreign languages and international studies. A study conducted by the Association of International Educators in 2006 to assess public attitudes towards international education revealed that most respondents agree that: (1) it is important to prepare future generations of Americans for a global society; (2) knowledge of other languages will give future generations a competitive advantage in career opportunities; (3) it is important for future generations to participate in study abroad programs while in college; and, (4) it is important for future generations to have knowledge of other countries and cultures. Given the social and economic impetus of the modern world, combined with the September 11, 2001, terrorist attacks on New York's World Trade Center and the ensuing wars on terror on different global fronts, it is not surprising to see that "globalization of the world continues to move at an accelerated rate with increasingly greater impacts."[2]

The Role of Higher Education

The role of higher education in globalization is not to be underestimated. In order for America to maintain a strong presence in the global economy, strengthen diplomatic relations, understand social, cultural, and political power of other nations' governments, as well as to enhance national security, the globalization of American higher education is absolutely necessary. American interest in the internationalization of education can be traced back to the late 1940s, that is, when a growing number of U.S. institutions began to engage in student and faculty exchanges and collaborative research projects with their counterparts throughout the world. Since the end of World War II, foreign language and area studies education have received substantial support from foundations, the federal government, and educational institutions themselves.[3]

By the 1990s, internationalization was part of the common rhetoric and, for the most part, an expected component of the curriculum of colleges and universities. In recent years, the rapid development of a highly globalized economic, social, and political environment has encouraged colleges and universities to focus more of their attention and resources on producing globally competent graduates and to internationalize their curriculum, research, and service. However, very little effort has been made to assess these efforts and their implementation. Data is lacking concerning how well higher education is preparing undergraduates for the demands of the contemporary world. Three studies conducted by the American Council on Education provide an overview of the state of U.S. undergraduate education's ability to foreign language training and knowledge about the rest of the world. They also reveal major gaps in undergraduates' international education. For example, Lambert noted that while many college presidents place high value on international studies, it ranks relatively low among their priorities when compared to other academic subjects. Lambert's report called for substantial changes in moving international studies higher up the list of priorities. In 2000, ACE began a series of studies, funded by the Ford Foundation, to examine the status of internationalization in the United States and to describe the changes in the fifteen years that had lapsed since the earlier studies. The data published in the *Preliminary Status Report 2000* suggested low levels of internationalization and showed very little improvement since the late 1980s. The Green, Luu, and Burris report on *Mapping Internationalization on U.S. Campuses* examined the state of internationalization of undergraduate education in the United States in comparison to prior data, along with the international experiences and attitudes of undergraduate students and faculty.[4]

Findings of this study disclosed a mixture of successes and weaknesses. The successes were: (a) the proportion of institutions offering education abroad opportunities for credit increased from 65 percent in 2001 to 91 percent in 2006; (b) a larger number of institutions began investing in international opportunities for faculty, such as travel to meetings and conferences, and showed willingness to offer workshops for faculty to learn a foreign language; (c) all stake holders in higher education (students, faculty, and the public) supported international education requirements and activities; and, (d) students and faculty reported a variety of international experiences and exposure to foreign language learning.

In contrast, the weaknesses were: (a) foreign language admission and graduation requirements decreased in the past five years, from 53 percent to 45 percent of participating institutions; (b) institutions demonstrated a low level of articulated commitment to internationalization in many of their policies and practices; (c) the level of undergraduate participation in international education programs and activities fell far below students' expressed interest in these same programs and activities; the same gap exists between faculty's professed interest and their actions; (d) foreign language enrollment as a percentage of total enrollment remained static since the mid 1970s. An increase in Spanish course enrollment was countered by a decrease in enrollment in other languages, particularly French and German. In general, students preferred foreign language and cultural learning focused on Western countries; (e) while numbers and participation rates had increased, still only a small portion of undergraduates participated in academic programs abroad and most of those who had short-term experiences; and, (f) internationally oriented extracurricular activities and academic programs abroad attracted only a small number of students. Most students were primarily exposed to international learning in the classroom.

Based on these findings, the following recommendations were made to institutions seeking to expand their internationalization efforts: (a) given the low level of student participation in internationally oriented extracurricular activities and academic programs abroad, colleges and universities should focus on the curriculum to ensure that students gain international skills and knowledge; (b) resources close to home are often underutilized, such as international students, faculty, and community members. Taking greater advantage of these resources can enhance internationalization efforts; (c) building upon and strengthening the strong support for internationalization among students, faculty, and the public can provide momentum for internationalization efforts and turn support into greater participation; (d) there is particularly strong support for foreign language learning and recognition of the need for foreign language skills and cultural literacy is at an all-time high; therefore institutions should seek ways to increase student participation in these areas, especially the study of less commonly taught languages and cultures; and, (e) institutions should make internationalization a priority by including it in their mission statements, making it visible in their strategic plans, and assessing their institutional efforts.[5]

Focus on the curriculum should be enforced to ensure students are exposed to international skills and knowledge. Even with a significant increase in the number of students who participate in academic programs abroad, the overwhelming majority of students surveyed did not go abroad nor participate in internationally oriented extracurricular activities on campus. If institutions want their students to graduate with international skills and knowledge, they will need to concentrate their efforts on the curriculum. Strategies that institutions could use to internationalize their curriculum include incorporating international courses into the general education requirements, strengthening foreign language academic program or international course graduation requirements, and providing faculty with support and incentives to internationalize their courses.

The Role of Historically Black Colleges and Universities

HBCUs were some of the first American colleges to develop international focuses. For example, during the 1880s Storer College taught rudimentary language skills in various Congolese languages in order to prepare students for missionary work. In the late nineteenth century, under the aegis of Booker T. Washington, Tuskegee sent agricultural experts to Togo for research and to develop the ways to increase cotton production. Moreover, HBCUs were in the forefront of providing undergraduate education to several African leaders and other professionals like Kwame Nkrumah, Nnamdi Azikiwe, James Thaele, and C. Cecil Denis (Lincoln University, Pennsylvania); Angie Brooks (Howard University); and Ellen Mills Scarborough (Shaw University).HBCUs such as Hampton and Tuskegee became academic models for various countries in Africa and the Caribbean. Marcus Garvey, as a component of his Black Nationalist movement, made numerous visits to Tuskegee and attempted to replicate the educational programs offered by the school in his native country Jamaica and in Africa. Likewise, Reverend James Henderson also for an "interracial association" in South Africa modeled on Tuskegee in mid–1920s.[6]

Professional schools also had a profound impact on the education of African students. Founded in the nineteenth century, Howard University and Meharry medical schools contributed significantly to the training of African physicians early on in fields that were beneficial to the continent: tropical medicine, bacteriology, microbiology, animal experimentation, and statistical epidemiology. Some notable Howard University Medical School graduates include:

J.H. Roberts, son of the first Liberian President.

E. Mayfield Boyle, a1902 graduate from Sierra Leone, human rights activist who challenged the exclusionist British medical policy in West Africa.

Malaku E. Bayan, a 1935 graduate from Ethiopia, who later became Emperor Haile Selassie's personal physician.

David E. Boye-Johnsona, a 1942 graduate from Sierra Leone, who became the nation's chief medical officer two years later.

Aderohunmau O. Laja, a 1955 graduate from Nigeria and was posted in the pathology department of the Federal Ministry of Health in Lagos.

Badejo O. Adebonojo, a 1955 graduate from Nigeria and served as the chief medical officer of the Lagos State Government of Nigeria.

Latunde E. Odeku, a 1954 graduate and dormitory roommate of Andrew Young at Howard, who established the first neurosurgical unit at the University of Ibadan, and became its first head. [7]

Likewise, Meharry kept a record of its influential graduates from Africa including:

Daniel Sharpe Malekebu, a 1917 graduate from Malawi who later became the Head of the Independent Providence Industrial Mission in Southern Malawi.

Hastings Kamuzu Banda, a 1936 graduate from Malawi who was the life president of the Republic of Malawi until his death in 1994.

Joseph Nagbe Togbe, a1944 graduate from Liberia who went on to become an important figure in the World Health Organization.

Henry Nehemiah Cooper, a 1954 graduate from Liberia who was head of the John F. Kennedy Hospital in Monrovia. [8]

HBCUs also took an active part in the formation of political linkages with Africa in the twentieth century. To cite an example, when Italian invasion and occupation of Ethiopia took place between 1935 and 1936, leading African American intellectuals and Pan-Africanists like W.E.B. Du Bois, Adam Clayton Powell, Sr., Ralph Bunche, Paul Robeson (an internationally known actor, singer and activist), and Mordecai Johnson organized the Council on African Affairs to "fight for Ethiopia." Most Black church leaders from such organizations as the National Baptist Convention, the Fraternal Council of Churches, the Colored Methodist Episcopal Church, and the African Methodist Episcopal Zion Church joined intellectual leaders not only by condemning Italy for its immorality, but also by preaching a pro–Ethiopian gospel based on Black Christian brotherhood. Many HBCUs adopted community service as part of their mission aligning with the church tradition of serving the needy throughout Africa including: raising funds, preaching the gospel, feeding the hungry, housing the homeless, and providing other forms of humanitarian support.[9]

Although Howard University taught Swahili in the 1920s, Rivers documented that French, German, Spanish and Italian were the most commonly taught languages on HBCUs and that students were not provided with opportunities to study abroad. Nyabongo conducted a survey on the number of faculty teaching foreign languages, the number of students enrolled in foreign language classes, and the language teaching method used from 1942 to 1944. Although the study showed an increased interest and enrollment in foreign language courses at HBCUs it concluded that little attention was paid to measuring and evaluating foreign language teaching and learning at HBCUs.[10]

A 1953 study by Miller on HBCU campuses found that teaching methods were an obstacle to greater competence in language acquisition among students at HBCUs but not an obstacle to participation in language study. LeBlanc studied foreign language programs at HBCUs and found that HBCU students felt that language study would be more relevant if it was specifically related to their academic majors. Students also expressed a desire to develop fluency in the languages they studied.[11]

Davis conducted a study with 57 HBCUs focused on attitudes towards foreign language programs. The study found that students generally held positive attitudes towards foreign language study and were aware of the practical and intrinsic value of second languages and cultural studies. As defined by Qiang, the organizational factor obstacles students identified to language study in the Davis study related to a lack of or insufficient (1) opportunity for developing conversational skills, (2) cross-cultural study and information provided in classes, (3) funding for study abroad opportunities, and (4) other extracurricular activities that promote the use of the language studied. Moore's study on the low enrollment of Blacks and African-Americans at a majority institution yielded to similar findings to that of Davis on HBCUs. Specifically, it also noted organizational factors as an obstacle to student participation in foreign language learning. Students recommended greater dissemination of information on the advantages of foreign language study and a requirement for foreign language study.[12] Comp completed a comprehensive literature review on diversity and study abroad. The review condensed findings from 131 different sources. Of these sources, Comp considered approximately 65 to be research-based. The obstacles identified in the literature review preventing minorities from participating in study abroad experiences included: (1) financial issues, (2) lack of family support and/or needing to remain close to family, (3) concerns about language, (4) concerns about discrimination, and (5) program sites not of interest. As a sample of the research included in Comp's literature review, Fels found that Black students assumed they would be treated as objects of fear abroad and that institutional efforts kept them ignorant of opportunities for study abroad.[13] The research included in the Comp literature review focused on minority participation in study abroad in general, rather than specifically on HBCU campuses. Similar observations to those of Comp were made by Norfles in his study with TRIO program faculty and students. Areas identified by Norfles included (1) cost, (2) lack of information, (3) family constraints, (4) individual limitations, and (5) language. Although this research was not specific to HBCUs, it did address underrepresented and underserved populations.[14]

Founded in 1940, the United Negro College Fund (UNCF) has taken some new initiatives in the 21st century. It created the United Negro College Fund Special Programs in the year 2000 with the funds of United States Agency for International Development (USAID) cooperative agreement. One of its major components is the International Development Partnerships (IDP) program. The IDP's primary goal is to fund Historically Black Colleges and Universities to work collaboratively with Institutions for Higher Education (IHE) in developing countries on social and economic development activities; thus, creating international partnerships between HBCUs and IHEs. The IDP funded 44 partnerships under three different program elements: (1) the core programs of IDP partnerships which are three-year grants of up to $200,000, intended to reach all geographic regions; (2) the Education for Development and Democracy Initiative (EDDI) partnerships which are limited to Africa and focus particularly on expanding education opportunities, particularly for girls; and (3) the Cross Hemispheric Partnership (CHP) element funded one-year grants of up to $50,000 to develop programs to educate K–12 teachers, particularly, but not exclusively, in the U.S., about Afro-Latino history and culture. The program, has generated several new ties between U.S. HBCUs and overseas universities. The resulting partnerships benefited both the HBCUs capacity to work internationally and left the IHEs with new or improved programs, sometimes with better equipment, than before the program, to enhance their capacity building.

Participating institutions believe that they have both contributed and gained from the experience. However, like any other project, these partnerships have had some challenges and lessons learned as summarized below.[15]

Challenges

1. Transfer of funding from the HBCUs to the IHEs; e.g., in some instances, IHEs had to wait for eight to nine months to clear checks, issued by their HBCU partners, in the banking system.
2. Communications (delayed, or poor, telephone, internet, and fax facilities, as well as language problems).
3. Travel and visa issues between countries of partnerships; e.g., security issues in the host country impacted travel from and to the countries of partnership as planned.
4. Limited/inadequate funding, budget reductions, and exchange rate problems.
5. Staff turnover at various levels in HBCUs and IHEs.
6. Financial reporting issues (understanding what was required and providing timely reports).
7. Arriving at shared goals and objectives between HBCUs and IHEs.
8. Intellectual property rights issues regarding books, videos and other products produced by the projects' partnership directors.

Lessons Learned

1. Spend sufficient time in planning phase to identify all logistics for successful implementation of project.
2. Develop a workable plan that is agreeable to both HBCUs and IHEs delineating the roles and responsibilities by each task from beginning to ending of the project.
3. Draw and execute a memorandum of understanding between HBCUs and IHEs.
4. Develop a backup plan as an alternative to the initial plan of operation.
5. Establish relationship with banking system to facilitate electronic transfer of funds in a timely manner.

6. Identify key communicators with bilingual communication skills.
7. Prepare and submit realistic budget estimates with narrative and justification.
8. Expand the support and participation by groups beyond university partners.

The UNCF Special Programs Study on HBCUs Study Abroad Programs

The United Negro College Fund Special Programs Corporation's Center for Assessment, Planning and Accountability (CAPA) and Komanduri S. Murty conducted a study in 2007, funded by the U.S. Department of Education, to examine undergraduate minority student participation in international education activities and programs at HBCUs. The study addressed two research questions: (1) what are the existing attitudes of minority undergraduates attending HBCUs toward international education activities and programs; and (2) what factors impact (i.e., promote or hinder) the participation of minority undergraduates attending HBCUs in international education activities and programs? A total of 1,346 students from sixty-two HBCUs completed a survey; seven focus groups were conducted on five college campuses to supplement the survey data. The study found that, for the general attitudes and abilities, over 80 percent of the respondents perceived that international skills (i.e., speaking a foreign language, understanding other cultures, and knowing about international events) would help them be successful in the job market in the future.[16]

A majority of HBCU students do not perceive that addressing international issues in the classroom distracts from instruction on the basics. At least 75 percent of the HBCU students also believe that all undergraduates should participate in a study abroad experience, be required to take courses covering international topics, and be required to study a foreign language. There is also vast agreement among HBCU students that studying international topics will help them better understand their own culture and values, increase their understanding of other cultures, and provide them with skills to work with people from diverse backgrounds. Fewer than half of the HBCU student respondents who had traveled abroad perceived that the experience would help them secure a better job in the future. As for the formal international education experiences, a vast majority of students who had traveled for academic purposes noted that the experience provided benefits in understanding other cultures, made them more well-rounded, increased their understanding of their own culture and values, provided life skills to work with people from diverse backgrounds, and increased their foreign language skills. At least 80 percent of all HBCU students perceived that it is important to study a foreign language, take a course focused on global themes, take a course on foreign cultures and religions, and study abroad. Positive attitudes were also noted in the reasons why students elected to participate in international education activities. Related to attitudes, the main reasons for participation were interest and planning to go abroad before graduating. Finally, regarding informal international education experiences, a vast majority of students who had traveled for nonacademic purposes noted that the experience provided benefits in understanding other cultures and made them more well-rounded. At least 75 percent of the HBCU students believed it would be important to have international-related internships, participate in local and foreign community service, and participate in international or foreign language clubs.[17]

At least 80 percent of the HBCU student survey respondents perceived that it is important to participate in international study trips or tours, international forums and discussions, and international travel for holiday or pleasure. Positive attitudes were also noted in the reasons why students elected to participate in informal international education activities. Less positive attitudes were expressed related to the benefits of nonacademic travel. Fewer than half of the HBCU student respondents who had traveled abroad perceived that the experience provided them with skills to work with other people from diverse backgrounds, increased their foreign language skills, or would help them secure a better job in the future.[18]

Recommendations for Enhancing HBCUs International Focus

Several recommendations are emergent from the study results. These recommendations guide the future steps appropriate for minority students to take, especially for those enrolled in HBCUs, to actively participate in international education.

Sustainability of Students' Interest: The vastly positive attitudes toward international education represent an opportunity for HBCUs. Students have expressed great interest in participating in international education activities and programs. HBCUs must, therefore, do all they can to sustain the level of student interest by developing appropriate programs within the existing resources and by acquiring additional resources, if necessary, in order to allow students to fulfill their interest in international education.[19]

Increasing Students' Motivation, Awareness, and Participation: Focus group results indicate that students have limited their definition of international education to study abroad experiences. HBCUs must increase the motivation and awareness of various international education opportunities among students on their home campuses by routinely organizing periodic events. Examples include an international education day, international fairs, and student international clubs, where students can be exposed to literature (flyers, pamphlets, etc.) on international educational opportunities, build partnerships with international students, and have opportunities to empathize with and understand various international cultures.[20]

Internship/community service opportunities with local organizations that work with people from foreign countries should also be explored and incorporated into academic programs. For example, the motivation and participation levels can also be boosted by developing additional recognition, incentives, and preferences in registration and graduation procedures for those who participate in international education and activities for a minimum number of specified hours (e.g., 150 clock hours or nine semester hours).[21]

Strengthening Study Abroad Programs: Study abroad programs teach important intercultural and language skills; but the true success of a program occurs within a student, when the student realizes that he or she can see the world from a different cultural viewpoint. This experience also has a lasting impact in that years after students return from abroad, they continue to learn languages, continue to foster interest in other cultures, and start to promote the importance of this experience to others. However, before this stage can be reached, HBCUs must strengthen their study abroad programs by undertaking the following three initiatives:. First, more financial assistance must be obtained from the federal government and study abroad providers. The survey data clearly shows that cost is a major obstacle for students who wish to participate in study abroad programs, as evidenced by the wide gap between perception and practice. Many students attending HBCUs depend on federal financial aid and student loans just to cover their basic college expenses (tuition, textbooks, and dormitory fees). Consequently, participating in programs like study abroad will remain a dream and beyond reach for many such students. HBCUs themselves are not wealthy and constantly face financial constraints just to meet infrastructure requirements. Therefore, it is inevitable that HBCUs must engage in strong fund-raising efforts to obtain finances to fund international and study abroad programs. Second, HBCUs must build partnerships with all stakeholders. Because any single HBCU cannot do it all by itself, they should form coalitions based on similar interests; develop partnerships with private corporations, governmental agencies, and international organizations, not only to pool their resources, but also to expand the program (fiscally and in terms of scope and curriculum content); and make the programs more economical and affordable. Third, HBCUs must pay more attention to the quality of study abroad programs. Administrators and program coordinators should develop standards and continually assess a program's impact to ascertain that the outcomes of the study abroad programs are rewarding and credit-worthy. Key performance indicators and proper monitoring techniques must be developed and implemented for evaluation and assessment purposes. These performance evaluations, in turn, help the HBCUs maintain and obtain additional funding in successive years.[22]

Increased Focus on Critical Languages: The *National Security Language Initiative* (NSLI) indicates that the United States has a need for more citizens to be fluent in critical languages (e.g., Arabic, Chinese (Mandarin), Hindi, Korean, Persian (Farsi), Russian, and Turkish). This study found, however, that the languages most spoken by HBCU students are Spanish and French. None of the critical languages are spoken by more than 2 percent of the HBCU students. HBCUs must, therefore, expand their foreign language departments by accommodating opportunities for students to learn these critical languages. In light of globalization, mastering critical languages will help pave the way for students to obtain higher-paying jobs in the future and becoming better citizens.[23]

Increased Focus on Male Students: Multiple areas of this study found that females have statistically significantly more positive attitudes and participation rates in international education. This is consistent with studies that have identified males as being underrepresented in international education. Efforts should be made at HBCUs to ensure that they include a focus on male students to increase their participation in international education activities.

Lessons to Learn from More Successful Campuses: HBCUs may opt to examine the international programs that are more successful on other college or university campuses, including those that are predominantly White, to gain knowledge of the logistics, scope, and measures that have contributed to the success of their programs. Once this knowledge is acquired, HBCUs can customize the programs to meet their own needs and resources. They can also use this knowledge for partnership purposes to develop similar programs.

Internationalizing the curriculum: Citing education as the single most critical element in enhancing an individual's contribution to society's long-term competitiveness, Ahmed and Krohn note that a lack of global awareness on the part of U.S. business school graduates has weakened U.S. business's ability to be competitive in the global economy. They also note that a global reason cannot be realized by adding a couple of courses on foreign lands into the school's curriculum. This points to a weakness in the existing international business and management curriculum at HBCUs. Total transformation of the learning approach of this curriculum is required to bring necessary change. In order to create the competency needed by multinational corporations, HBCUs must offer sound international business and management programs. HBCUs have to realize that business, management, and the entire global enterprise is not static. It is a dynamic process of constant change and innovative techniques. The projections of Gregerson, Morrison, and Black. indicate that the international business at the current growth rate is so diverse that trade between nations will exceed total commerce within nations by 2015.[24]

Therefore, educating students with an American view of supply chain management and finance is not sufficient for us to become successful in a global economy. HBCU students graduating with a degree in international business and management must be equipped with a global mindset that prepares them for the diversity of global management, business, and organization. They must be prepared to live and work in foreign countries, and elevate their emotional intelligence to adequately adjust to a foreign environment. Thus, the major focus of international studies program should be to: (a) develop and promote academic exchange initiatives; (b) forge international collaborations and alliances with institutions worldwide; and, (c) offer opportunities that equip students with skills vital for international studies, such as communicating in other languages, knowing other cultures and markets, and understanding the increasingly fluid economic, social and political realities of globalization.

Leadership Training: Globalization requires leadership of global competence. Since the end of the Cold War, American institutions and organizations have been working to identify and acquire the resources needed for leadership skills, traits, and characteristics to effectively work through global politics and economy. HBCUs are trying to implement global leadership development into their international art, music, management, business, justice, and other curricula. Such traditional syllabi are not enough to prepare globally professional leaders. The question is: how to create such leaders?[25] Unlike traditional and legal theories which emphasized rational processes, there are some recent theories like task versus relations-oriented leadership, autocratic versus participative leadership, and leadership versus management, for example, Bass argued that transformational leadership must be grounded in moral foundations because the morality process reflects the legitimacy of both influence processes on the part of the leaders and empowerment processes on the part of followers as they engage in dynamic self-transformation. Moreover, a global leader, in any industry or corporation, needs to have a personal commitment and interest to enjoy and adapt to diverse cultures. In addition, an important mindset for global leaders to have is that of patience: patience to work through language and cultural difference, and the desire to value those differences. Global leaders must understand that their native way of conducting business may spell disaster in other nations. So an early exposure to different cultures goes a long way toward the development of global leadership competence.[26]

Conclusion

Despite all the positive steps that HBCUs are taking to increase their presence on the international stage, the road ahead is "still very long and sometimes tortuous," because: (1) international education programs are very expensive; (2) some HBCU administrators do not realize the urgent necessity to institutionalize international education on their respective campuses; and, (3) sustainability problems continue to exist in HBCUs due to their dependence on soft monies (grants and contracts from government agencies). Jacqueline Howard-Mathews of United Negro College Fund Special Programs Corporation says that the barriers to international education at black colleges were greater than the challenges of staffing study abroad offices. She observed that too many study abroad programs at black colleges were "pass throughs" in which students were applauded for travel but failed to integrate overseas experiences into the curricula at the home institutions. Development of study abroad must accompany improved foreign language and foreign area studies.[27]

Notes

1. American Council on Education. *Educating Americans for a World in Flux: Ten Ground Rules for Internationalizing Higher Education* (Washington, D.C.: American Council on Education, 1995), p. 3.

2. National Association for International Education, *Americans Call For Leadership on International Education* (Washington, D.C.: National Association for Foreign Student Advisers, 2006); Jan A. Scholte, *Globalization: A Critical Introduction* (New York: Palgrave Macmillan, 2005), p. 59; Carnegie Endowment for International Peace, "Globalization 101: What is Globalization?" http://www.globalization101.org/What_is_Globalization. html. NAFSA originally stands for National Association of Foreign Student Advisers. However, since its inception in 1948 the name has been changed to NAFSA: Association for International Educators, to reflect the expanding roles of its members into all aspects of international education and exchange.

3. Hayward, Fred M. *Preliminary Status Report 2000: Internationalization of U.S. Higher Education* (Washington, D.C.: American Council on Education, 2000); Charles Anderson, *International Studies for Undergraduates* (Washington, D.C.: American Council on Education, 1988); Richard Lambert, *International Studies and the Undergraduate* (Washington, D.C.: American Council on Education, 1989); Madeleine Green, Dao Luu and Beth Burris, *Mapping Internationalization on U.S. Campuses: 2008 Edition* (Washington, D.C.: American Council on Education, 2008).

4. Green, Luv and Burris.

5. Ibid.

6. Casandra R. Veney, "The Ties That Bind: The Historic African Diaspora and Africa," *African Issues* 30:1 (2002), pp. 3–8; Paul B. Rich, "The Appeals of Tuskegee: James Henderson, Lovedale, and the Fortunes of South African Liberalism, 1906–1930," *The International Journal of African Historical Studies* 20:2 (1987), pp. 271–292.

7. Adell Patton Jr., "Howard University and Meharry Medical Schools in the Training of African Physicians, 1868–1978," in Joseph E. Harris, ed., *Global Dimensions of the African Diaspora*, 2d ed. (Washington, D.C.: Howard University, 1993), pp. 109–120.

8. Ibid.

9. James Hunter Meriwether, "The African Connection and the Struggle for Freedom: Africa's Role in African-American Life, 1936–1963" (Ph.D. dissertation, University of California, Los Angeles, 1995), p. 48; C. Eric Lincoln and Lawrence H. Mamiya, *The Black Church in the African-American Experience* (Durham, NC: Duke University Press, 1990); and William R. Scott, *African-Americans and the Italo-Ethiopian War, 1935–1941* (Bloomington: Indiana University Press, 1993).

10. W. Napoleon Rivers, "A Study of Modern Foreign Languages in Thirty Negro Colleges," *Journal of Negro Education* 2 (1933): 437–493; and Virginia S. Nyabongo, "Modern Foreign Language Study in Negro Colleges," *French Review,* 20 (1946):153–58.

11. James Davis, "A Study of Student Attitudes Toward Language Study at Historically

and Predominantly Black Institutions" (unpublished Ph.D. dissertation, University of Maryland, College Park, 1990); Kenneth C. Miller, "The Teaching and Learning of Modern Foreign Languages in Colleges for Negroes" (Ph.D. Thesis, Ohio State University, 1953); and Helen G. LeBlanc, "An Exploratory Study on the Responses to Students' Needs in Foreign Language Instruction in Colleges and Universities Predominantly Attended by Afro-American Students" (Ph.D. Thesis, University of Minnesota, 1972).

12. Zena Moore, "African American Students' Opinion About Foreign Language Study: An Exploratory Study of Low Enrollments at the College Level," *Foreign Language Annals, 38*(2) (2005), pp. 191–200; and Zha Qiang, "Internationalization of Higher Education: Towards a Conceptual Framework" *Policy Futures in Education,* 1, no. 2 (2003), pp. 248–270.

13. Michael D. Fels,"Assumptions of African-American Students about International Education Exchange," (unpublished paper, Convention of the Communication Association, Miami, Florida, 1993); and Nicole Norfles, "Toward Equal and Equitable Access: Obstacles and Opportunities in International Education," 2003, http://www.jhfc. duke.edu/ducis/globalchallenges/pdf/.

14. Nicole Norfles, "Toward Equal and Equitable Access," and Komanduri S. Murty, *UNCFSP Global Center Partnerships Evaluation Report* (Washington, D.C.: United Negro College Fund for Special Programs, 2003).

15. Komanduri S. Murty, "UNCFSP Global Center."

16. Ibid.

17. Ibid.

18. Ibid.

19. Ibid.

20. Ibid.

21. Ibid.

22. Ibid.

23. Ibid.

24. Hal Gregerson, Allen J. Morrison, and J. Stewart Black. "Developing Leaders for the Global Frontier," *MIT Sloan Management Review* 40(1) (1998): 21–32; Zafar Ahmed and Franklin B. Krohn, "Internationalizing Business Programs at Non-Accredited Collegiate Institutions," *Journal of Education for Business* 66, no. 2 (1990), p. 5.

25. Gary Yukl, "An Evaluation of Conceptual Witnesses in Transformational and Charismatic Theories," *Leadership Quarterly* 10, no. 2 (1999), p. 285.

26. Roya Ayman, Noel A. Kreicker, and Jaci J. Masztal, "Defining Global Leadership in Business Environments," *Consulting Psychology Journal: Practice and Research* 46, no. 1 (1994), pp. 64–77.

27. Ingrid Norton, "International Education Remains a Challenge at Historically Black Colleges," *Chronicle of Higher Education* (2008); and Olusoji Akomolafe, "Africanizing HBCUs: Problems and Prospects of International Education in Historically Black Institutions," *African Studies* 28, no. 1–2 (2000), pp. 103–107.

7

Business, Finance and Fund-Raising

VANN R. NEWKIRK AND DANIEL WIMS

Since the first historically black college opened, raising money to keep the doors open has been a constant challenge. As indicated by former Morehouse College President Benjamin Mays, "the ever-present necessity of raising funds is particularly difficult for the Negro college, since money owned and controlled by whites flows more freely and more abundantly from white to white than it does from white to black. Moreover, the Negro president of a Negro college is almost daily confronted by stumbling blocks, hurdles and personal embarrassments that rarely it ever clutter the path of his white counterpart." Perhaps due to this fact nearly forty years after Mays published his prophetic words, John Wilson, the executive director of the White House Initiative on HBCUs said, "There seems to be a tendency [among the media] to emphasize and accentuate all the bad things, all the negative news coming at us [meaning HBCUs]. Someone gets injured, or a faculty member gets in trouble, or a lot of students are leaving for financial reasons, then there are big headlines. But when there is breakthrough research going on or students winning special awards, or major gifts coming in then there isn't as much publicity." In addition to these challenges, most black colleges face persistent funding shortfalls caused by the failure of state governments and denominational groups to provide adequate funding.[1]

Despite the hurdles, most of America's historically black colleges continue to weather the storm as they have for more than a century. Yet, with the economic meltdown of 2008, HBCUs now face greater challenges in securing the resources needed to support operations and student aid. For instance, in many southern states where most HBCUs are located, budget deficits have led to a reduction of state allocations to public and private HBCUs. It has also led to calls, in a number of states, for the merger of HBCUs as a means of saving money. The last decade also has seen many church groups, such as the United Methodist, Presbyterian Church U.S.A., and the Episcopal Churches, who are suffering from declining membership, to reduce the already meager support provided for denominational HBCUs.

As if these issues were not enough, many HBCUs must also cope with the consequences of poor strategic decisions made years earlier. Several of these decisions, such as the use of overcollateralized loans to support capital construction and the addition of high cost athletic teams now threaten institutional viability. This chapter examines the challenges of fund-raising, inadequate state and denominational funding, and problematic business practices that endanger America's historically black colleges. The chapter also looks at emerging practices and strategies that HBCUs might implement to develop more productive approaches to fund-raising, and operations.

The Historic Perspective of HBCU Fund-Raising

Born in the turbulent days at the close of the Civil War, many HBCUs owed their existence to northern missionary groups. These groups provided one of the most significant early sources of financial support for black education contributing approximately $15,000,000 for the construction and maintenance of schools and colleges for African-Americans. Another source of support for the early HBCUs came from Freedmen themselves. Freedmen provided much of the money, labor and land for the construction of black colleges. Black church groups such as the AME, AMEZ and CME also played their part by establishing more than two dozen colleges. They also supported the schools by providing operational support, scholarships for students and funds to construct buildings.[2]

The most important early source of support for the early HBCU was the Freedmen's Bureau. Although the bureau never taught a single former slave, it organized the assorted groups connected with African-American education. The Bureau also supplied transportation to teachers of freed people, paid for salaries, books, and other learning aids. The Freedmen's Bureau secured space for schools by confiscating the property of former Confederates. Most importantly, the Bureau distributed more than $5,000,000 for the construction and support of black schools and colleges. By 1870, the Freedmen's Bureau supervised more than 4,000 schools, employing 9,000 teachers and enrolling more than 247,000 students.[3]

At the turn of the century, HBCUs gained new supporters, namely Northern industrialists. The basis for this support lay in America's Negrophobic past. Throughout the period from 1619 through 1865, blacks occupied a position at the bottom of America's social hierarchy. At the end of the Civil War, the nation's four million slaves suddenly gained their freedom. Yet, as former Stanford University official J.M. Stephen Peeps observed, freedom "did not give America's ex-slaves all that much." Most social gains were small and, economically, freedmen remained at the bottom of the nation's social hierarchy. However, to many southern whites, any gain, no matter how small, was "immense in symbolic significance." Nothing garnered more white anger than black schools. "Keep the spelling book and the land from the possession of the Negro if you hope to control him," warned a prominent Southern senator. Hence, holding back black education and wages was deemed crucial to the maintenance of the new social order with which white supremacists sought to replace slavery.[4]

Accompanying this basic intolerance was the "quasi-scientific" movement of Social Darwinism which promoted the view that blacks were an inferior race. Such a view made it a much easier to justify the suppression of black college education. Indeed, even if one held no fear of menacing blacks there was no reason to support higher education for former slaves who were by birth naturally fitted only for manual labor. As a result, upon returning to power, white supremacists limited "Negro college education to the preparation of the few professionals needed to insure a hermetic casts system."[5]

The impact of this development was a general lack of interest in black collegiate education. Instead, all turned their focus toward vocational training.[6] As indicated by William H. Baldwin, the first chair of northern industrialist's John D. Rockefeller's General Education Board,

"The Negro should not be educated out of his environment. Industrial work is his salvation; he must work ... at trades and on the land.... Except in the rarest of instances, I am bitterly opposed to the so-called higher education of Negroes." Due to these developments, there was little incentive for HBCU leaders to be innovative or to organize any significant fund-raising apparatuses. The key to obtaining support lay not in innovation but in developing programs that supported the narrow-minded directives of others. For example, when Fisk University faced financial ruin at the turn of the century the school established a vocational department, and through the intercession of Booker T. Washington, Fisk secured support from two foundations. Unfortunately, this had lasting ramifications in that it produced generations of unimaginative HBCU leaders, and passive boards with little skill in securing the resources needed to support operations.[7]

HBCU Support After the Brown Case

With the landmark *Brown vs. Topeka* ruling, in 1955, most philanthropic support for black colleges dried up as many whites questioned the continued relevancy of HBCUs. However, during this dark period, Congress passed several important pieces of legislation.[8] The first of the acts, the National Defense Education Act of 1958, provided funding to institutions of all types by allocating scholarships, grants, and loans to increase the number of students attending college and majoring in the sciences.

Seven years later, Congress passed the Higher Education Act of 1965. This program contained two provisions that provided direct support for HBCUs: Title III which sought to strengthen black colleges through a series of formula grants, and Title IV which provided student financing through grants, loans and work-study opportunities.[9] Another important development occurred in 1972, when Congress passed the Pell Grant program. Originally known as the Basic Education Opportunity Grant (GEOG), Pell grants awarded need-based aid to low income students who enrolled at least part-time at an accredited college. Hence, the law provided access to higher education for millions of students who heretofore could not attend college.[10]

Although federal programs, such as the Pell grant program, relieved much of the financial stress faced by historically black colleges they also rekindled old issues by installing new kingpins. These kingpins, in the form of federal regulators and their proxy agents, regional accrediting bodies, set agendas and determined the structure and type of degree programs to be offered by black colleges. Federal assistance also led to a new problem: increased institutional dependency on soft money.[11]

The Development of Professional Fund-Raising Offices

During the early to mid–1970s, HBCUs established their first professional fund-raising offices.[12] The majority of these offices consisted of little more than a chief fund-raising officer, and a few support staff. Few of the so-called fund-raising professionals had the requisite training, or support infrastructure to undertake their assigned mission. As indicated by Alice Green Burnette, former president of Advanced Solutions, a fund-raising consulting firm in Palm Coast, Florida, most HBCU leaders, frequently "put all of their eggs in one basket, having one good person who was highly qualified and cutting corners on support staff."[13]

However, for many HBCUs, failure to invest in a development office was not the result of failure to understand the importance of fund-raising but more a product of institutional capability. For example, at cash-strapped Fisk University, total staffing in the development office in 2010 consisted of four professionals plus a support staff member. This level of staffing however was the same as 1999, when the University raised $5,000,000. According to Robert Poole, who served as vice president of advancement at Fisk University, in 1999, in order to increase office productivity, Fisk University needed at least four more professionals who specialized in "planned giving, corporate and foundation relations, donor research, and major gifts and the support staff and computer resources to back them up." To get the big gifts, Poole maintained, "you have to court donors over time, it is labor intensive activity." Despite Poole's admonition, in the years since 1999, limited institutional resources prevented Fisk University from expanding staffing levels in the office of development.[14]

Unfortunately, the failure or financial inability to invest in the fund-raising office has led to the institutionalization of fund-raising failure and constant turnover at many smaller HBCUs. For example, the inability to support the fund-raising office led to the departure of seven chief fund-raising officers between 1990 and 2000 at Barber-Scotia College.

Perhaps due to this fact the college only raised $1,750,000 of a $5,100,000 capital campaign. In similar fashion, Talladega College had five development officers between 2000 and 2010.* This undoubtedly played a role in the Southern Association of Colleges and Schools' decision to place the institution on probation twice, during the period, for poor finances. Commenting on the situation, Dr. William Harvey, president of Hampton University said, "a lot of people don't understand that you have to spend money to get money." As explained by Gail Perry, the former director of fund-raising for the Kenan-Flagler School of Business at the University of North Carolina at Chapel Hill, spending money on fund-raising operations is a venture that pays dividends repeatedly. The institutions that put money into raising money bring in the most capital. "Organizations that think they cannot afford to invest resources in fund-raising are the ones that don't raise money. They stay right where they are because they never changed a thing." Unfortunately, change is the one area many HBCU leaders are unable to embrace. Said one former HBCU development officer, "changing established processes is hard at an HBCU, until black college presidents embrace new fund-raising paradigms most will never be successful in raising money."[15]

Despite this grim forecast, over the last decade, a number of HBCUs have revamped outdated organizational frameworks and created more coherent approaches to fund-raising. The list of opportunities that HBCUs are now delving into consist of: non-alumni donor development, collaborative partnerships, online contributions, online relationship building via Facebook, Twitter and other social networks, alumni giving, endowment development; challenge grants; faculty and staff giving; student and parent giving; estate-planned-giving; major gifts; and foundation and corporate gifts. Properly coordinated with public relations, communications, marketing, direct mail and government relations, such activities can yield significant returns. For example, between 1990 and 2010, a number of HBCUs, such as Spelman College, Johnson C. Smith, Hampton and Howard universities, conducted fund-raising campaigns that set records at the time each concluded.† In the case of Johnson C.

---

*Turnover in the development office, however, was not unique to HBCUs. For example, between 2000 and 2010 five vice presidents of development served North Carolina Wesleyan College a small traditionally white institution.

†In addition to these well-known campaigns a number of smaller HBCUS such as Harris Stowe College, Claflin, and Prairie View A&M University concluded major campaigns that set records for each institution.

Smith University, between 1993 and 2007, the institution launched two capital campaigns. The first campaign, unveiled in 1993, combined an effective message, of developing new programs and renovating buildings with the coordinated actions of public relations, communication and marketing to raise $63.8 million in 1998. The same formula allowed the University to raise $81.5 million between 2005 and 2007.[16]

In contrast, Howard University's successful $275,000,000 capital campaign, which ended in 2008, was especially notable for how the University involved its alumni. In the years prior to the campaign, annual giving by alumni at Howard University averaged approximately four percent. However, during the campaign, alumni giving increased to twenty percent per annum. According to former Howard University President H. Patrick Swygert, the key to increasing alumni giving, "was to reengage them [alumni] with Howard by showing them the University's key asset: its students." Consequently, Howard ran ads in local and national newspapers featuring their best and brightest students. The University also sent postcards to alumni that featured Howard's Rhodes, Marshall and Fulbright scholars. The postcards also contained features about distinguished alumni. In addition to these features, the University updated its web site, alumni magazine and advancement offices. It also updated alumni databases to ensure a greater penetration of the campaigns marketing materials. Subsequently, the number of identified alumni and potential donors grew from 30,000 to 60,000.[17]

Howard University trustees also played a major role in the fundraising campaign by enhancing enthusiasm for giving early on. For example, Frank Savage, an alumnus, and former chair of the Board of Trustees gave $5,000,000 to the campaign. Another Trustee, Richard D. Parson, Chair of Time Warner, gave more than $1,000,000. James Silcott, a Los Angeles architect, alumnus, and Trustee gave $3,000,000 while Swygert contributed $2,000,000. The Trustees also went on the road appearing at alumni events across the nation. At several of the larger events alumni pledges took on a competitive spirit. For example, in Philadelphia, one alumnus pledged $1,000,000; in Miami, the school raised $8,000,000; while an event in New York raised $25,000.000. According to Howard University's Vice President for Development, Virgil E. Ecton, the early gifts of the Trustees, "sent a clear signal to the giving community that we were serious about the campaign." At the end of the campaign, thirty-three percent of the money raised was from alumni.[18]

During the same period, Hampton University used a heavy dose of corporate and foundation gifts to raise $264,000,000. Major gifts from foundation and corporations included $6,500,000 from the Scripps Howard Foundation; $5,000,000 from John T. Dorrance Jr., chief executive of the Campbell Soup Company; $4.1-million from the Pepsi Bottling Group; $3,000,000 from the Kellogg Foundation; $1.1 million from the Alfred P. Sloan Foundation; and $1,000,000 from the Bush Foundation. Other substantial gifts came from the school's national alumni association in the amount of $5,000,000 and $1,000,000 from University President William Harvey and his wife. Said Henry Ponder, the former president of the National Association for Equal Opportunity, "Its not surprising to me that Hampton would raise that because their president and others have been very astute in the fund-raising business."[19]

Yet, direct fund-raising only forms part of the puzzle. Over the past few years, a number of HBCUs have formed collaborative relationships that have linked colleges to industry, government, and major research institutions. Such partnerships have allowed institutions to increase opportunities for students, while also increasing revenue raised from corporate and governmental sources. One such program is the Cooperative Development Energy Program (CDEP), established by Fort Valley State University in 1993. According to the program's founder, Isaac Crumbly, "the CDEP program is a pre-collegiate/collegiate technical work force program that concentrates primarily on diversity for the private and public sector of the energy industry." Students enrolled in the program spend their first three years at Fort Valley State University (FVSU), majoring in mathematics, chemistry, or biology. After completing three years of study at FVSU, students transfer to a partnering research university to complete a second degree in engineering, geosciences or health physics. Once students have met the requirements of both programs, they receive two bachelor's degrees, one from FVSU and a second from a partnering university. Since its inception, CDEP has graduated 72 engineers, 25 geoscientists, and four health physicists. However, most importantly, since its inception, the program has raised more than $28,000,000.[20]

Another innovative fund-raising idea is Hampton University's Hampton Harbor shopping Center and apartment complex. Constructed in 1990, Hampton Harbors consists of a commercial shopping center, a Chick-Fil-A, a private catering service and a 246-unit apartment complex. Since its completion, the project has generated nearly $1,000,000 annually in profits. According to the university president,

William Harvey, "such projects can be economic drivers, providing an additional source of revenue for the institution and jobs for the community." This in turn serves as a conduit for increasing community support and revenue generation from government and private philanthropy.[21]

The success of Hampton University's economic development program, Fort Valley State University's CDEP program, as well as novel fund-raising campaigns at Johnson C. Smith University, Spelman College, Hampton University, Howard University and a handful of other black colleges clearly show that HBCUs must adopt new strategies to secure financial support. Listed below are the components of a new development model that incorporates many of the successful strategies described above:

1. **Identify Clearly Defined Goal(s).** Successful fund-raising starts with the development of clearly defined goals. Goals must persuasively describe why colleges need money. Goals must also provide realistic targets for long range planning.

2. **Identify Sources of Gifts and Fund-raising Methods.** For any given fund-raising project, it is essential to determine the best potential sources of support (i.e. alumni, foundations, community stakeholders, trustees, grants, or estate). Compiling data of past fund-raising efforts along with comparisons of peer institutions provides institutions with essential information as to which set of objectives and/or strategies to implement for maximum success. Upon adopting a strategy, colleges must incorporate the methodology into the fund-raising planning process. Although most profitable fund-raising occurs through person-to-person contact, a balanced approach is most suitable. A balanced fund-raising approach will likely include some combination of direct mail, phonations, and special events.

3. **Identify/Promote a Viable Product.** For many black colleges, marketing is a process of highlighting an institution's glorious past and its successes in educating underserved students. However, for many donors this message no longer resonates. In 2009, the Associated Press released an article entitled "Men Struggling to Finish at black colleges." The article revealed that just 37 percent of the black students at HBCUs finished a degree within six years. That is four percentage points lower than the national graduation rate for black students. Donors are no longer satisfied with pouring money into an institution simply because it staked out a

particular niche or serves a particular group. To enhance fund-raising efficiency colleges must promote success. This means improving graduation and retention rates. Identifying and promoting unique or distinctive strengths and putting resources into these key programs.[22]*

4. Assemble a Suitable Team. Perhaps the most important aspect of a successful fund-raising program is hiring a skilled and well-trained fund-raising staff. In today's environment, a staff for a small institution (3,000 and under) might consist of a vice president of development assisted by two development officers; full-time development officers for each academic school of the institution; governmental and a private resources grant writers; an Alumni Affairs Coordinator; a director for donor research; a director of sponsored research; a team of skilled professional who focus on corporate relations; a team of public relations officers; as well as attendant support staff. In support of these efforts, colleges must also involve key stakeholders – namely trustees, faculty, staff, students, alumni, and community supporters. However, as indicated by Wesley Wilmer in *Advancing Small Colleges Strategies for Success in Alumni Relations*, "The idea structure and operation for each institution's development office depends on the evaluation of many factors including:

- How long the institution has existed;
- The institution's history of raising money;
- Where it is located and whether there are competing institutions nearby;
- The culture of the institution and the community in which it operates;
- What constituencies have vested interest in the institution;
- The level of board support;
- The level of alumni support, and;
- How much of the budget has been allocated for the fund-raising operation."

5. Enhance Trustee Giving and Participation. For any college, trustee giving is key to an institution's success in meeting funding goals. All

*To raise perceptions of quality, colleges also must be more deliberate about highlighting their academic gems. Hence, it is important to arrange typical academic activities so as to garner media interest This means thinking deliberately about what instructors are doing in the classroom, in the research lab, or at academic meeting, and not being shy about supporting these activities in public.

trustees must provide substantial annual financial gifts and set an example for others (Since substantial is defined differently for this study, the sum is defined as $10,000 and above). After making their own gifts, board members should be involved in solicitation activities.

6. Undertake Entrepreneurial Efforts to Reduce Tuition Dependency. Business ownership is an important tool for educating students and in increasing capital for the institutions. The African American and urban markets in the United States are a trillion dollar market. Yet, the mainstream continues to ignore these communities. Today a number of HBCUS, including Hampton, Howard, Tuskegee, and Clark-Atlanta Universities, are among a group of historically black colleges that have business ownership ventures. These businesses not only benefit the universities but educate future entrepreneurs and businessmen. Although such ventures have the potential for substantial rewards "it is important to investigate each venture before risking an institution's capital."[23]

The Crisis of Reduced State and Denominational Funding

Black colleges and universities also face a stern test in the form of reduced state and denominational funding. These cuts threaten to widen the funding gap between TWIs and HBCUs as state governments grapple with record budget deficits.* Cut also have led to the adoption of a number of controversial policies. For example, in Louisiana the legislature adopted performance funding as a means of shrinking state allocations

---

*Historically, Southern legislatures established policies that allocated unequal resources and allowed rampant discrimination against public HBCUs. Indeed, between 1890 and 1940 Georgia's HBCUs received only 2 percent to 5 percent of the total state appropriation for higher education. During the period, African-Americans made up approximately 30% of the state's population. Yet Georgia was not alone throughout the 1920s: Florida allocated appropriately $7,600 annually for its land-grant HBCU while Louisiana limited its black college allocation to $10,000. As if this was not enough until the 1940s most states refused to provided the funding needed to conduct research, military training, or extension services as stipulated by the Morrill and Smith-Level Acts. Yet, by 1937, Southern state governments received more than $13,000,000 annually in extension funding. All of this funding, however, went to predominately white institutions. Perhaps due to these facts by the late 1930s the average Black land-grant institution had a value of $700,000. In contrast, the average white land-grant value exceeded $4.5 million. At the same time, the average state expenditure per student at the HBCUs was $138 compared to $234 per student at white land-grant colleges. The system remained substantially the same for the next thirty years.

to higher education. Performance funding allocates funding to colleges based on the institution's ability to retain and graduate a predetermined number of students. However, for many HBCUs which serve large numbers of first-generation students, such approaches are problematic. Students from these groups often require costly remedial assistance. As a result, such students may take longer to complete degree programs. The hurried implementation of performance funding formulas fails to consider situations such as this. Yet, performance-based budgeting has already started to take a toll on HBCUs. For example, in Louisiana, the new performance based budget approach takes 25 percent of the state allocation for higher education and reallocates it based on graduation rates. According to Southern University Chancellor Kofi Lomotey, "the formula has cost the state's HBCUs millions, and at [his] school, jeopardized its mission."[24]

However, in Mississippi, state officials proposed a more controversial measure to close the state's budget deficit. This measure, unveiled by the Governor Haley Barbour in the summer of 2009, included a proposal to merge the state's eight public universities into five. Specifically the plan called for the merger of Mississippi University for Women into Mississippi State University and it consolidated the state's three public HBCUs, Mississippi Valley State University and Alcorn State University into Jackson State University. According to Barbour, consolidating the schools would save money by reducing administrative jobs and eliminate duplication in academic offerings. Said Barbour, "sometimes you have to look your friends in the eyes and tell them something they don't want to hear."[25]

The proposal, however, unleashed a whirlwind of opposition. Upon receipt of the proposal, members of the state's black Legislative Caucus vowed to block any proposed merger. "I am opposed to any measure that would reduce access and opportunity to quality education at any level," said the Chair of Mississippi's House Universities and Colleges Committee Chairman Kelvin Buck. However, former North Carolina Central University Chancellor Julius Chambers was even more blunt: "This is obviously a slap at black colleges. I think this would be another act of discriminating against black colleges." Chambers also noted that the mergers of HBCUs in the south have historically not gone well for students and faculty of black colleges. "What happens to the faculty at black colleges," if campus and programs are consolidated? He also maintained that if the merger led to smaller branch campuses where comprehensive HBCUs now exist in Lorman and Itta Bena, Mississippi, "How do you ensure that the same number of minority students end up in college? Why aren't they asking questions about minority enrollments?"[26]

Yet, as opposition grew, a bigger surprise emerged when the Jackson, Mississippi, newspaper, the *Clarion-Ledger*, revealed that behind closed doors the president of Jackson State University, Ronald Mason Jr., also proposed a plan to merge Alcorn State University and Mississippi Valley State University into his institution. In an article published in *Inside Higher Education*, Mason maintained this was not how he planned to talk about his proposal. Indeed, news about his plan leaked to the press while Mason was on a trip to Washington. However, in a response to the *Clarion Ledger*, the Jackson State University president claimed that he was, "against the governor's proposal. It's a bad idea, and we'll be fighting for generations with that kind of forced merger." Yet in the same vein, Mason maintained that all mergers are not fundamentally bad. For a merger of HBCUs to work he claimed that the inspiration for consolidation would need to come from the black college community and not from the outside. Surprisingly, Mason failed to explain why his plan, created without the input of these very constituents would garner support as opposed to a plan from the outside.[27]

Mason also maintained that Mississippi's HBCUs are in real danger of closing if they don't do something different. "There is a real possibility that Mississippi's HBCUs may disappear within our lifetime," particularly in light of a history of discriminatory funding and the current budget cuts proposed by the state government. These proposed cuts reduce funding at Jackson State University by 23 percent between 2011 and 2013.[28]

Opposition arose immediately to Mason's controversial proposal. In the Mississippi legislature, members of the black legislative caucus threatened to block any proposal calling for the merger of the state's three public HBCUs. Black legislators also held a news conference and rally, on the steps of the state capital, to denounce the idea. During this rally, black state representative Bryant Clark, said he was "appalled" that any president of an HBCU would even consider such a merger. Representative Alice Harden said she was shocked by Mason's announcement: "For me, it was a betrayal because he said he wasn't in favor of a merger and now all of a sudden he's kicked it in high gear." Mason has lost credibility within the HBCU community. Perhaps due to this opposition and the backlash again his proposal, Mason subsequently departed Mississippi for the friendlier confines of a presidency in Louisiana and the plan to merge Mississippi's HBCUs quietly died.[29]

In addition to the crisis created by poor state budgets, funding gaps still exist between HBCUs and TWIs. For example, in 2006, North Carolina's five public HBCUs enrolled 63 percent of the African-American students in the University of North Carolina system. Yet, in the fall of 2006, North Carolina allocated $15,700 for each African-American student at the University of North Carolina–Chapel Hill (UNC) and North Carolina State University (NCSU) compared to only $7,800 per African-American student at North Carolina Agricultural & Technical and Fayetteville State universities. Collectively, UNC and NCSU enrolled approximately 4,145 students in 2006 while North Carolina A&T State University enrolled nearly twice as many alone. Closing this funding gap is a challenge HBCU leaders must confront. However, in today's poor economic climate, the funding gap is likely to persist as state governments seek ways to balance budgets.[30]

Finally, the issue of adequate funding is also a concern of the private church-related HBCUs. As indicated in Chapter I, white church denominations and missionary groups played major roles in establishing the HBCUs at the end of the Civil War. Unfortunately, as with the public HBCUs, Jim Crow tempered the level of support the colleges received. Hence, in many cases, black colleges received just enough funding to keep their doors open. However, starting in the 1960s, many churches reduced or ended support for the HBCUs that they established. The result has been disastrous. For example, during Reconstruction, agents of the Northern Presbyterian Church established more than a dozen black colleges and schools including Knoxville, Mary Holmes, Barber-Scotia, Stillman Colleges, and Johnson C. Smith University.[31]

Unfortunately, with the reunification of the Northern and Southern Presbyterian churches in the mid–1980s, church leaders citing declining membership; an oversupply of church supported colleges and schools; and, the need to pay pensions for aging ministers as reason they redirected funds away from the church supported HBCUs. In part, due to this decision, Mary Holmes College closed in 2004; Knoxville and Barber-Scotia colleges lost regional accreditation; and another, Stillman College, faces the possible loss of accreditation due to poor finances. Despite these issues, in 2010, the Presbyterian Church announced the implementation of a new funding formula which allocates funding based on the number of students enrolled in each school. Such a policy however, fails to take into account years of discriminatory church funding that greatly contributed to the low enrollments by failing to provide enough support to upkeep campus infrastructure, which has contributed greatly to rundown and outdated physical plants. This, in turn, has impacted the ability of each school to recruit students. The implementation of the new policy threatens the future of all of the Presbyterian church-related HBCUs except Johnson C. Smith University. Similar problems face many HBCUs supported by the Episcopal, Lutheran, and United Methodist churches. To overcome this issue it is essential that the leaders of church-related HBCUs forge bonds with church fathers and mobilize supportive parishioners to push for increased funding.[32]

Challenges of Tuition Driven Enrollment

The challenges of reduced state and denominational funding are only a small segment of the total picture. Many HBCUs, as are many TWIs, are tuition-driven, meaning that the institutions are heavily dependent upon student tuition to survive.* Unfortunately, the need to enroll a certain number of students has led many colleges to enroll students who have little chance of completing a course of study. The ramifications of such policies are significant. On one hand, the decision to admit poor students affects student retention, graduation, and loan default rates (see Table 7.1). On the other hand, it has led to charges that the graduates of such institutions completed watered-down curriculums.[33] Unfortunately, when institutions produce poor graduates or weaken curriculum to enhance graduation rates donors notice.

---

*Many traditionally white institutions also are tuition driven. The Council of Independent Colleges identifies an institution that relies on tuition for more than 60 percent of its budget as tuition dependent.

Table 7.1: Student Graduation/Retention and
Default Rates at Select Open Admission HBCU*

Institution	2007 Graduation Rate	Ave. Freshman Retention Rate	Student Loan Default Rates		
			2007	2006	2005
Southern Univ. New Orleans	8%	45%	11%	7.4%	7.4%
Edward Waters College	9%	40%	22.8%	20.2%	19.8%
Jarvis Christian College	10%	49%	40%	40%	37%
Texas Southern University	12%	59%	18%	19%	15%
Texas College	12%	20%	41%	41%	37%
Paul Quinn College	16%	36%	23.4%	3.3%	2.3%
Philander Smith College	18%	60%	14%	20%	15.2%
Saint Paul's College	25%	48%	15%	19%	17.8%
Benedict College	27%	58%	34%	33%	34%

*Data compiled from the National Center for Education Statistics: IPEDS Data Center, U.S. Department of Education; U.S. News America's Best Colleges 2009 edition; and Diplomas and Dropouts.

Today donors want to be assured that gifts are used effectively, that the institutions they support are well managed and accountable for performance.[34]

Indeed, moving students through the educational pipeline is a problem that tuition-driven HBCUs must confront. For example, to improve student graduation and retention rates the state of Ohio has created a framework of "stackable" certificates that incorporates developmental education courses into a sequence of professional skills certificates. In this model, all courses successfully completed, "build so that certificates stack on top of one another and the credits count towards a two_year degree." Such a process might be the key to enhancing HBCU retention and graduation rates. For instance, stackable certificates would build into general competency and occupational associate's degrees, which would serve as springboards into baccalaureate degree programs, thus enhancing HBCU retention and graduation rates.[35]

Challenges of Tuition Discounting

Another problem facing many HBCUs is tuition discounting, a process that uses institutionally funded grants to defray student college costs. Institutions generally use tuition discounts for a number of reasons — namely to attract better students or increase campus diversity. The most common purpose of tuition discounts at many small private HBCUs is to shore up declining enrollments or support expensive athletic programs. However, the increasing use of tuition discounts has led to considerable concern among many higher education experts. On one hand, a number of authorities maintain that "universities which offered the steepest tuition discounts tended to have lower enrollments, less revenue from tuition, and less money for instructional and other vital services to students."[36]

On the other hand, many professionals feel that tuition discounting could "pay off as a short-term tactic if it is part of a strategic enrollment plan and accompanied by good marketing." Both sides however agree that the best method to determine if tuition discounts are successful is to "look at how much tuition money [discounting] is adding to the operational budget and whether that amount is increasing and how it compares with the cost of educating students."[37] For example, DePauw University, a small Midwestern TWI, with relatively high costs, discounted tuition by 59 percent in 2009 and netted only $14,000 per student for the 2,400 student institution. However, according to Moody's Investor's Service the College was moving in the right direction as DePauw saw 28 percent increase in net tuition over the last five years. According to Moody's: "As long as more tuition money is flowing toward

Table 7.2 HBCU Tuition Discount Rate Comparison Table (Fall 2009)

School	Tuition	Tuition Discount Rate	Real Impact of Discount Tuition (net tuition)	Per. Below Net Tuition Ave. for peer Southern Institutions
Stillman College	$13,890	31%	$9,585	30%
Edward Waters College	$9,990	31%	$6,954	50%
Saint Paul's College	$13,130	25%	$9,848	29%
Livingstone College	$13,658	25%	$10,244	26%
Bethune Cookman University.	$13,452	25%	$10,089	27%
Benedict College	$15,590	22%	$12,161	12%
Paine College	$11,794	21%	$9,318	32%
Talladega College	$8,940	20%	$7,152	48%
Shaw University	$11,696	16%	$9,825	29%
Voorhees College	$10,164	12%	$8,945	35%
Tuition Average for private Southern colleges and universities†	$21,526	36%*	$13,777	0

*Does not include "high cost" elite privates such as Baylor, Duke, Emory, Vanderbilt, Wake Forest, Rice or Tulane Universities.
†Data from the National Association of college and University Business Officers Tuition Discount Survey indicated that the average tuition discount rate for independent college in the southern states of Alabama, Arkansas, Florida, Georgia, Kentucky, Louisiana, Mississippi, North Carolina, South Carolina, Tennessee, Virginia, and West Virginia was 43% in 2007.

Source: Stillman College Office of Fiscal Affairs; Edward Waters College Vice President for Finance; St. Paul's College Office of the Comptroller; Livingstone College Office of Institutional Research; Bethune Cookman University Office of Fiscal Affairs; Benedict College, Office of Institutional Research; Paine College, Office of Academic Affairs; Talladega College Office of Fiscal Affairs; Shaw University Vice President for Finance; Voorhees College, Office of Fiscal Affairs.

the University's budget, high discounting might not be a problem." Yet, tuition revenues at Depauw only covered 38 percent of the $36,000 needed to educate each student. Fortunately, the college's $425,000,000 endowment allowed the university to bridge the gap between tuition revenue and the cost of educating each student. However, few HBCUS have endowments the size of Depauw's. Thus, it is difficult to bridge the gap between tuition revenue and the cost of educating students which averages $35,000 for private colleges nationally.[38]

Despite this fact, over the last decade, tuition discounts at private HBCUs increased from an average of 17% in 2000 to 29% in 2008. However, it is important to note that tuition discounts, at colleges of all types, increased from 37 percent in 2000, to 41.8 percent in 2008. During the same period, nationally, net tuition revenue declined two percent. Hence, tuition discounts outpaced total gross tuition and fee increases.[39]

Listed, in table 7.2, are the tuition discount rates for a select sample of private HBCUs. Although all of the HBCUs in the sample have lower discount rates than the average rate of independent southern TWIs, the average gross cost of each HBCUs is 43% lower than that for the TWIs. As a result, discounts have a greater impact on the HBCUs shown in the table. For example, the average net tuition of the HBCUs is $9,412 compared to $13,777 for comparable TWIs. This is a gap of $4,365. It is essential that most of the HBCUs in the sample close the net tuition gap and reduce tuition discount rates.

However, reducing tuition discounts is easier said than done. What works well at one institution might not work at another. One institution might be willing to reduce aid to high need students, while another college might limit or eliminate aid given to merit scholars "willing to suffer lower yields on students with low or no need." Still eliminating aid to any particular group brings with it its own set of problems. For instance, if an institution decided to lower the amount of merit aid to top achievers most students in the lower categories would not see much change in their institutional aid. Hence, the impact of such a decision would lower the overall quality of incoming students.

Unfortunately, at many HBCUs, tuition discounts are concentrated on supporting expensive athletic programs. Any reduction or plan of reduction runs the added risk of impacting athletic programs, upon which many HBCU leaders assume much of their enrollment is dependent. Thus far, few HBCU leaders have been willing to make such reductions. Perhaps one of the reasons for this reluctance is a failure by many

HBCU leaders to understand or appreciate the important role of admissions and enrollment management in the construction of student bodies that fit the financial and academic needs of an institution.

As indicated by the *Education Encyclopedia* the role of admissions and enrollment management is to systematically influence the number and characteristic of new students as well as influence the persistence of students to continue their enrollment from the time of their matriculation to graduation. Unfortunately, at many HBCUs, offices of admissions often poorly perform this vital function. As a result they flounder aimlessly, enrolling students with little chance of completing a course of study. Predictably, such practices have led to poor retention and low graduation rates. They have also raised questions about the future relevancy of HBCUs. One solution put forth by John Wilson, the head of the White House Initiative on black colleges, is to alter the message and purpose of HBCUs from a concentration of accepting the least-prepared students to a focus on graduating students who are well-prepared for the work-force. "We do want to stop saying that we enroll the kids that nobody wants."[40]

However, for many HBCU leaders, adjusting age-old admission practices is difficult since many HBCU leaders lack the resources to adjust such admissions practices. An examination of admissions practices of private, church-related, HBCUs in Alabama, Florida, Georgia, South Carolina, and North Carolina revealed that most of the black colleges lagged in the utilization of modern enrollment management technologies in comparison with similar private TWIs (see Table 7.3). According to Edward Alexander, the director of admissions at Edward Waters College, "The challenge is lack of resources." Indeed, Wallace Keese, a former official with the college Board, revealed that despite extensive outreach, including deep pricing discounts, few HBCUS use the College Boards Student Search Service. Keese cited two main factors for this outcome: limited resources and a failure by HBCU officials to understand, "that to recruit good students you have to spend money." However, as Alexander maintained, "Often HBCU leaders don't look at the return to investment.[41]

Yet, in today's increasingly competitive environment, it is essential that HBCUs improve the effectiveness of their admission and enrollment management functions. This means embracing new technologies and tools, such as social media. It also means: (a) increasing the number of full-time admissions office staff members to levels comparable with

Table 7.3: Comparison: Enrollment Management
Policies of Select Private HBCUs in Alabama, Georgia,
North Carolina, South Carolina, Florida, and
Texas with Similar Private Southern TWIs

	Number of Admissions Office Staff			Purchase SAT/ ACT Names as a Recruitment Tool		Use of Social Media and Electronic Communication To Recruit Students	
Institution	Full-Time	Part-Time	Student Workers	Yes	No	Yes	No
Allen University.	2	—	—		X		X
Benedict College.	4	2	6	X		X	
Edward Waters Coll.	4	0	10		X		X
Voorhees College.					X		X
Paine College					X		X
Florida Mem. Coll.	5	2	11		X		X
Stillman College	2		10	X		X	
Shaw University	5		6		X		X
Morris College	2				X		X
Saint Paul's College	2	—	—		X		X
Bethune Cookman	6	—	20		X		X
Texas College	2	—	—		X		X
Traditionally White Institutions							
North Car. Wes. Coll.	7	2	8	X		X	
Chowan Univ.	10	—	15	X		X	
Ferrum Univ.	6	—	10	X		X	
Greensboro Coll.	5	—	10	X		X	
Lenoir Rhyne Coll.	7	—	9	X		X	
Catawba Coll.	8		12	X		X	
Brevard Coll.	11	—	9	X		X	
Carson Newman Coll.	7	—	11	X		X	
Newberry College	8	—	8	X		X	
North Greenville Coll.	5	—	7	X		X	

Source: Paine, Florida Memorial, Voorhees, Stillman, Shaw, Morris, St. Paul's, Texas, North Carolina Wesleyan, Chowan, Ferrum, Greensboro, Lenoir Rhyne, Catawba, Brevard, Carson Newman, Newberry, North Greenville, Edward Waters, Benedict Colleges, and Allen, and Bethune Cookman offices of admissions.

national averages; (b) developing effective methodologies to identify candidates for early acceptance; (c) implementing an efficient automated candidate identification process; (d) building a cadre of high performing students to serve as campus leaders; (e) increasing opportunities for international study and internships; (f) increasing the number of opportunities to do research; and (g) forming collaborative partnerships that allow an institution to expand its degree program offerings. However, building infrastructure costs money. One way many colleges are overcoming these obstacles is to increase the use of technology as a recruiting tool, outsourcing of key elements to contractors, and the formation of collaborative partnerships in which two or more HBCUs pool resources to purchase current enrollment management tools and services.

Challenges of Building, in the Hope of Attracting Students

Adherence to the belief that the construction of new facilities will increase student enrollment is another challenge faced by HBCU leaders. Since the mid–1980s, colleges across the nation have constructed a host of new facilities in the hope of attracting students. For example, in the early 1990s, officials at Elon University, a small liberal arts college in North Carolina, undertook a massive effort to transform the institution. Consequently, the University built a new library; a science building; an 8,000-seat football stadium; ten new residence halls; six new Greek houses; a new student center; and, a new dining hall. The total cost of the construction exceeded $150 million.[42]

In addition, to these changes, the university upgraded its athletic programs moving from the National Association of Intercollegiate Athletics' (NAIA) Division I to the National Collegiate Athletic Association's Division I, the top tier for intercollegiate athletic competition. As a result, the university's enrollment increased from 3,845 in 1998, to 5,628 in 2008, a growth rate of 32 percent. In the process of increasing enrollment, the university also enhanced student quality. For example, in 1998, the average grade point average and SAT score for entering freshmen was 3.28 and 1090 respectively. By 2005, the average high school GPA of entering students was 3.72 while SAT scores reached 1208.[43]

Another institution that used construction and new programs to transform itself was Claflin University, a small HBCU in Orangeburg, South Carolina. In the decade between 1998 and 2008, Claflin, then a struggling tuition-driven college, invested more than $50,000,000 into renovating and constructing several new buildings, such as a new living and learning center, a residential complex, a new music center, and a new dining hall. The college also opened a new chapel. In addition to these enhancements, institutional leaders moved the college's athletic programs from NAIA to the more prestigious NCAA Division II. Due to these efforts, and an aggressive push by institutional leaders to increase quality, enrollment increased from 1,000 students in 1995, to 2,400 students in 2007. The quality of students also improved from an average SAT of 620 in 1995 to 920 in 2010. In conjunction with these developments, and the school's fundraising prowess that included a successful $30,000,000 capital campaign, the college's governing board moved the institution to university status. When asked about the transformation, Claflin University President Henry Tisdale, credits the change to strong student development programs and a commitment to excellence.[44]

Yet, for many HBCUs, as well as a number of TWIs, treading a similar path has been problematic. For example, in the early 1970s Wilberforce University constructed a new campus in the hope of increasing enrollment from 800 to 1,500 students. Although the college completed the construction with few glitches, enrollment never reached 1,500. The resulting debt left years of problems that continued to reverberate. For example, in 2001 the North Central Accrediting Association levied sanctions against the school due to weak finances caused, in part, by the construction of the new campus. Although Wilberforce removed the sanctions, lingering effects remain. In 2009, the debt forced the college to cut administrative pay by 15% and to implement an 11-week furlough for all staff.[45]

Another school that faced the "If you build it they will come" syndrome is Morris Brown College. The problems started in 1977, when the college constructed new residence halls in the hope of boosting enrollment. However, upon opening the dorms, enrollment growth stalled, which made repaying the construction loans difficult. Consequently, between 1977 and 2000, Morris Brown officials refinanced the loans numerous times; each time the new loan carried a higher interest rate. By 2001, the original $7,000,000 debt ballooned to $16,000,000.[46]

Yet, the debt on the residence halls was not the only problem. In the late 1990s, institutional leaders, despite increased costs, made a decision to move the athletic program from the NCAA's Division II to Division I. Although this effort increased student enrollment from 2,170 in 1997, to 2,700 in 2003, it overtaxed campus housing. As a result, college officials rented hotel rooms for more than 400 students. Undoubtedly, such practices weakened institutional finances and contributed to the loss of accreditation in 2004.[47]

The quest to increase enrollment also played a role in a decision by officials at Barber-Scotia College to borrow funding from the Department of Education's Capital Financing Program in 2001. However, for Barber-Scotia College this decision was perhaps one of the worst

Barber-Scotia College's Faith Hall. In 2001, the college borrowed $7 million to renovate Faith Hall and to conduct campus improvements. To secure the loan the Capital Financing Program placed a lien on the entire college campus valued at $15,000,000. However, the legality of the lien has been in contention as many Barber-Scotia College officials maintain that authorization was never given to secure the entire campus. Whatever the case, the loan has been a burden in the college's efforts to regain regional accreditation (courtesy of Barber-Scotia College).

decisions in institutional history. Congress established the Capital Financing Program in 1992, under Title III, Part D of the Higher Education Act of 1965. The program sought to lend money to eligible HBCUs with qualified capital projects. Officials at Barber-Scotia College, which had a total enrollment of 500 students, borrowed $7,000,000 to cover the renovation cost of Faith Hall, a historic residence hall unoccupied since 1985, and to upgrade campus infrastructure. In this regards a major controversy arose. Officials at Barber-Scotia College agreed to use the renovated residence hall and student housing fees as collateral for the loan. However, administrators with the Capital Financing Program insisted on using the entire campus as collateral. Resulting from this disagreement was a loan document that contained particulars that favored each side. For example, the security deed given to Barber-Scotia College's governing board only listed Faith Hall as security for the loan.

However, the documents recorded by the Cabarrus County Register of Deeds listed the entire campus as collateral.[48]

Unfortunately, the tendency by officials at the Capital Financing program to overcollateralize the value of real estate pledged as security has been constant problem of the program. Many HBCU officials maintain that overcollateralization, "presents a problem for schools trying to obtain additional financing," since without sufficient assets remaining most financial institutions refused to advance additional capital (see Table 7.4). Indeed, "one nonparticipant cited the collateral required as a reason for its decision not to participate."[49]

In response to these charges, officials with the Department of Education maintained that the value of the collateral needed to guarantee a loan under the Capital Financing Program varied based on the particular conditions of an institution. For example, an institution with a, "relatively large endowment and stable tuition revenue," might need less collateral than an institution with a small endowment and few physical properties. "Education officials further noted that requiring the value of the collateral to be greater than the value of the loan was not an uncommon business practice."[50] Indeed such practices are not restricted to black colleges. In 2009, when Greensboro College, a small TWI in North Carolina, faced financial ruin, institutional leaders negotiated a $16,000,000 loan with bank of America. For collateral, the Bank secured the entire campus along with the president's $1,200,000 house. In addition, the bank required college officials to move a $12,000,000 endowment from Wachovia Bank to The Bank of America as collateral. Said the school's controller, "they definitely have more collateral value than we have debt."[51]*

Yet, for the Capital Financing Program, criticism about the collateral requirements led the Department of Education to revise security requirements. According to the program's director Don Watson, since 2007, the Capital Financing Program has not required any of the colleges

---

*In the period before 2007 the Capital Financing Program (see Table 7.3)required no collateral beyond the net revenues of various facilities for any public institution, despite the fact that many of these institutions had minuscule endowments and declining enrollments that impacted the stability of tuition revenue. At the same time the agency required all private HBCUS, regardless of endowment size or tuition stability, to provide substantial collateral for all loan awards. For example, between 1995 and 2006 enrollment at South Carolina State University fell from 4,993 to 4,384 while the school's endowment, $5,000,000, stood well below many of the private HBCUs that were forced to pledge major collateral.

Table: 7.4: Select Institutions Participating in the Capital Financing Program

School	Type Inst.	Amount Borrowed	Year	Project	Security on Capital Commerce Loan	Term	Endowment
Bennett College	Private	$9,500,000	2010	Refinancing of outstanding indebtedness	Secured by general obligation of the college and lien on college endowment	20 Year Fixed	$8,965,780
Tuskegee Univ.	Private	$68,000,000	2010	Financed new student housing facility; Financed new science building; Financed renovation of academic buildings and student housing facilities.	Secured by lien on unrestricted portion of University endowment.	30 Year Rate	$102,000,000
Shaw University	Private	$30,100,000	2010	Refinanced outstanding debt	Secured by five parcels: Talbert O. Shaw Living/Learning Center (considered two parcels), Fleming/Kee Residence Hall, Dimple Newsome Residence Hall, and Gary Student Union.*	20 Year Fixed	$24,000,000
Harris Stowe St. Univ.	Public	$17,315,000	2010	Financed new student housing	Secured by Student housing revenue	30 Year Fixed	$1,000,000
Lane College	Private	$29,000,000	2010	Refinancing of outstanding indebtedness		20 Year Fixed	$2,000,000
Bennett College	Private	$21,000,000	2009	Program loan financed new student housing, academic buildings, and renovations	Secured by general obligation of the college and pledge of student housing revenue	30 Year Fixed	$8,965,780
Talladega College	Private	$12,000,000	2009	Renovation of existing facilities; new student housing; refinance outstanding debt.	Secured by general obligation of the college	30 Year Fixed	$4,500,000
Florida Memorial Univ.	Private	$28,000,000	2009	Program financed new student housing facility; Refinancing of outstanding indebtedness	Secured by general obligation of the college and pledge of all revenue from new housing facility	30 Year Fixed	$6,700,000
Allen University	Private	$19,000,000	2007	New student housing and residence hall improvements	Secured by general obligation of the University, net revenue of entire student housing and a first mortgage on five buildings.	30 Year Fixed	$307,322

Institution	Type	Amount	Year	Purpose	Security	Terms	Amount
Tougaloo College	Private	$28,560,000	2007	Refinancing outstanding indebtedness; Renovation of existing facilities; modernization of campus facilities	General obligation of university, secured by mortgages, lien on all revenue	30 Year Var. Rate	$8,021,483
Tuskegee Univ.	Private	$28,000,000	2007	Renovation of existing facilities, modernization of campus facilities.	Revenues of mortgage facilities, General obligation of the university, secured by mortgages, lien on all revenue.	30 Year Fixed	$102,000,000
Xavier University	Private	$165,000,000	2007	Refinanced outstanding indebtedness. Renovation of existing facilities.	Secured by mortgages on campus, lien on residence hall revenue, and portion of endowment.	30 Year Fixed	$90,000,000
Dillard Univ.	Private	$160,000,000	2007	Refinance outstanding indebtedness, Renovation of existing facilities; construction of science and professional school building	Secured by university campus, secured by mortgages, lien on all revenue, portion of endowment.	30 Year Fixed capped at 1%	$42,000,000
Clark Atlanta Univ.	Private	$20,000,000	2007	Renovation of existing facilities, campus modernization.	Secured by general obligation of the University, pledge of all revenue and mortgages	30 Year Fixed	$44,200,000
Southern Univ. at New Orleans	Public	$44,000,000	2007	New Student Housing	A pledge of net revenues of the Southern Univ. of New Orleans Housing System.	30 Year Var. Rate capped at 1%	$3,867,059
Harris Stowe St. Univ.	Public	$15,500,000	2006	Financed new student housing facility	Secured by all student housing revenue.	30 Year Fixed	$1,000,000
South Car. State Univ.	Public	$42,000,000	2005	Construction of new 780 bed housing facility; refinanced existing student housing revenue bond.	Secured by net revenue of entire student housing revenue system.	30 Year Fixed	$5,052,804
Miles College	Private	$7,835,000	2004	New men's residence hall	Secured by general obligation of the college, lien on revenues of student housing facility and mortgage on facility.	30 Year Fixed	$13,107,245
Tuskegee Univ.	Private	$12,056,000	2004	Refinanced taxable bond issued to finance the university's Kellogg Conference Center.	Secured by a mortgage on the Kellog conference Center	23 Var. rate Financing	$102,000,000

Table: 7.4: Select Institutions Participating in the Capital Financing Program (*cont.*)

School	Type Inst.	Amount Borrowed	Year	Project	Security on Capital Commerce Loan	Term	Endowment
Shaw University	Private	$10,015,000	2004	Refinanced bond issue, refinanced a note on a satellite campus, refinanced existing Department of Education mortgage, provided small amount of new money.	Secured by college campus.	20 Year Variable	$24,000,000
Clark Atlanta Univ.	Private	$23,905,000	2003	Financing structured primarily to offer substantial debt service savings.	Secured by general obligation of the Univ.,pledge of all revenue and mortgages.	13 Year Fixed/ Var. rate amort. 2020	$44,200,000
Virginia Union Univ.	Private	$8,218,000	2002	Building Renovation, HVAC upgrades, Refinancing	Secured by general obligation of the university, a first lien on revenues and a mortgage 30-year fixed rate financing.	30 Year Fixed	$14,600,00
Tuskegee Univ.	Private	$23,875,000	2002	Financing for campus infra-structure projects and residence hall improvements	Loan secured by general obligation of the University, a first lien on certain student housing revenues and mortgages.	30 Year Fixed	$102,000,000
Bennett College	Private	$8,700,000	2001	Roof repair, storm drains, network telephone upgrades	General obligation of the college and lien on all revenue	30 Year Fixed	$8,965,780
Livingstone College	Private	$13,000,000	2001	Student Housing renovation, Administrative classroom reno-vation, Refinancing ($7 Million)	Secured by a mortgage on campus, and lien on all revenues refinancing,	17 Year Fixed on 30 Year fixed on new projects	$1,300,311
Barber-Scotia * College*	Private	$7,000,000	2000	Renovation of Faith Hall	Secured by lien on entire campus and a lien on all revenue from Faith Hall	30 Year Fixed	$4,000,000*
Bethune Cookman Univ.	Private	$15,500,000	1999	Project included student center, auditorium, and mass com-munication bldg.	Secured by general obligation of the college, lien on all revenues and a mortgage	30 Year Fixed	$30,366,000

Institution	Type	Amount	Year	Purpose	Security	Terms	Amount
Tougaloo College	Private	$8,200,000	1999	Four new housing facilities	Secured by general obligation of the college, and net revenues of the financed dormitories and a mortgage	10 Year Fixed/30 Year fixed	$8,021,483
Lincoln University	Private	$13,850,000	1999	Refinancing and renovation of university's urban center; deferred campus maintenance and computer software and hardware upgrades	Secured by general obligation of the University and secured by a mortgage on the Urban Center.	25 Yr Fixed for Urban Center. 15 Yr Fixed deferred maint.	$23,000,000
Bethune Cookman Univ.	Private	$4,795,000	1997	Provided financing for a new 200 bed student housing facility	Secured by lien on all revenues and a mortgage on building and a covenant to maintain minimum level of unrestricted net assets equal to 150% of debt.	30 Yr. Fixed	$30,366,000
West Virginia State College	Public	$3,5000,000	1996	Renovation of Student housing	Secured by pledge of net revenues on student housing.	30 Year Fixed	$3,200,000

*Source: Historically Black College and University Capital Financing Program, Awards: http://www2.ed.gov/programs/hbcucapfinance/awards.html#96 and interview with Don Watson, director of Capital Financing Program, December 14, 2010. Capital Financing Program.

seeking assistance to collaterize loans at 100 percent. He also maintained that the agency has launched new programs that offered better terms and rates than many private commercial lenders. For example, in 2010 the Capital Financing Program (CFP) refinanced Shaw University's $30,000,000 debt. For collateral, the agency used five campus buildings instead of the entire campus (65 parcels) as had the previous lender the Bank of America.[52]

Nonetheless, the recent actions of the officials at the Capital Financing Program still does not explain why the burden of overcollaterization fell so heavily upon private HBCUs in the first place. The actions of the program, during the period before 2007, caused irreparable damage to a number of smaller HBCUs. For example, in the case of Barber-Scotia College, the loss of accreditation in 2004 created serious problems, namely by making the students attending the college ineligible to receive federal financial aid on which 96 percent, of students depended. This reduced enrollment from approximately 700 to 99 students. As a result, institutional revenues dropped from approximately $8,000,000 to approximately $740,000. This led college officials to launch an effort to refinance the institution's debt by securing a loan on the school's gym and student union: which were valued at more than $10,000,000. However, the lien held by the Capital Financing Program quashed this effort. Although college officials tried several times to get officials with the Department of Education to release various parcels of land held as collateral, each time the agency refused. As a result Barber-Scotia College was pushed to the brink of insolvency. The institution was also unable to garner support from corporate and philanthropic supporters.[53] Hence, the program originally created to help HBCUs fund capital projects has, in many cases, been problematic.[54]*

Moreover, the current stance taken by the Capital Financing Program since 2007 also appears risky. For example, since revising its collateral policy, the Capital Financing Program has provided funding for nearly a half dozen residential facilities, mainly, at small private HBCUs. Unfortunately, at many of the schools, enrollment has fallen or remained stagnate despite the presence of new facilities. Consequently, residence hall profits that the institution once received, have evaporated, as a large

---

*Unable to secure financing, the College's Governing Board hired prominent Washington, D.C., attorney William Bud Blakey to investigate the legality of the lien. However, the outcome of the investigation is unknown due to the untimely illness and subsequent death of Blakey.

Above and next page: Recent projects financed by the Capital Financing Program on HBCUs. Although the program was designed to help HBCUs, collateral policies used by the program have caused problems for a host of small private black colleges. *Top:* South Carolina State's Hugine Suites Residence Halls. *Bottom:* New residence halls at Allen University.

Top: New Global Learning Center at Bennett College. *Bottom:* New residence hall at Bennett College.

Mini-residence hall at North Carolina Wesleyan College. Buildings such as this one cost approximately $1 million to build. Each facility holds 48 students. For small colleges such buildings are cost-effective and provide savings in both debt service and energy costs.

portion of the new residence hall rental fees now go to pay debt-service on loans financed by the Capital Financing program, while older facilities sit empty or nearly empty. For small institutions, such as Bennett College, which has not seen any substantial enrollment growth over the last thirty years, such loans have the potential to threaten institutional viability and financial stability.

Although building infrastructure in the hope students will come is a strategy that contains many pitfalls, it is nonetheless essential that historically black colleges maintain modern facilities that serve the needs of contemporary student. While the cost of construction and maintenance of such facilities continues to escalate, a small number of institutions have developed programs that reduce costs and the need for external financing. This new blueprint calls for colleges to construct residence and classroom buildings of sizes 10,000 square feet and under instead of the mammoth buildings found on most campuses. Such a strategy has meant cost savings for North Carolina Wesleyan College, a small college located in Rocky Mount, North Carolina. In the mid–1990s, officials at North Carolina Wesleyan College constructed mini-residence halls composed of single rooms of approximately 100 square feet each. The college paid slightly over $1,000,000 for each residence hall.(According to Belinda Faulkner, former vice president of fiscal affairs at the college, "the idea was to build dorm space that would house 40 people – we could grow incrementally without sinking a fortune into a larger residence hall that might be half empty until we grew into it." However, the long-term savings on the building were even more significant as the annual upkeep on the mini-halls was proportionally only 30% of the cost of a full-sized residence hall. For many HBCUs, following such a course presents a better option than the highly collateralized, revenue extracting loans from private lenders and the Capital Financing Program. Moreover, such a course allows institutions to grow incrementally ensuring that growth is long-term and that institutional resources are not tied to capital projects for decades.[55]

The Challenge of
Intercollegiate Athletics

Since the early 1900s, intercollegiate athletic programs have been an integral component of HBCU campus life. For example, in 1912, administrators from Shaw University, Virginia Normal and Industrial Institute, Lincoln University, Virginia Union University, Howard University, and Hampton Institute formed the Colored Intercollegiate Athletic Association (CIAA). One-year later administrators from Alabama State, Morris Brown, Jackson State, Morehouse, and Clark Colleges plus Fisk University, Tuskegee Institute and Atlanta University formed the Southeastern Intercollegiate Athletic Conference. In the years since this early period, intercollegiate athletics have become a ticket for advancement for countless numbers of student athletes. For example, between 1900 and 1954, the names of players that formerly graced the campuses of black colleges reads like a cornucopia of greats including: Buck O'Neal (Edward Waters College); Satchel Paige (Knoxville College); Charlie Joyner (Grambling); Althea Gibson (Florida A&M); Tank Younger (Grambling); and Wilma Rudolph (Tennessee State).

In addition to legendary athletes, HBCU athletics spawned a number of premier sporting events such as the Vulcan Bowl, a New Year's Day game in Birmingham; and the Orange Blossom Bowl in Florida,

which featured the Florida A&M Rattlers football team versus teams
from one of the other four black college conferences and the CIAA basketball tournament. However, after the passage of the Civil Rights Act
of 1964, TWIs aggressively recruited black athletes. The impact of this
development was significant in that HBCUs, which previously had sole
access to black athletes, were now forced to compete with TWIs and
offer costly scholarships to remain competitive. Unfortunately, the
increased cost of scholarships and athletic support came just as philanthropic support waned amidst questions about the future relevance
of black colleges. As a result, between 1960 and 1979 many smaller
HBCUs dropped expensive football programs and tightened athletic
budgets (see Table 7.5 below). During the same period, a number of the
larger HBCUs, mainly state-supported institutions, elevated their athletic
programs from the National Collegiate Athletic Association's (NCAA)
Division II to Division I. Resulting from these initiatives were two Division I HBCU athletic conferences, the Mid-Eastern Athletic Conference,

Benedict College's Bolden Football Stadium. In 2004 Benedict College borrowed $10 million to construct a new football stadium. The cost of the stadium
and the land on which the stadium sits ($6.3 million) greatly increased the
college's debt, pushing the institution to the brink of insolvency.

Table 7.5: HBCU Football Cancelations
and Revivals, 1940-2011

College	Date Football Team Originally Discontinued	Date Football Program Resumed	Date Football Dropped Second Time	Current Level of Athletic Competition
Barber Scotia Coll.[b]	N/A	2003	2004	N/A
Wiley College	1969	-	-	NAIA
Xavier Univ. (LA)	1961	-	-	-
Tougaloo Coll.	1961	-	-	NAIA
Tillotson[d]	1961	-	-	**
Texas College	1961	2004	-	NAIA
Shaw Univ.	1979	2003		NC Div II
Rust Coll.	1965	-	-	NCAA
Philander Smith Coll.	1965	-	-	NAIA
Paul Quinn Coll.[b, c]	1961	2000	2007	***
Morris College	1965	-	-	NAIA
Mississippi Ind. Coll.[a]	1965	-	-	-
Maryland East. Shr	1980	-	-	NC Div I
Lincoln Univ. (Pa)	1961	2008	-	NC Div II
Lemoyne-Owen Coll.[e]	1951	2011	-	NC Div II
Leland (LA)[a]	1960	-	-	Unk
Knoxville Coll.[b]	1996	-	-	NC Div. III
Jarvis Christian Coll	1967	-	-	NAIA
Fisk Univ.[c]	1984	-	-	NC Div. III
Florida N&I	1959	-	-	Unk
Dillard Univ.	1965	-	-	NAIA
Claflin Univ.	1965	-	-	NC Div II
Bishop Coll.[a]	1987	-	-	NC Div. III
Allen Univ.	1969	2001	2006	NAIA
Benedict College	1967	1995	-	NC Div II
Edward Waters College[e]	1968	2002	-	NAIA
Morris Brown Coll.[b]	2003	-	-	NC Div I
Concordia Coll.[c]	N/A	2003	-	NAIA
Central State Univ.	2005	2005	-	NAIA
Friendship College[a]	1970	-	-	Unk
Selma Univ.	1940	-	-	Unk
Talladega Coll.	1940	-	-	Unk
Univ. Dis. Col.	1990	-	-	NC Div II
Bluefield State Coll.	1980	-	-	NC Div II
St. Paul's College[c]	1988	2005	-	NC Div II
St. Augustine's Coll.[e]	1966	2002	-	NC Div II
Miles College	1989	1990	-	NC Div. II
Stillman Coll.[c, e]	1951	1999	-	NC Div II
Lincoln Univ. (Mo)	1990	1999	-	NC Div II
Arkansas Baptist Coll.	??	2010	-	NCJC
Uni. Arkansas Pine Bluff	??	1993	-	NC Div. I

[a]College Now Closed/ [b]Lost Regional Accreditation/ [c]Under Sanction by Regional Accreditor/ [d]Merged / [e]Under Sanction by Regional Accreditor for Finances 2003-2008. Source: NCAA Added or Discontinued Programs; and Craig T. Greenlee, "There's a Football Revival Going On — College Football Programs Reappear- Statistical Data Included," *Black Issues in Higher Education*, August 2, 2001.

composed mainly of public institutions along the Eastern Seaboard, and the Southwestern Athletic Conference made up of public institutions in Texas, Louisiana, and Mississippi.[56]

On the heels of these developments, in 1995, administrators at Benedict College, as a means of boosting enrollment and revenue at the tuition-driven school, resumed the college's long-dormant football team. According to the school's president, "I don't consider this a risky move. If this is the most difficult risk I have to take I'm in pretty good shape." Swinton also maintained that he expected football to have a significant impact on the school's five-year enrollment, citing students who choose a college, in part, because of a, "vibrant, vital athletic environment." Indeed, the college's enrollment jumped from 1,207 in 1992, to 2,966 in 2000, an increase of 145 percent.[57]

Yet, the resumption of football played a major role in pushing the school's finances to the brink. Three years after resuming football, the college borrowed $6,300,000 to purchase commercial property as a home for a football stadium. Six years later, college officials borrowed $10,000,000 to build a stadium. In addition to these expenses, officials added the operating costs of the football team which totaled approximately $13,000,000 for the period between 1995 and 2009 to the college's growing debt. Coupled with these expenses were additional costs caused by the construction of new facilities and the employment of faculty and staff to serve the needs of the growing enrollment. By 2005, Benedict College's total debt stood at $101,000,000 while the college's endowment hovered around $19,000,000. In response, in 2003, Moody's Investors Service downgraded Benedict College's creditworthiness to below investment grade. The next year Standard & Poor downgraded its rating on the college's long-term bonds to below investment grade. Standard & Poor also noted that Benedict College's spending exceeded revenue by $2,600,000 and that college officials projected deficits for 2005 and 2006. Said College President Swinton after the ruling, "The rating agencies were primarily concerned that the college stabilize its enrollment," which had fallen from 2,966 in 2000 to 2,531 in 2006, a 15% decrease."[58] To stabilize enrollment, in 2004, administrators adopted the controversial Success Equals Effort policy (SEE). This policy required faculty to calculate freshmen grades on a 60/40 formula with effort counting for 60% and academic performance 40%. In the sophomore year, the formula moved to 50/50. In the junior year, the formula required faculty to judge students strictly on academic policy. According to Swinton, "We don't feel that we are doing anything that's not sound educational policy. If anything, the policy raises the academic standards at the college. It's doing this by getting students to work harder and by committing more effort to learning."[59] However, many faculty members and former students objected to the policy maintaining that SEE cast doubt not only on their work but on the overall ability of students, "as well as the quality of an education received at, Benedict College." In response to such criticism, college officials dismissed a number of dissenting faculty. This led to two lawsuits in which former faculty members claimed wrongful termination, breach of contract, and defamation stemming from their opposition to the SEE program. In 2007, the college settled the lawsuits in a confidential agreement, and both sides claimed victory.[60]

On the heels of these developments, the school's poor finances improved slightly after officials restructured $24,900,000 of short-term debt. However, the reprieve was only temporary. In the summer of 2009, the U.S. Department of Education, upon reviewing Benedict College's audits, indicated that the "school must take extra precaution to ensure that the college is financially viable." The Department also required college officials to make financial aid disbursements to eligible students and parents before the college could request funds from the government to cover financial aid, and then only for the amount actually disbursed. As a final stipulation, federal officials required Benedict administrators to notify the Department of Education within ten days of any negative changes in the college's finances or its status with oversight agencies such as SACS. According to the Swinton, "The school's failure to meet the required 2008 federal financial ratio for student aid is attributable to the recent downturn in financial markets [which caused a drop in the value of the school's endowments] and more than $8,000,000 in write-offs of student loans."[61]

Unfortunately, for many small private HBCUs, news about Benedict College's financial challenges came too late. Between 1995, the date Benedict's College kicked off its football team, and 2002, newspapers across the nation chronicled Benedict College's rapid growth. Indeed, many of these articles heralded the addition of football as a panacea for fixing all that ailed small private colleges. For example, in an article published in *Black Issues In Higher Education* Craig T. Greenlee wrote that the addition of football, "has an alluring upside as a main attraction and moneymaker," while Joe Humphrey, a reporter for the *Florida Times Union*, stated that the addition of football, "helps build a robust student body."[62]

With such pronouncements, it is little wonder that the leaders of cash-strapped HBCUs, such as Allen University, Barber-Scotia College, Stillman College, Edward Waters College, St. Paul's College, Shaw University, and Paul Quinn Colleges as well as a number of TWIs launched or revived morbid football teams.* Said former Allen University Official Bob Smith, football is a "drawing card," and larger enrollment means more money for the school. Rosemary Lewis, the former Vice President for Student Affairs at Allen University agreed, "football helped us recruit more students." However, Johnny B. Watson, LeMoyne-Owen College's President was even more optimistic, when talking about efforts to revive the college's dormant football program, he maintained that the startup cost for a team would not come from the "school's operating budget, but rather from revenue generated by increased enrollment."[63]

Yet, the attempted revival of football has been problematic, for most HBCUs, since the expected enrollment gains only lasted briefly (see Table 10.6 below). Unfortunately, during the brief enrollment upsurges, many schools built new facilities. This, increased operational costs which led to financial and accreditation problems.[64]

One college caught in this trend was Stillman College. In 1999, the institution revived its football team, built a 9,000-seat stadium, constructed two new classroom buildings, and a residence hall to house the expected influx of students. Initially enrollment increased from 1,017 in 1998, to 1,530 in 2,000. However, in the years since this milestone enrollment at Stillman College, has undergone a steady decline. By 2005, only 804 students enrolled for the fall semester. This number was 213 students

---

*In many cases, the drive to start football teams ranged between the comical to the outrageous. For example, in one case, institutional leaders of a small unidentified HBCU unable to afford the cost of starting a football team, made a deal with the institution's cafeteria vendor to suspend payments for one year. This allowed the College to obtain enough money to start a football team. According to several former officials, administrators hoped to repay the food vendor with resources garnered from the expected enrollment boom. Unfortunately, the expected boom never came and the institution was stuck with more than a $1,000,000 debt from the food vendor. Things worsened several years later: the college canceled its season opener when it was revealed that the institution was unable to provide helmets or shoulder pads for its players. According to school officials the helmets had been shipped to the manufacturer for a scheduled reconditioning and had not been returned. However, according to the manufacturer the helmets were not returned due to the fact the school had not paid outstanding bills totaling more than $150,000. Yet, despite these serious financial problems the school refused to cancel football. In part due to outstanding obligations caused by the addition of football in 2010 led the Southern Association of Schools and Colleges placed the institution on probation, its toughest sanction short of loss of accreditation.

Table 7.7: Institutional Enrollment of Private Colleges that Started or Revived Intercollegiate Football Teams, Fall Semesters, Years 1–10 before the Start of Intercollegiate Football Teams and Fall Semesters 1–5 After the Start of Teams

	Enrollment by Institution Fall Semesters Years 1-10 Prior to the Start of Intercollegiate Football Teams										Start of F/ball	Enrollment by Institution Fall Semester Years 1–5 after the Start of Intercollegiate Football Teams					% enrollment change from fall sem. Preceding start of football	Curr. Status w/ Accredit. Agency
	1	2	3	4	5	6	7	8	9	10	FB	1	2	3	4	5		
Edward Waters	680	773	540	568	405	482	704	800	987	1320	811	1300	1206	836	839	811	-39%	**
Paul Quinn	1004	933	789	670	667	803	653	641	742	670	674	828	567	858	966	769	15%	SACS Prob.
Benedict College*	1495	1469	1474	1448	1616	1478	1422	1207	1266	1501	1862	2138	2208	2405	2750	2966	98%	
Stillman College	770	822	888	953	913	842	1014	1035	1017	1458	1530	1513	1441	1200	1116	804	-47%	SACS Warning
St. Paul's College	681	675	658	602	606	518	555	700	475	627	717	681	700	645	584	550	-12%	SACS Prob.
St. Augustine's Coll.	1918	1745	1673	1637	1584	1639	1598	1492	1465	1360	1577	1629	1395	1163	1247	1284	-6%	**
Texas College	262	328	293	271	261	294	92	511	617	1035	757	807	755	774	705	936	-10%	
Concordia	472	473	525	564	564	525	532	781	968	851	905	850	827	555	579	651	-23%	SACS Warning
Shaw University	2504	2432	2485	2262	2327	2569	2670	2527	2523	2683	2616	2709	2882	2822	2856	2629	-2%	
ave enrollment	1087	1072	1036	1088	1101	1017	1027	1077	1118	1278	1272	1384	1331	1251	1294	1267	-1.47	

Table 7.6: Institutional Enrollment of Private Colleges that Started or Revived Intercollegiate Football Teams, Fall Semesters, Years 1–10 before the Start of Intercollegiate Football Teams and Fall Semesters 1–5 After the Start of Teams (W/O Benedict College)

	Enrollment by Institution Fall Semesters Years 1-10 Prior to the Start of Intercollegiate Football Teams										Start of F/ball	Enrollment by Institution Fall Semester Fall Semesters Years 1-5 after the Start of Intercollegiate Football Teams					% enrollment change from fall sem. Preceding start of football	Curr. Status w/ Accredit. Agency
	1	2	3	4	5	6	7	8	9	10	FB	1	2	3	4	5		
Edward Waters	680	773	540	568	405	482	704	800	987	1320	811	1300	1206	836	839	811	-39%	**
Paul Quinn	1004	933	789	670	667	803	653	641	742	670	674	828	567	858	966	769	15%	SACS Prob.
Stillman College	770	822	888	953	913	842	1014	1035	1017	1458	1530	1513	1441	1200	1116	804	-47%	SACS Warning
St. Paul's College	681	675	658	602	606	518	555	700	475	627	717	681	700	645	584	550	-12%	SACS Prob.
St. Augustine's Coll.	1918	1745	1673	1637	1584	1639	1598	1492	1465	1360	1577	1629	1395	1163	1247	1284	-6%	**
Texas College	262	328	293	271	261	294	92	511	617	1035	757	807	755	774	705	936	-10%	
Concordia	472	473	525	564	564	525	532	781	968	851	905	850	827	555	579	651	-23%	SACS Warning
Shaw University	2504	2432	2485	2262	2327	2569	2670	2527	2523	2683	2616	2709	2882	2822	2856	2629	-2%	
ave enrollment	1036	1023	981	1037	1019	959	977	1061	1099	1251	1198.4	1290	1222	1107	1111.5	1054	-16%	

Source of Data for tables 7.6 & 7.7: IPEDS Peer Report; UNCF Statistical Guides 1996, 1995, 1997, and Various Institutional Fact Books.

*Allen Univ. started a football team in 2001. Enrollment increased from 323, the semester before launch of team, to 592. Over next two years enrollment increased to 624 before school dropped football in 2006. However, since dropping football enrollment has continued to increase. Currently, the school enrolls 825 student.

**SACS Sanction between 2004–2007

In 1999 Stillman College revived its football team and constructed a new football stadium. Unfortunately, the addition of football failed to generate the expected enrollment boom. This has led to persistent financial problems.

less than the fall semester of 1998, one year before the college launched its football program.[65]

For Stillman College, the enrollment decline caused severe financial problems. By 2008, the college's net assets decreased $4,400,000 to $29,380,000, down from $37,740,000 in 2004 according to the college's tax returns. As a result, in the summer of 2010, the Southern Association of Colleges and Schools (SACS) placed the college on "warning" for six months. According to the commission, Stillman College's recent financial history did not demonstrate financial stability. Nor did it appear that the institution had the necessary resources to support the mission and the scope of its programs and services.[66]

Yet, the problems of Stillman and Benedict Colleges are not unique to HBCU startups. For example, in 1999 Birmingham-Southern College (BSC), a small private TWI with an enrollment of 1,500, moved its athletic programs from the NAIA to the NCAA's Division I, the highest level of competition for college athletic teams. To meet the NCAA requirements

Birmingham-Southern added women's basketball, softball, rifle and golf teams. The college also joined the Big South Athletic Conference and won eight conference titles and competed in five NCAA Division I tournaments. However, the cost of participation in Division I was problematic. For one, the move to Division I, did not enhance the school's reputation or increase its enrollment. In fact, enrollment declined from 1,500 students in 1999, to 1,300 in 2007. By 2006, the college was spending about 15% of its $42,000,000 operational budget on athletics. As a result, by 2007, the college was running a $6,000,000 annual deficit.[67]

Participation in Division I athletics also led officials at BSC to promote athletic programs at the expense of academics. A study conducted by the school's Board of Trustees in 2007, revealed that the college offered just one academic scholarship in 2006, compared with 116 for athletic teams. With that track record, it should have been no surprise that between 2003 and 2006 Moody's Investors Service downgraded the college's debt three times. Hence, in 2007 the College abandoned Division I for the more friendly confines of Division III, which offers no athletic scholarships. Yet, instead of taking time to digest the move, college officials announced that the school would add football and four other intercollegiate sports. According to former Birmingham-Southern College President David Pollick, the addition of new teams at the lower level would allow Birmingham-Southern to increase enrollment and balance its budget. Moreover, to house the expected influx the college also announced a number of expensive capital projects including the construction of a large pond near the dorm quad, a new dorm, a football stadium, a new welcome center, and several new athletic facilities.[68]

The new athletic teams, capital construction, and increased tuition discounts created a perfect storm for disaster. By 2008, the school's deficit stood at $22,100,000. To cover this shortfall, institutional leaders borrowed liberally from the school's endowment, which fell from $114,000,000 in 2004 to just over $60,000,000 in 2009. Consequently, in the fall of 2010 institutional leaders took drastic steps to cut almost $10,000,000 from the institution's budget by terminating 29 faculty members, five majors, and 51 staff positions. The school also cut pay by 10 percent for the remaining employees and gave staff members two weeks of unpaid furlough. Despite these draconian measures, the future of Birmingham-Southern is still very much in doubt. However, with an endowment that still totals approximately $60,000,000 it appears the school will survive this crisis. Yet, few HBCUS have endowments the size of BSC. Hence, the impact of athletic enhancements on institutional viability is much greater. For this reason, many private HBCUS would be better served de-emphasizing athletics. Moving all athletic programs to NCAA Division III or NAIA Division II, where no team offers athletic scholarships, dropping football Programs or canceling the construction of expensive athletic facilities and residence halls, are several of the more visible options. Whatever the case, in the near future, many smaller HBCUs will have to make decisions as to whether athletic enhancements are worth the risk or long-term costs.[69]

Notes

1. Benjamin Elijah Mays, *Born to Rebel: An Autobiography* (Athens, University of Georgia Press, 2003), p. 96; and John S. Wilson, "America's Historically Black Colleges and Universities and the Third Transformation," *The Presidency*, December 19, 2009, 16–17.

2. Henry N. Drewy and Humphrey Doermann, *Stand and Prosper: Private Black Colleges and their Students* (Princeton, NJ: Princeton University Press, 2002).

3. David Augustus Stroker, *The New South Investigated* (Detroit: Ferguson Printing Company, 1888), p.215.

4. Ibid.

5. Raymond Wolters, *The New Negro on Campus: Black College Rebellions of the 1920s* (Princeton, NJ: Princeton University Press, 1975), pp. 5–7. In this way, vocational training became a corollary of white supremacy, with black men and women expected to learn the elementary lessons of carpentry, gardening, and homemaking that would make them useful helots.

6. Stephen S. Peeps, "Northern Philanthrophy and the Emergence of Black Higher Education Do-Gooders: Compromise, or Co-Conspirators?" *Journal of Negro Education* (Summer 1981), pp. 266–267.

7. Peeps, p. 266.; Leland Cozart, *Venture of Faith* (Ann Arbor: University of Michigan Press, 1967); James Lyons, "In the Beginning Faith: Oral History of Barber-Scotia College" (unpublished paper, Barber-Scotia College, 1976); and interview with Dr. Mabel Parker McLean, former president of Barber-Scotia College, August 15, 2006. As late as the 1930s many white supporters of black higher education still favored the industrial education model. For example in 1930, officials of the Northern Presbyterian Church agreed to merge Barber Memorials College of Anniston, Alabama, and Scotia Women's College. For officials at Scotia Women's College, the proposed site of the merged institution, the prospect of a merger seemed particularly appealing. Barber Memorial College had a cash endowment of $250,000. However, church officials seized Barber Memorials College's endowment before the merger as there was concern among church officials that school administrators might implement programs wholly unsuited to the education of black women — namely, liberal-arts programs. That church officials held such beliefs in surprising given the fact the president of the merged Barber-Scotia Junior College for Women was a white church official as were most faculty members. Since the merger of the two schools in 1930 Barber-Scotia College officials have launched several attempts to recover the endowment that by 2004 totaled more than $4,000,000. However, church officials countered that a clause in the endowment did not restrict he funds to Barber-Memorials College. The only restriction on the money was that its use be limited to black women which since the mid–1960s can take place at dozens of church related Presbyterian colleges.

8. Marybeth Gasman and Noah D. Drezner, "Fundraising For Black Colleges During the 1960s," *Nonprofit and Voluntary Sector Quarterly* (April 2010).

9. Brian Harper, "African American Access to Higher Education: The Evolving Role of Historically Black Colleges and Universities," *Academic American*, 3, no. 109, p. 113.

10. Ibid.

11. Ibid.

12. Henry N. Drewy and Humphrey Doermann, *Stand and Prosper: Private Black Colleges and their Students* (Princeton, NJ: Princeton University Press, 2002), pp 258–259. A large number of institutions also added the position director of institutional research to their fund-raising efforts. Although institutional research had little to do with fund-raising and more to do with assessment and accreditation, at the time, many HBCU presidents especially those at small colleges considered the position essentially as grant writers. Unfortunately, the result of this development was detrimental. In the years since 1980, despite having established offices of institutional research, HBCUs consistently garnered sanctions from accreditors in the areas in which institutional research was responsible.

13. Cheryl D. Fields, "HBCUs Get Savvy About Fund Raising," *Black Issues in Higher Education*, August 30, 2001, pp. 38–44.

14. Kit Lively, "Grants Help Black Colleges Build Fund-Raising Capacity Semifinalists in Kresge Program," *Chronicle of Higher Education*, May 7, 1999; and Joye Mercer, "Black College Aim Higher With Fund-Raising Campaigns," *Chronicle of Higher Education*, November 20, 1998; Fisk University Staff Listing for the Office of Institutional Advancement, December 2010, http://www.fisk.edu/AlumniAndFriends/OfficeOfInstitutional-Advancement/Staff.aspx.

15. Eugene Perr, interview by author, Roanoke, Virginia, 24 November 2010; and Gail Perry, *Fired-up Fundraising: Turning Board Passion into Action* (Hoboken, NJ: John Wiley, 2007), p. 190; *Barber-Scotia College Catalog 1993–1997* (Concord, NC: Barber-Scotia College, 1994); *Statistical Guide of the United Negro College Fund 1994* (Fairfax, VA: United Negro College Fund, 1994); *Statistical Guide of the United Negro College Fund, 1995* (Fairfax, VA: United Negro College Fund, 1995); *Statistical Guide of the United Negro College Fund, 1996* (Fairfax, VA: United Negro College Fund, 1996); *Statistical Guide of the United Negro College Fund, 1997* (Fairfax, VA: United Negro College Fund, 1997); *Talladega College Catalog 2000–2003* (Talladega, AL: Talladega College, 2000); *Talladega College Catalog 2003–2008* (Talladega, AL: Talladega College, 2003); resume of James Perkins, Ph.D., former vice president for advancement at Talladega College, http://www.jsums.edu/~sst/cset/Resume11_Jim_Perkins.pdf; *North Carolina Wesleyan College Catalog 2000–2001* (Rocky Mount NC: North Carolina Wesleyan College, 2000); *North Carolina Wesleyan College Catalog 2002–2003* (Rocky Mount, NC: North Carolina Wesleyan College, 2002); *North Carolina Wesleyan College Catalog 2006–2007* (Rocky Mount, NC: North Carolina Wesleyan College, 2006).

16. "Dr. Dorothy Cowser Yancey," http://www.shawuniversity.edu/press_releases/Dr_Yancy.pdf .

17. Kathryn Masterson, "Howard Assembles Fundraising Juggernaut," *The Chronicle of Higher Education*," June 27, 2008.

18. Ibid.

19. Kit Lively, "Hampton U. Campaign Raises $216 Million, Shattering Record for Black Colleges," *Chronicle of Higher Education,* December 5, 2000; and "Hampton University Reaches Goal of $200 Million Three Years Early," *Black Issues in Higher Education*, January 4, 2001; and "Hampton University: Educating For Life in The New Century: Virginia Institution Celebrates 135th Anniversary," *Ebony,* September 1, 2003.

20. Interview with Isaac Crumley, Director of the CDEP Program, Fort Valley State University, November 15, 2010.

21. Arelis Hernadez, "HBCU's Explore Ways to Move Beyond Tuition Dependence," *Diverse Issues in Higher Education*, April 15, 2020.

22. "Men Struggling to Finish at Black College," Associated Press, March 28, 2009.

23. Arelis Hernadez, "HBCU's Explore Ways to Move Beyond Tuition Dependence," *Diverse Issues in Higher Education*, April 15, 2020.

24. Reginald Stuart, "Ready for Battle," *Diverse Education*, August 19, 2010.

25. Emily Wagster Pettus, "Mississippi Governor Wants to Merge State's 3 HBCUs into One," *The Grio*, November 19, 2009.

26. Scot Jaschik, "Threat to Black Colleges," *Inside Higher Education*, November 17, 2009; and "Mississippi Plan to Consolidate Black Colleges Facing Opposition," *Diverse Issues in Higher Education*, November 18, 2009.

27. Scot Jaschik, "Threat to Black Colleges," *Inside Higher Education*, November 17, 2009; and "Mississippi Plan to Consolidate Black Colleges Facing Opposition," *Diverse Issues in Higher Education*, November 18, 2009; and Sheila Byrd, "JSU President Defends Black College Unity Plan," *Diverse Issues in Higher Education*, February 1, 2010.

28. "Letter to the HBCU Community," [Jackson] *Mississippi Link*, January 27, 2010.

29. "Letter to the HBCU Community," [Jackson] *Mississippi Link*, January 27, 2010; and "Mississippi Plan to Consolidate Black Colleges Facing Opposition," *Diverse Issues in Higher Education*, November 18, 2009.

30. James T. Minor, "Contemporary HBCUs: Considering Institutional Capacity and State Priorities," http://steinhardt.nyu.edu/scmsAdmin/uploads/002/151/MINOR_Contemporary_HBCU_Report_2008.pdf.

31. Vann Newkirk, "Barber-Scotia College: A Case for Faith Based Education," paper presented to Barber-Scotia College Board of Trustees, October 2005.

32. Ibid.

33. Ibid.

34. Michael Worth, *New Strategies for Educational Fundraising* (Westport, CT: Praeger, 2002), p. 293; R. Michael Haynes, "The Impact of Financial Aid on Postsecondary Persistence: A Review of the Literature," *NASFAA Journal of Student Financial Aid* vol. 37, no. 3 (2008), p. 30. Another problem created by tuition dependency crisis created by the reliance of large number of low performing low-income students on federal student loans. This is problematic since students in this group are more likely not to attain a bachelor's degree. The resulting lower earning power of these students increases the likelihood they will default on their student loan debt. Under current federal rules, colleges with default rates of 25 percent or greater for three consecutive years face the loss of eligibility in the federal student aid program. Students with a default rate greater than 40 percent in the latest year may lose eligibility to participate in the federal loan program.

35. Jeremy Offenstein, Collen Morre and Nancy Shulock, "Pathways to Success Lessons From the Literature on Career Technical Education," December 2009, The Institute for Higher Education Leadership and Policy.

36. John Pulley, "New Report Warns of the Danger of Tuition Discounting," *Chronicle of Higher Education* January 26, 2001.

37. Paul Fain, "Why Deep Tuition Discounts May Not Spell Financial Doom," *Chronicle of Higher Education*, May 2, 2010.

38. Paul Fain, "Why Deep Tuition Discounts"; Daniel Luzer, "How Colleges Spend," *Washington Monthly*, July 10, 2010; and "Trends in College Spending: Where Does the Money Come From? Where Does it Go?" American Institutes for Research, 2009.

39. Paul Fain, "Tuition Discount Rate Hits Record High, NACUBO Survey Finds, *Chronicle of Higher Education*, March 30, 2010.

40. Ibid.

41. Edward Alexander, interview by author, Jacksonville, FL, December 27, 2010; Wallace Keese, interview by author, Fort Valley, GA, December 14, 2010.

42. George Keller, *Transforming a College: The True Story of a Little Known College's Strategic Climb to National Distinction* (Baltimore, John Hopkins University Press, 2004), p. 27; *Elon University Fact Book: 2009–2010* (Elon College, NC: Elon University, 2010); *Elon University Fact Book 2005–2006* (Elon College, NC: Elon University, 2006).

43. George Keller, *Transforming a College*, p. 27; *Elon University Fact Book 2009–2010*; *Elon Universtiy Fact Book 2005–2006*.

44. "Tisdale Leads Claflin on Journey of Excellence," *Educational Pathways Magazine*, Vol. 11, Issue 2, (2007–2010), pp. 48–55.

45. Gabriel Adebayo Omolewu, *President Rembert Stokes of Wilberforce 1956 to 1976* (Bloomington, IN: AuthorHouse, 2009), pp. 114–115; and "Wilberforce University Needs $3 Million by June, Black America Web, http://www.Blackamericaweb.com/?q=print/news/the_state_of_Black_america_news/14791.

46. "Morris Brown Faces Increased Pressure to Solve Financial Crisis, Pay Back Money," *Black Issues in Higher Education*, November 21, 2002.

47. "Morris Brown Faces Increased Pressure."

48. Vann Newkirk, "Barber-Scotia College: A Case For Faith Based Education."

49. "Capital Financing: Department Management Improvements Could Enhance Education's Loan Program for Historically Black Colleges and Universities"(Government Accountability Office, October 2006); and Vann Newkirk, "Barber-Scotia College: A Case For Faith Based Education."

50. "Capital Financing: Department Management Improvements Could Enhance Education's Loan Program for Historically Black Colleges and Universities," Government Accountability Office, October 2006.

51. Lorraine Aheam, "Greensboro College Puts Up Campus to Back Loan," *Greensboro News and Record*, July 18, 2009.

52. Don Watson, interview by author, Washington, D.C., December 14, 2010; and "Capital Financing: Department Management Improvements Could Enhance Education's Loan Program for Historically Black Colleges and Universities," Government Accountability Office, October 2006

53. Vann Newkirk, "Barber-Scotia College: A Case For Faith Based Education."

54. "Capital Financing: Department Management Improvements Could Enhance Education's Loan Program for Historically Black Colleges and Universities," Government Accountability Office, October 2006.

55. Interview with Belinda Faulkner, former vice president for academic affairs at North Carolina Wesleyan College, December 2, 2010.

56. "The CIAA Celebrates Its 77th Year," *Ebony*, May 1989, pp. 176–178; "CIAA Celebrates Golden Anniversary," *Ebony*, December 1962, pp. 93–98; and Central Intercollegiate Athletic Association, http://en.wikipedia.org/wiki/Central_Intercollegiate_Athletic_Association.

57. Neil White, "Benedict Kicks Off Again: Officials Hope Revival of Football Will Give Boost to School Spirit," Columbia, *The State*, June 1, 1995; and Craig T. Greenlee, "There's a Football Revival Going On–College Football Programs Reappear; Statistical Data Included," *Black Issues in Higher Education*, August 2, 2001.

58. Gina Smith, "Benedict Grading Is Under Scrutiny," [Columbia] *State*, September 18, 2004; Williams Gunn, "Benedict Policy May Harm School's Good Name," [Columbia] *State*, September 24, 2004; James T. Hammond, "Benedict Professor Settle Academic Lawsuit," [Columbia] *State*, April 17, 2007; Scott Smallwood, "Faculty Group Censures Benedict College Again, This Time Over A for Effort Policy, *Chronicle of Higher Education,* January 21, 2005.

59. Gina Smith, "Benedict Grading Is Under Scrutiny," [Columbia] *State*, September 18, 2004.

60. Ibid.; "Benedict College Professor Settles Academic Lawsuit," South Carolina Lawyer Blog, http://www.southcarolinalawyerblog.com/2007/04/benedict_college_professor_set_1.html; and "Professors Take Benedict to Court," *Columbia Free Times*, Issue 20.5, January 31, 2007–February 6, 2007.

61. Gina Smith, "Benedict Grading Is Under Scrutiny," [Columbia] *State*, September 18, 2004; and Roddie Burris, "Benedict Struggling Financially," [Columbia] *State*, July 27, 2009.

62. Craig T. Greenlee, "There's a Football Revival Going On–College Football Programs Reappear; Statistical Data Included," *Black Issues in Higher Education*, August 2, 2001; Joe Humphrey, "EWC Pushes its Game Plan, but Football Money Lagging," [Jacksonville] *Florida Times Union*, January 23, 2001.

63. Craig T. Greenlee, "There's a Football Revival Going On–College Football Programs Reappear; Statistical Data Included," *Black Issues in Higher Education*, August 2, 2001; Joe Humphrey, "EWC Pushes its Game Plan, But Football Money Lagging," [Jacksonville] *Florida Times Union*, January 23, 2001; Marior W. Morgan, "LeMoyne-Owen Closer on Football: Committee Favors Starting in 2012; President, Board Still Must Approve," [Memphis] *Commercial Appeal*, October 21, 2010.

64. Roddie Burris, "Benedict Struggling Financially," [Columbia] *State*, July 27, 2009.

65. National Center for Education Statistics, "1997–1998: Integrated Postsecondary Education Data System," United States Department of Education, 1998; National Center for Education Statistics, "1998–1999: Integrated Postsecondary Education Data System," United States Department of Education, 1999; National Center for Education Statistics, "2004–2005: Integrated Postsecondary Education Data System," United States Department of Education, 2005; National Center for Education Statistics, "2005–2006: Integrated Postsecondary Education Data System," United States Department of Education, 2006; National Center for Education Statistics, "2006–2007: Integrated Postsecondary Education Data System," United States Department of Education, 2007; Wayne Grayson, "Accreditation Groups Extend Stillman College Warning," *Tuscaloosa News*, December 10, 2010; Adam Jones, "15 Jobs Cut at Stillman College," *Tuscaloosa News*, September 1, 2010; Adam Jones, "Credit Agency Rated Stillman Stable," *Tuscaloosa News*, July 18, 2010; Adam Jones, "Accrediting Agency Warns Stillman," *Tuscaloosa News*, June 29, 2010; Jimmy Boone, "Danzy Aims to Keep Building Stillman Program," *Tuscaloosa News*, June 27, 2000; Jimmy Boone, "Stillman Getting Its Tradition," *Tuscaloosa News*, September 6, 1999.

66. Adam Jones, "Credit Agency Rated Stillman Stable," *Tuscaloosa News*, July 18, 2010; Adam Jones, "Accrediting Agency Warns Stillman," *Tuscaloosa News*, June 29, 2010.

67. Greg Garrison, "David Pollick Resigns as President of Birmingham-Southern College Amidst Turmoil; Mark Schantz Named Interim President," *The Birmingham News*, August 12, 2010; Audrey Williams June, "After Costly Foray Into Big-Time Sports, a College Returns to Its Roots," *Chronicle of Higher Education*, May 18, 2007; Brad Wolverton, "A Costly Move," *Chronicle of Higher Education*, June 22, 2010; "Birmingham-Southern College Plans 20% Budget Cut, Citing Costly Student-Aid Errors," *Chronicle of Higher Education*, June 15, 2010; Audrey William June, "Layoffs at Birmingham-Southern College Highlight a Workplace Paradox," *Chronicle of Higher Education*, July 27, 2010; Daniel Luzer, "Extraordinary," *Washington Monthly*, July 17, 2010; Paul Fain, "Birmingham-Southern's President Resigns While Trustees Explain College's Financial Meltdown," *Chronicle of Higher Education*, August 11, 2010; Kyle Whitmire, "BSC Tax Records Show Years of Red Ink," http://weldbham.com/secondfront/2010/07/26/bsc-tax-records-show-years-of-red-ink/; Asher Hawkins, David Randall, Archana Rajan, and Christina Fierro, "Private College Financial Health Rankings," *Forbes,* April 20, 2010.

68. Greg Garrison, "David Pollick Resigns as President of Birmingham-Southern College Amidst Turmoil; Mark Schantz Named Interim President," *The Birmingham News*, August 12, 2010.

69. Audrey William June, "Layoffs at Birmingham-Southern College Highlight a Workplace Paradox," *Chronicle of Higher Education*, July 27, 2010.

8

Summary and Thoughts for the Future

Vann R. Newkirk and Daniel Wims

Historically Black Colleges and Universities continue to play an important role in the education of African-Americans in the United States. For over 176 years institutions like Storer, Edward Waters, Bluefield State, Arkansas Baptist Colleges and Langston University have educated countless numbers of African American professionals. These institutions also served as the birthplaces of social change, playing key roles in the creation of the black middle class, and the civil rights movement. Despite these accomplishments, HBCUs continue to face questions about their continued relevancy. As indicated by Marybeth Gasman and Christopher Tudico, "Early on those who fundamentally believed that African-Americans were not worthy of education challenged black colleges (or tried to dilute their curricula); since Brown v. Board, those who believe that these institutions perpetuate segregation have called for this closure."[1] Today, although federal courts have affirmed the right of HBCUs to exist and to receive funding to address historic inequities, governors and members of state legislatures, faced with difficult choices in trying to cope with a weak economy have issued proposals that called for the consolidation or merger of HBCUs with nearby traditionally white institutions. Moreover, with the recent decision by the Louisiana Higher Education Commission to approve a proposal that seeks to merge Southern University of New Orleans with the University of New Orleans it appears that the opponents of HBCUS, who now control cash-strapped state governments, have put the anti-HBCU rhetoric into action.

Contributing to the actions of Southern politicians are biased reports by newspapers and other public media. Instead of highlighting institutional accomplishments, it appears that the focus of most newspapers and media outlets in regards to black colleges has been based on their flaws. This has led to a virtual torrent of articles, editorials, and television reports that highlight problems with accreditors, financial shortcomings, and academic deficiencies. Most of these reports never point out that many of the "so-called" issues facing HBCUs vary little from challenges facing regional public, and private church related TWIs. Nor do these articles show that many of the challenges faced by HBCUS stem from the historical discrimination faced by HBCUs since their establishment.

For example, most HBCUs originated during the negrophopic period at the end of the Civil War. Although, in the early years, most offered few college-level courses they nonetheless garnered the wrath of whites who deemed the education of blacks a threat to white hegemony. In this regard the opponents of black colleges and white supremacists faced a dilemma. For one, opponents of HBCUs lacked the political strength to roll back all of the gains won by blacks as a result of the Civil War. As a result, the foes of black colleges as well as Northern industrialists limited Negro education to the lowest level.

For HBCUs however these challenges led to the development of governmental systems at that focused on survival. At the core of this development were weak governing boards dedicated to the maintenance of the status quo. Such boards did little to provide direction or financial support. Instead, such boards interfered in the daily administration of the institution.

In conjunction with this development, the period saw the rise of dictatorial presidents who saw little need to be resourceful or innovative. Instead the early HBCU presidents managed black colleges like autocrats, tolerating no disobedience. Although such developments differed little from TWIs of the period, at many HBCUS such traits continued into the present.

As a result of these historical developments many HBCU developed institutional cultures that are resistant to change. This has led to the continued utilization of outdated practices which undoubtedly impact student and faculty recruitment as well as efforts to garner increased financial support from donors and foundations. In addition, many black colleges face challenges related to shared governance in which governing boards occasionally infringe on faculty rights and responsibilities, or meddle in the daily operations of an institution. For example, at many HBCUs there is a complete unwillingness by administrators to engage faculty and staff in the governance process. Yet, inclusiveness and shared governance are important aspects of any effective higher-education management model. Top professors and students are not likely to tolerate a management style that restricts their ability to play a role to the well-being of the institution when they have opportunities to go to or teach at other institutions with more inclusive forms of governance. "Effective leadership in the presidency and strong board governance, along with a commitment to work together to fulfill the mission of the institution, are crucial to the success of a college or university. A president who dominates his or her board, or a board that usurps its president will invariably lead to failure."[2]

For HBCU governing bodies, the problems are just as alarming. At most private colleges and universities management boards are self-perpetuating. They may represent church groups that established the institution, or trustees might serve without regard to term limits. Such factors make it difficult to enlist individuals with new point of views and different experiences. Perhaps the biggest challenge is enlisting trustees who know and understand the roles and responsibilities of the governing board, as well as the functions of the president. Such members must also be prepared to provide the intellectual capital, and resources needed to be productive.

Perhaps, due to the factors above it is easy to understand why scores of HBCU leaders engage in risky business practices that threaten the future viability of the institution that they serve. For example, since the mid–1990s many cash-strapped HBCUS have launched high-cost football teams as a cure-all for long-term institutional ills. By and large these efforts have not succeeded. Enrollment at eight of the nine private HBCUs that launched football teams, between 1995 and 2005, suffered enrollment declines instead of increases. Unfortunately, many of the schools borrowed heavily to construct new stadiums for the football team, and residence halls to house the expected enrollment increases. This has placed strains on already tight budgets and has led to a number of problems with regional accreditors. Indeed six of the nine private HBCUs that launched football teams from 1995 to 2007 have received sanctions from the Southern Association of Colleges and Schools for financial problems and two others received public downgrades of institutional bonds, thus limiting the ability of the institution to access capital.

Another problem facing HBCUs today stems from the tendency to construct new facilities in the hope of increasing enrollment. Since 2001, the Department of Education's Capital Financing Program has been a major source of funding for HBCU construction. Unfortunately, for much of the Capital Financing Program's history the agency has operated under guidelines that threaten the future well-being of HBCUs. Most troubling was the tendency of officials at the Capital Financing Program to overcollateralize loans by securing the entire campus of client institutions. The result of this policy has been disastrous for a number of smaller HBCUs who as a result of such policies are unable to leverage campus facilities to access capital despite the fact in many cases campus properties exceeded the value of loans received through the Capital Financing Program. Although criticism of the policy by members of Congress and HBCU supporters led to changes in the lending policies of the Capital Financing Program the agency still conducts practices that threaten the future of many smaller HBCUS. For example, since 2006 a number of smaller HBCUS have borrowed funds from the Capital Financing Program to construct new residence halls. The loans are secured by the new residence halls and by guarantees of specific occupancy and facilities revenue. Unfortunately, at many of the schools enrollment has fallen or remained stagnate despite the presence of new facilities. Consequently, residence hall profits that many smaller institutions once received evaporated as large portions of residence hall fees now go to pay debt-service on loans financed by the Capital Financing Programs while older facilities sit empty or nearly empty thus weakening already weak financial infrastructures.

To overcome the challenges and remain viable HBCUS must adopt more productive approaches to operations and fund-raising. Foremost in these changes include a revision of board governance structures and the (a) development of governing bodies that work together for the advancement of the institution; (b) deconstruction of governing boards dominated by church or special interest groups; (c) promotion of boards that clearly understand the role of trustees; (d) the development of and adherence to policies that ensure the governing body does not intrude into the daily operation of the institution; (e) identification of goals and objectives that allocate resources accordingly; (f) development of merits for measuring the achievement of these objectives; and (g) the development of real and meaningful committees that tackle issues.

In addition to these changes, HBCUs must find ways to overcome their financial shortcomings. Over the past decade a number of HBCUs have completed highly successful fund-raising campaigns. Key components of these campaigns were the identification of clearly defined goals; the identification of sources of gifts and fund-raising methods; enhancement of trustees giving and participation; the assembly of a suitable fund-raising team; and the development of entrepreneurial efforts to reduce tuition dependency. However, perhaps the most important factors in fund-raising success of these institutions was marketing of a viable product. In this regards institutions must promote success. This means improving graduation and retention rates. One proposal put forth in this study calls for the creation of a program of stackable certificates that incorporate developmental education courses into a series of professional skills certificates. In this model, all courses successfully completed build so that certificates stack on top of one another and the credits count towards a two_year degree and could serve as springboards into baccalaureate degree programs, thus enhancing HBCU retention and graduation rates.

Yet, these changes only represent part of the puzzle, and perceptions about the purpose and worth of HBCUs won't change without purposeful effort and commitment. Such change must not only build up weak operational and governance structures, but upgrade institutional fund-raising systems, and improve the educational performance of graduates. The continued success and sustainability of both public and private HBCUs requires that these changes be undertaken to ensure black colleges remain a viable educational option for all students.

Summary

1. Marybeth Gasman and Christopher L. Tudico, *Historically Black Colleges and Universities: Triumphs, Troubles and Taboos* (New York: Macmillan, 2008), p. 1.

2. Jack L. Ezzell Jr. and Alvin Schexnider, "Leadership, Governance, and Sustainability of Black Colleges and Universities," *Trusteeship* (May/June 2010), pp. 25–28.

Appendix:
Profiles of Closed HBCUs

DAWN J. HERD-CLARK

Avery Institute, 1865–1947.

Avery Normal Institute, named after the estate of Reverend Charles Avery of Pittsburgh, Pennsylvania, was established in 1865. The American Missionary Association school became the first accredited secondary school for African-Americans in Charleston. Francis Cardozo expanded the school's curriculum to include a normal department. Avery Normal Institute flourished as a private school for area African-Americans until 1947, when the city of Charleston began to meet its educational obligation to its African-American citizens. However under the context of abiding by the *Brown v. Board of Education* in 1954, Avery was closed by the county school board due to the lack of finances.

Drago, Edmund L., and Eugene C. Hunt. *A History of Avery Normal Institute from 1865 to 1954*. Charleston, S.C.: Avery Research Center, 1991.

Bishop College, 1881–1988.

Established by the Baptist Home Mission Society in 1881 as South-Western Baptist College, Bishop College began when New Yorker Nathan Bishop worked to establish an institution of higher education for African-American Baptists in Texas. Initially located in Marshall, the school became known as Bishop College when additional funds from the Bishop family were secured. As a religious institution that provided liberal arts instruction, the financially struggling school persevered. By 1948 Bishop College earned a Class A accreditation from the Southern Association of Colleges and Secondary Schools. As the school grew, including the formation of a junior college branch in Dallas in 1947, as well as a graduate program, it was thought that the school might prosper if it moved permanently to Dallas. Funds from the Hoblitzelle Foundation, along with those raised by area Baptists, led to the completion of the Bishop College in 1961. Problems at the school began in the 1970's when the American Association of University Professors blacklisted the school due to the firing of a white faculty member. Then embezzlement charges were made against several Bishop College administrators, and although cleared, enrollment began to drop, causing financial strains. In December 1986, the Southern Association of Colleges and Schools stripped Bishop College from membership. The following year the school attempted to file Chapter 11 bankruptcy but was unsuccessful in doing so. Thus the school closed in 1988. The grounds and facilities were then occupied by African Methodist Episcopal Church sponsored Paul Quinn College.

Heintze, Michael R. *Private Black Colleges in Texas, 1865–1954.* College Station: Texas A&M University Press, 1985.

Boggs Academy, 1906–1984.

Established by Reverend John Lawrence Phelps and the Presbyterian Church in 1906, Boggs Academy was founded in Keysville, Burke County, Georgia. Boggs Academy secured accreditation from the Southern Association of Colleges and Secondary Schools in 1943. Boggs Academy closed in 1984 due to financial constraints.

Campbell College, 1887–1965.

Campbell College, the first college to be established by African-Americans in Mississippi, was established by the African Methodist Episcopal Church in 1887. Initially the school had two Mississippi campuses, one in Vicksburg, while the other was located in Friars Point. Under Bishop W. B. Derrick the two campuses merged into one in 1898, in Jackson. During the modern civil rights movement Campbell College student body president, Charles Jones, led area college students in a Easter boycott of businesses in the Capitol Street area in Jackson. When students at McComb, Mississippi's Burgland High School were expelled for not signing a letter barring them from future Civil Rights protests, Campbell College granted them an education. The modern civil rights movement took a toll on the school's finances and in 1964, the indebted and deteriorating campus was seized through eminent domain by the State of Mississippi. The land from this seizure was turned over to Jackson State College, thus merging the two campuses.

Williamson, Joy Ann. "'Quacks, Quirks, Agitators, and Communists': Private Black Colleges and the Limits of Institutional Autonomy." History of Higher Education Annual 2003–2004 Vol. 23, ed. by Roger L. Geiger. New Brunswick, NJ: Transaction, 2005. *http://westjxn.com/2011/02/10/westerday-trivia-answer-campbell-college/,* accessed February 27, 2011.

Central City College, 1899–1956.

Organized by the General Missionary Baptist Convention of Georgia, under the advice of Revered E. K. Love, after African-Americans choose to form their own institution to rival the Atlanta Baptist Seminary when their voices in the institution continued to be ignored, Central City College, located outside Macon, Georgia, was established in 1899. Since the school was owned and controlled by African-Americans they felt a sense of pride in their institution of higher education that trained preachers and teachers. In 1938 the school was renamed the Georgia Baptist College. Throughout the history of the school monetary problems plagued the school which caused it to close in 1956.

Coleman College, Bienville Parrish, Louisiana, 1887–1937.

Founded by Oliver Lewis Coleman in 1887, Coleman College was established to provide educational opportunities for African-American youth in rural north Louisiana. Coleman's school received assistance from white northern philanthropists, area Baptist churches who formed the Springfield Baptist Association to support his school, white northern Baptists, and in time the Bienville Parrish School Board. The school grew until Coleman's in 1927, and that event, along with the Great Depression, caused the school to cease operation in the late 1930's.

Faircloth, Adam. *A Class of Their Own: Black Teachers and the Segregated South.* Cambridge, Massachusetts: Belknap Press of Harvard University Press, 2007

Fort Worth Industrial and Mechanical College, 1909–1929.

Founded as Hearne Academy, in 1881, outside of Hearne, Texas, by Baptist Lincoln Association for African-American youth, the school was moved and renamed Fort Worth Industrial and Mechanical College 1909. The school's offered elementary, secondary, college-preparatory, and industrial courses. Although funded by the American Baptist Home Mission, as well as the Texas Baptist Missionary and Education Fund, the school struggled financially. In 1929, Fort Worth Industrial and Mechanical College closed due to the lack of adequate finances.

Montgomery, William E. "Hearne Academy," Handbook of Texas Online, (http://www. tshaonline.org/handbook/online/articles/kbh16), accessed February 19, 2011.

George R. Smith College, 1894–1925.

Named after the founder of Sedalia, MO, George R. Smith, George R. Smith College was established in 1894 by the Freedmen's Aid Society of the Methodist Episcopal Church with a of land from Smith's daughters. George R. Smith College's curriculum had normal and four year college tracts. The school flourished until 1925, when it was destroyed by a fire. In 1933 the school's assets were merged with Philander Smith College in Little Rock, AR.

Christensen, Lawrence O., and Gary R. Kremer. *A History of Missouri: Vols. IV, 1875– 1919.* Columbia: University of Missouri Press, 1997.

Guadalupe College, 1884–1936.

Founded in Seguin, Texas, by the Guadalupe Baptist Association in 1884, Guadalupe College sought to educate African-American Baptists for the education and preaching fields. The school's first session took place in 1887, and African-Americans continuously raised funds to keep their school open. In 1914, Guadalupe College moved to another part of town when turmoil plagued the school due to lawsuits, financial crises, declining enrollment, which led to a loss of accreditation. By 1929 the college had resumed its prominence and had been rated senior college by the Texas Department of Education. However the Great Depression took its tool on the school and it reverted to a junior college in 1931, and in 1936 a fire destroyed the campus' main building. Although able to rebuild, the college was never able to regain its accreditation. The school was granted a new charter in 1971, however collegiate level classes never returned to the school.

Brawner, Anne. "Guadalupe College: A Case History in Negro Higher Education, 1884– 1936." M.A. thesis, Southwest Texas State University, 1980.

_____. "Guadalupe College." *Handbook of Texas Online,* (http://www.tshaonline. org/handbook/online/articles/kbg19), accessed February 10, 2011.

Lancaster Normal and Industrial College, 1887–1923.

In 1879 the Reverend Charles Pettey, an African Methodist Episcopal Zion pastor opened Pettey High School at the Lancaster Court House in Lancaster, South Carolina. When the church began to support the school in 1880, it was renamed Lancaster High School. In 1887 the school was renamed Lancaster Normal and Industrial

College, where it operated as a boarding school providing African-American youth educational opportunities, including normal certification. The school closed in 1923.

Mitchell, Henry H. *Black Church Beginnings: The Long-Hidden Realties of the First Years.* Grand Rapids, MI: Wm. B. Eerdmans, 2004. *http://www.sctravel.net/African_American_Sites_Brochure.pdf,* accessed February 27, 2011.

Leland University, 1870–1915/1960.

Leland University was founded by Holbrook Chamberlain, a resident of Brooklyn, New York, who went to the state to establish an institution of higher education for African-Americans in Louisiana. From its inception Leland University did not discriminate, all people, regardless of gender or race, were encouraged to attend. Initially a primary school, it evolved into a college that trained preachers and teachers, and operated an industrial department. The school closed in 1915 when a hurricane hit New Orleans; however it moved to Baker, Louisiana, in 1923 and continued as an institution of higher learning until its closure in 1960.

Mary Allen College, 1886–1942.

Mary Allen's origins trace back to the first school in the area for freedmen, Crockett Presbyterian Church Colored Sabbath School, established in 1871 by Reverend Samuel Fisher Tenney. In 1785 the school had transitioned into a parochial day school, Moffatt Academy. When the Presbyterian Church expressed an interest in establishing an institution of higher education in Texas, Tenney encouraged the church to build it in Crockett. Named after Mary E. Allen, the wife of Richard H. Allen, secretary to the Presbyterian Board of Missions for Freedmen, who worked hard to ensure that the Presbyterian Church established a school for women in Texas, Mary Allen Seminary secured Southern Association of Colleges and Schools accreditation in 1932. In 1932 the school formally changed its name to the Mary Allen Junior College, and began accepting male students. In 1942 an attempt was made to make the school a four-year state institution of higher education for African-American students, and although the Presbyterian Church agreed to do so, World War II prevented the transfer, causing the school to close in 1943. Although the Missionary Baptist Convention of Texas purchased the property and reopened the school in 1944, the school closed permanently in 1972.

Hendrick, John R. "Mary Allen Junior College." *Handbook of Texas Online* http://www.tshaonline.org/handbook/online/articles/kbm08, accessed February 11, 2011.

Mississippi Industrial College, 1905–1982.

Mississippi Industrial College was established in 1905 by the Mississippi Colored Methodist Episcopal Church under Bishop Elias Cottrell. In 1906 the Holly Springs Mississippi school admitted its first students. Founded to educate African-Americans in a Christian environment, the college was always under funded, and struggled once integration took place; African-American students could now attend less expensive state supported community colleges. Mississippi Industrial College ceased operating in 1982. In 2008 Rust College purchased the property of Mississippi Industrial College.

Morristown College, 1881–1988.

The origins of Morristown College began when Almyra H. Stearns established a Freedmen's Bureau school for the newly emancipated freedmen in 1868. In 1881 the Methodist Episcopal Church expanded upon Stearns' school and Morristown College, in Morristown, TN, commenced. Initially charged with supplying ministers for black Methodist congregations and teachers for black schools, the two year school became known as Morristown Normal and Industrial College when industrial education was introduced to the curriculum. In the 1930's the school's curriculum transition from industrial to a liberal arts curriculum. Morristown College prospered until the modern civil rights movement, when African-American students could attend all state institutions that cost less. The school struggled financially until the campus was acquired by Knoxville College in 1989, and operated it as a junior college. Knoxville College's financial struggle during the 1990's forced the school to cease operation of the Morristown College campus in 1995.

Payne College, Cuthbert, Georgia, founded 1879.

On June 5, 1912, Payne Institute was changed to Payne College and it became part of Morris Brown University, which also included Morris Brown College in Atlanta, GA and Central Park Normal and Industrial Institute in Savannah, GA.

Smith, Charles Spencer, and Daniel Alexander Payne. *A History of the African Methodist Episcopal Church*. Philadelphia: Book Concern of the A.M.E. Church, 1922.

Roger Williams University, 1864–1929.

Founded in 1864 in Nashville, TN, Roger Williams University began as an educational institution for African-American Baptist preachers. The school's first classes were held in the home of Daniel W. Phillips, a white minister and freedmen's missionary from Massachusetts. In 1866 the school was renamed the Nashville Normal and Theological Institute under the auspices of New York's American Baptist Home Mission Society. In 1883 the school was incorporated as Roger Williams University, and in 1886 Roger Williams expanded the curriculum to include a master's degree program. In 1905 the school was closed when a fire destroyed most of the campus. African-American Baptists lead the effort to relocate and reopen the school in 1908, with matching from the American Baptist Home Mission Society. Financial problems forced the campus to close in 1929; however the students and teachers merged with Howe Institute, now known as LeMoyne Owen College, in Memphis.

TeSelle, Eugene. "The Nashville Institute and Rover Williams University: Benevolence, Paternalism, and Black Consciousness, 1867–1910." *Tennessee Historical Society Quarterly* (December 1982).

Seldon Normal and Industrial Institute, 1903–1933.

Seldon Normal and Industrial Institute was founded by Carrie E. Bemus in 1903 in Brunswick, Georgia. In 1933 the school merged to form the Gillespie-Selden Institute in Cordele, Georgia.

Trinity College/Trinity School, 1865–1942.

Trinity College was established in 1865 by the Western Freedman's Aid Commission when Mary Frances Wells, a Union Army nurse, began to educated freedmen in Athens, AL. The American Missionary Association soon added the school as a mission when the Western Freedmen's Aid Commission ceased functioning. Known for its normal program , Trinity sought to provide a cadre of African-American teachers. A series of fires plagued the school including ones in 1879, 1907, 1913, however the African-American community made a commitment to support the school and it continued to prosper. In 1943 the Limestone County Board of Education agreed to finance a public high school for African-American youth and took over the operation of Trinity High School. The final transfer of Trinity to the state of Alabama took place in 1956.

Amistad Research Center. "Trinity School (Athens, Ala.)." http://www.amistadresearch center.org/archon/?p=creators/creator&id=53.

Walden University, 1868–1925.

Founded in 1865 as a school for freedmen by the northern Methodist Episcopal Church, Walden University was initially chartered in Nashville, TN as Central Tennessee College in 1867. In the 1870's the school expanded to include normal and medical departments and in the 1880's, Central Tennessee College added even more programs to the school's curriculum including law, industrial art, dentistry, and pharmacy; in 1892 nursing was added. In 1900, the school was renamed Walden University in honor of Bishop John Morgan Walden. When the state of Tennessee funded a state supported institution of higher education, Tennessee Agricultural, Industrial, and Normal State School, in Nashville in 1912, Walden University's attendance dropped. Then in 1915 Meharry Medical College broke away from Walden. The school was moved and renamed Walden College in 1922, and became a junior college. The financial prosperity of the 1920's did not help Walden College, forcing the school to close in 1925.

Lovett, Bobby L. "Walden University *(1868–1925)*," 1995. http://www.tnstate.edu/library/ digital/walden.htm.

Walker Baptist College, Augusta, Georgia, 1898–1938.

Initially located in Waynesboro, GA as a day school in the early 1880's, the Walker Baptist Association, led by Rev. Dr. Charles T. Walker, expanded the school's curriculum and renamed the school Walker High School in 1886. Walker thought the school would have a greater impact on African-Americans by moving to a more populous community, and he wanted to rival the educational gains being made by the Methodists and Presbyterians, thus in 1892 it was moved to Augusta and renamed the Walker Baptist Institute. Also known as the Walker Baptist College, the school closed in the late 1930's.

Floyd, Silas Xavier. *Life of Charles T. Walker, D. D., ("The Black Spurgeon"), Pastor of Mt. Olivet Baptist Church, New York City.* Nashville: National Baptist Publishing Board, 1902. Gardner, Robert G. "Baptist Educational Institutions in Georgia." Jack Tarver Library, Mercer University, Macon, Georgia, 2007.

Western College and Industrial Institute, Macon, MO, founded 1890.

Established by African-American Baptists in Independence, MO, Western College and Industrial Institute moved two years later to Macon. In 1920 the school moved to Kansas City Missouri; however the Great Depression caused the school to cease operation during the 1935–1936 school term. The college was reorganized in 1937 and renamed the Western Baptist Bible College, and currently offers a variety of degrees in graduate programs in religious studies.

Bibliographical Essay

JUONE BROWN

Until the late 1960s, HBCUs garnered little attention from main-stream scholars. During this early period, two distinctive types of HBCU literature emerged. The first genre grew out of efforts by the federal government and private foundations to determine the number and types of institutions that served African-Americans. Most of these studies were similar to William T.B. Williams, *Report on Negro Universities* (1922), sponsored by the John F. Slater Fund. This report listed important details about private HBCUs such as enrollment, location, types of programs offered, and size of endowments. Other important works of this genre include: John F. Slater Fund, *County Teacher Training Schools for Negroes* (1913); Thomas Jesse Jones, *Negro Education: A Study of the Private and Higher Education Schools for Colored People in the United States* (1917); Leo Mortimer Favrot, *A Study of County Training Schools For Negroes in the South* (1923); Oscar F. Galloway's, *Higher Education for Negroes in Kentucky* (1933); David Lane, "The Junior College Movement Among Negroes," *Journal of Negro Education* (1933); and Fred McCuistion, *Higher Education of Negroes* (1933).[1]

The early period also saw the development of a second category of HBCU literature, written by former students and black college administrators. These authors chronicled the origin, development and growth of the historically black colleges. Many of these works also provide analysis of institutional operations and offer suggestions for the improvement of programs and services. Perhaps the most important of these examinations is Oliver Wendell Holmes, *The Evolution of the Negro College* (1934). In this study, Holmes, the first African-American president of historically black Morgan State University, describes the chaotic conditions in which HBCUs developed. The study also identifies and highlights the roles of the groups that were responsible for founding and expanding HBCUs — namely the federal government, white Protestant church groups, black religious denominations, state governments and private philanthropists. As a final component, Holmes employs historical analysis to provide a series of recommendations to improve the quality of education and the viability of HBCUs. Other studies of this type include William Newton Hartshorn, *An Era of Progress and Promise 1863–1910: The Religious, Moral and Educational Development of the Negro American* (1910); John W. Davis, *Land-Grant Colleges for Negroes* (1934); John W. Davis, *Problems in the Collegiate Education of Colleges of Negroes* (1937); Felton Clark, "The Development and Present Status of Publicly Supported Higher Education for Negroes," *The Journal of Negro Education* (1958); Charles Spurgeon Johnson, *The Negro College Graduate* (1938); Benjamin Mays, "Black College: Past, Present and Future," *Black Scholar* (1975); Nathan Carter Newbould, *Five North Carolina Negro Educators* (1938); Jeanne L. Noble, *The Negro Woman's College Education* (1956); Walter Dyson, *Howard University, the Capstone of Negro Education, a History 1867–1940* (1941); Ambrose Caliver, *Postwar Problems of Negro Colleges* (1943); John Irving Scott, *Negro Students and Their Colleges* (1949); Fredrick Chambers, "Histories of black Colleges and Universities," *Journal of Negro History* (1972); Williard Range, *The Rise and Progress of Negro Colleges in Georgia 1865–1949* (1951); Frenise Logan, "The Movement in North Carolina to Establish a State Supported College for Negroes," *North Carolina History Review* (1958); Horace Mann Bond, *The Education of the Negro in the American Social Order* (1966); Aaron Brown, "Graduate and Professional Education in Negro Institutions," *The Journal of Negro Education* (1958); and Frenise Logan, "The Evolution of Private Colleges for Negroes," *Journal of Negro Education* (1958).[2]

In the 1950s, important legislation changed the landscape in which HBCUs operated. For example, in 1950 the United States Supreme Court outlawed segregation in public institutions of higher education in the landmark case *McLaurin v. Oklahoma State Regents*. Several years after this ruling, the Supreme Court, overturned the constitutionality of racial segregation in the famous *Brown v. Board of Education of Topeka* case. Following these rulings, the percentage of African-Americans who attended HBCUs declined significantly. Perhaps due to these factors in the mid 1960s a number of mainstream scholars published studies that examined the future of HBCUs. Important studies of this type include James Earl McGrath, *The Predominately Negro College and University in Transition* (1965); and Abram Jaffe, *Negro Education in the 1960s* (1964). However, perhaps the most controversial of these works was Christopher Jencks and David Riesman's 1967 commentary "The American Negro College," published in the *Harvard Educational Review*. This study, which called HBCUs "academic disaster areas," argued for the closure of HBCUs.[3]

In response to this article, two distinctive types of literature developed. The first strain called for the closure of HBCUs. Many of these studies were similar to Gerald Foster, *Is There a Conspiracy to Keep Black Colleges Open?* (2001), in which he calls for black colleges to relinquish the crutch of slavery and its harmful effects and learn to embrace a standard of academic excellence that transcends race. Furthermore, Foster claims that if "there is one basic criticism of far too many black colleges it is that their admission decisions are driven by the need for tuition and federal aid rather than seeking high-quality students who are ready to engage in serious study." Other important studies in this genre include Christopher Jencks and David Riesman, *Academic Revolution* (1968); Douglas Decator McAdoo, "America's Black Colleges: Survival or Demise: Do They Still Have a Place?" Ph.D. thesis (1974); and Gerald Anthony Foster, *Are Black Colleges Needed? An At-Risk/Prescriptive Guide* (1996).[4]

The second strain of literature attempted to promote the value of HBCUs by highlighting their contributions. These studies also addressed why these institutions exist, how effective they have been, and if the 103 HBCUs in existence are still necessary. In addition, many give special attention to the years since 1954 and to desegregation cases such as *Brown v. Board of Education*, *United States v. Fordice*, and other judicial decisions. Important studies of this school include: Carlos H. Vernon, "A Current History of Black Colleges," *Black World/Negro Digest* (1973); Patricia Gurin and Edgar Epps, *Black Consciousness, Identity, and Achievement: A Study of Students in Historically Black Colleges* (1975); Addie Louise Joyner Butler, *The Distinctive Black College: Talladega, Tuskegee and Morehouse* (1977); Ian Kenrick Gransison, "Negotiated Space: The Black College Campus as a Cultural Record of Postbellum America," *American Quarterly* (1999); Miles Mark Fisher, *The Historically*

Black Colleges and Universities: A Crucial Resource (1978); Marian E. Brazziel, *Black Colleges and Universities: How They Started and What They Do* (1987); Albert Whiting, *Guardians of the Flame: Historically Black Colleges Yesterday, Today and Tomorrow* (1991); Julian Roebuck and Komanduri S. Murty, *Historically Black Colleges and Universities: Their Place in American Higher Education* (1993); Harold Wenglinsky, *Students at Historically Black Colleges and Universities: Their Aspiration and Accomplishments* (1997); InJay, *Black Colleges and Universities: Charcoal to Diamonds* (1999); Henry Drewy, *Stand and Prosper: Private Black Colleges and Their Students* (2003); and Frank W. Hale, *How Black Colleges Empower Black Students: Lessons for Higher Education* (2006).[5]

During the mid–1980s, scholars began to reevaluate the traditional form of supportive HBCU literature. From this re-evaluation emerged a new literature that attempted to promote HBCUs by critically examining the operations of black colleges in an effort to improve the efficiency and effectiveness of these institutions. Many of these studies also contained modal frameworks that identified potential roles which historically black colleges may choose to implement in the near future in order to maintain a viable position in the sphere of American higher education. Important studies of this nature include Andrew F. Brimmer, "The Future Outlook of Black Colleges," *Daedalus* (1971); Daniel Calbert Thompson, *Private Black Colleges at the Crossroads* (1973); Louis Augustus Venson, "Trends in Black College: Strategies for Improvement of Educational Opportunities in Selected Areas," Ph.D. thesis (1975); Derrick A. Bell, *Black Colleges and the Desegregation Dilemma* (1979); Katherine Harris White, "Black Colleges Since 1954 Brown v. Board of Education," Ph.D. thesis (1983); Antoine M. Garibaldi, *Black Colleges and Universities: Challenges for the Future* (1984); Robert Lewis Albright and George Neely, *Challenges for the Traditionally Black College: A New Look*, (1987); Wilma J. Roscoe, *Accreditation of Historically and Predominately Black Colleges and Universities* (1989); M. Starita Boyce, "Fund-Raising and Marketing Effectiveness at Historically Black Colleges," master's thesis (1992); Vinetta L. Wesley, "Leadership at Historically Black Colleges and Universities: Impact on Student Outcomes," master's thesis (1997); Carolyn O. Wilson Mbajekwe, *The Future of Historically Black Colleges and Universities: Ten HBCU Presidents Speak Out* (2006); and Marybeth Gasman and Christopher L. Tudico, *Historically Black Colleges and Universities: Triumphs, Troubles and Taboos* (2008).[6]

Although the literature that covers HBCUs has varied, there has been no singular attempt to develop a comprehensive study that includes key elements of early descriptive studies with that of the later works which examine the future of HBCUs and those that promoted black colleges. Most of these works also fail to critically examine the evidence of studies that called quickly for the closure of HBCUs. Furthermore, in evaluating the extant literature on HBCUs, researchers Allen and Jewell (2007) report that a large portion of the initial publications about HBCU's continue to be either biographical or autobiographical with a tendency towards focusing heavily on social function HBCUs served within the African American community.

Hence the historical nature of such information, while valuable, does not lead to solutions for the problems faced by HBCUs today.[7] Partly due to the previously mentioned oversights, a group of HBCU administrators gathered in San Antonio in the winter of 2008 to discuss the current literature and its impact on the future of HBCUs. From these discussions, a group of Fort Valley State University faculty and administrators set out to develop a new, inclusive, approach for examining HBCUs. According to Dr. Julius Scipio, vice president of academic affairs at Fort Valley State University, the goal of this group was "to study and merge the demographic, historical and predictive data found in today's HBCU literature with speculative analyses that called for the closure of HBCUs." Through such an analysis, the Fort Valley group seeks to provide new insights into ensuring that HBCUs continue to play an important role in the education of Americans of all races for many years to come.[8]

Notes

1. T.B. Williams, *Report on Negro Universities* (Baltimore: John F. Slater Fund, 1922); John F. Slater Fund, *County Teacher Training Schools for Negroes* (New Orleans: Tulane University Press, 1913); Thomas Jesse Jones, *Negro Education: A Study of the Private and Higher Education Schools for Colored People in the United States* (Washington, D.C.: Government Printing Office, 1917); Leo Mortimer Favrot, *A Study of County Training Schools for Negroes in the South* (Charlottesville, VA: John F. Slater Fund, 1923); Oscar F. Galloway, *Higher Education for Negroes in Kentucky* (Lexington: University of Kentucky Press, 1933); Fred McCuistion, *Higher Education of Negroes* (Nashville, TN: Committee on Approval of Negro Schools, 1933); and David Lane, "The Junior College Movement Among Negroes," *Journal of Negro Education* (1933), 272–283.

2. Oliver Wendell Holmes, *The Evolution of the Negro College* (New York: Teachers College, Columbia University, 1934); William Newton Hartshorn, *An Era of Progress and Promise 1863–1910: The Religious, Moral and Educational Development of the Negro American* (Boston, MA: Pricilla, 1910); John W. Davis, "Land-Grant Colleges for Negroes," *Journal of Negro Education*, vol. 21, no. 3 (Summer 1952); Charles Spurgeon Johnson, *The*

Negro College Graduate (New York: Negro Universities Press, 1969); Nathan Carter Newbould, *Five North Carolina Negro Educators* (Chapel Hill: University of North Carolina Press, 1938); Walter Dyson, *Howard University, the Capstone of Negro Education, A History 1867–1940* (Washington, DC: Howard University, 1941); Ambrose Caliver, *Postwar Problems of Negro Colleges* (Raleigh: North Carolina Negro College Conference Proceedings, 1943); John Irving Scott, *Negro Students and Their Colleges* (Boston: Meador, 1949); Williard Range, *The Rise and Progress of Negro Colleges in Georgia 1865–1949* (Athens: University of Georgia Press, 1951); Frenise Logan, "The Movement in North Carolina to Establish a State Supported College for Negroes," *North Carolina History Review*, vol. 35 (April 1959), 167–180; Frenise Logan, "The Evolution of Private Colleges for Negroes," *Journal of Negro Education*, vol. 28 (Summer 1958), 213–220; Horace Mann Bond, *The Education of the Negro in the American Social Order* (New York: Octagon, 1966), Aaron Brown, "Graduate and Professional Education in Negro Institutions," *Journal of Negro Education*, 27, no. 3 (summer 1958), 233–242; Fredrick Chambers, "Histories of Black Colleges and Universities," *Journal of Negro History* (1972), 370–275; Felton G. Clark, "The Development and Present Status of Publicly Supported Higher Education for Negroes," *Journal of Negro Education*, 27, no. 3 (summer 1958), 221–232; Benjamin E. Mays, "Black College: Past, Present and Future," *Black Scholar* (1974), 32–37; and Jeanne L. Noble, *The Negro Woman's College Education* (New York: Teachers College, 1956).

3. James Earl McGrath, *The Predominately Negro College and University in Transition* (New York: Columbia University Press, 1965); Abram Jaffe, *Negro Education in the 1960s* (New York: Praeger, 1964); and Christopher Jencks and David Riesman, "The American Negro College," *Harvard Educational Review*, vol. 37 Winter (1967), 3–60.

4. Gerald Foster, *Is There a Conspiracy to Keep Black Colleges Open?* Dubuque, IA: Kendell/Hunt, 2001; Christopher Jencks and David Riesman, *Academic Revolution*, Garden City, NY: Doubleday, 1968; Douglas Decator McAdoo, "America's Black Colleges: Survival or Demise: Do They Still Have a Place?" Ph.D. thesis, University of Massachusetts, 1974; and Gerald Anthony Foster, *Are Black Colleges Needed? An At-Risk Prescriptive Guide* (Kearney, NE: Morris Publishing, 1996).

5. Carlos H. Vernon, "A Current History of Black Colleges," *Black World/Negro Digest* (February 1973), 26–33; Patricia Gurin and Edgar Epps, *Black Consciousness, Identity, and Achievement: A Study of Students in Historically Black Colleges* (New York: Wiley, 1975); Addie Louise Joyner Butler, *The Distinctive Black College: Talladega, Tuskegee and Morehouse* (Metuchen, NJ: Scarecrow, 1977); Miles Mark Fisher, *The Historically Black Colleges and Universities: A Crucial Resource* (Washington, D.C.: Howard University Press, 1978); Marian E. Brazziel, *Black Colleges and Universities: How They Started and What They Do* (Atlanta: Marian Brazziel, 1987); Albert Whiting, *Guardian of the Flame: Historically Black Colleges Yesterday, Today and Tomorrow* (Washington, D.C.: American Association of State Universities, 1991); Julian Roebuck and Komanduri S. Murty, *Historically Black Colleges and Universities: Their Place in American Higher Education* (Westport, CT: Praeger, 1993); Harold Weglinsky, *Students at Historically Black Colleges and Universities: Their Aspirations and Accomplishments* (Princeton, NJ: Policy Information Center, Educational Testing Service, 1997); Injay, *Black Colleges and Universities: Charcoal to Diamonds* (Princeton, NJ: Princeton University Press, 1999); Henry Drewy, *Stand and Prosper: Private Black Colleges and Their Students* (Princeton, NJ: Princeton University Press, 2003); Frank W. Hale, *How Black Colleges Empower Black Students: Lessons for Higher Education* (Sterling, VA: Stylus, 2006); and Ian Kendrick Grandison, "Negotiated Space: The Black College Campus as a Cultural Record of Postbellum America," *American Quarterly* (1999), 539–579.

6. Andrew F. Brimmer, "The Future Outlook of Black Colleges," *Daedalus* (Summer 1971); Daniel Calbert Thompson, *Private Black Colleges at The Crossroads* (Westport, Ct: Greenwood, 1973); Louis Augustus Venson, "Trends in Black College: Strategies for Improvement of Educational Opportunities in Selected Areas," Ph.D. thesis, University of Michigan, 1975, Derrick A. Bell, "Black Colleges and the Desegregation Dilemma,"

Emory Law Journal, vol. 28 (1979); Katherine Harris White, "Black Colleges Since 1954 Brown v. Board of Education," Ph.D. thesis, University of Pittsburgh, 1983; Antoine M. Garibaldi, *Black Colleges and Universities: Challenges for the Future* (New York: Praeger, 1984); Robert Lewis Albright and George Neely, *Challenges for the Traditionally Black College: A New Look* (Atlanta: Southern Education Foundation, 1987); Wilma J. Roscoe, *Accreditation of Historically and Predominately Black Colleges and Universities* (Lanham, MD: University Press of America, 1989); M. Starita Boyce, "Fund-Raising and Marketing Effectiveness at Historically Black Colleges," master's thesis, State University of New York at Albany, 1992; Vinetta L. Wesley, "Leadership at Historically Black Colleges and Universities: Impact on Student Outcomes," master's thesis, George Peabody College for Teachers of Vanderbilt University, 1997; Carolyn O. Wilson Mbajekwe, *The Future of Historically Black Colleges and Universities: Ten HBCU Presidents Speak Out* (Jefferson, NC: McFarland, 2006); Marybeth Gasman and Christopher L. Tudico, *Historically Black Colleges and Universities: Triumphs, Troubles and Taboos* (New York: Palgrave Macmillan, 2008).

7. W. Allen and J. Jewell, "A Backward Glance Forward: Past, Present, and Future Perspectives on Historically Black Colleges and Universities," *The Review of Higher Education,* 25, no.3 (2002), 241–261.

8. Julius Scipio, interview by author, Fort Valley, Georgia, October 7, 2009.

Bibliography

Archival Materials

Caldwell, B.C. "Report to the Conference of State Agents for Negro Rural School." In General Education Board Papers, Box 28, Folder 1998, Rockefeller Archive Center, Pocantico Hill, New York.

Newspapers

Abilene Report-News, 1977
Beckley, WV *Post–Herald*, 1969
Birmingham News, 2010–2011
Bluefield Daily Telegraph, 1946, 1968
Boston Daily Advertiser, 1890
Brownsville Herald, 1977
Charleston, WV *Daily Mail*, 1968.
Charleston, WV *Farmer's Advocate*, 1940, 1948
Chicago Daily Defender, 1959–1969
Cincinnati Daily Gazette, 1869
Chicago Defender, 1920-1967
Cleveland Gazette, 1890–1906, 1913
Columbia Free Times, 2007
Columbia, SC *State*, 1997–2010
Corpus Christi-Times, 1977
Daily Kennebec Journal, 1894
Durham *Herald-Sun*, 1997
Enis TX Daily News, 2011
Fort Pierce, FL *News Tribune*, 1955
Fort Worth, TX *Daily Gazette*, 1890
Fredrick Post, 1955
Galveston, TX *Flake's Bulletin*, 1870
[Greensboro, NC] *Carolina Peacemaker*, July 7, 2011
Hampton, VA *Southern Workman*, 1870–1900
The Harvard Crimson, 1954
Indianapolis *Freeman*, 1893–1898

Iowa State Bystander, 1899
[Jackson] *Mississippi Link*, 2010
Jacksonville *Florida Times Union*, 1997–2008
Kansas City Advocate, 1916, 1924, 1925
Langston *Journal-Record*, 2005
Little Rock *Plaindealer*, 1906–1910.
Los Angeles Times, 1978
Los Angeles Tribune, 1943
Memphis *Commercial Appeal*, 2010
Milwaukee Star, 1969
Negro Star, 1943
New York Times, 1982, 1984
Newport Mercury, 1893
Orangeburg, SC *Times and Democrat*, 2010
Pacific Stars and Stripes, 1965
Raleigh, WV *Register*, 1963, 1968
Savannah Tribune, 1892, 1912
Springfield, MA *Republican*, 1890, 1899, 1913
Texarkana, AR *Freeman*, 1891, 1894, 1902, 1912
Topeka, Kansas *Plaindealer*, 1891–1958
Tuscaloosa News, 1998–2011
Washington Bee, 1906, 1910, 1914
Washington, D.C. *Daily Critic*, 1876
Wichita Times, 1974–1975
Williamsport *Homeland*, 1993

Government Documents

Li, X. "Characteristics of Minority-Serving Institutions and Minority Undergraduates Enrolled in These Institutions." U.S. Department of Education, 2007.
National Center of Education Statistics. "Digest of Education Statistics." U.S. Department of Education, 2005.
National Center for Education Statistics. "Employees in Postsecondary Institutions." United States Department of Education, 2007.
National Center for Education Statistics. "1994–2009: Integrated Postsecondary Education Data System." United States Department of Education, 1994–2009.
National Center for Education Statistics. "2007–2008 Integrated Postsecondary Education Data System." U.S. Department of Education, 2008.
United States Bureau of Education, "Industrial Education in the United States." U.S. Government Printing Office, 1883.
United States Department of Education, "Historically Black Colleges and Universities: 1976 to 1994." National Center for Education Statistics, 1996.
United States Department of Education, "The Traditionally Black Institutions of Higher Education: Their Development and Status, 1860 to 1982." In *Historical Report* Washington, D.C.: National Center for Education Statistics, 1985.
United States Department of the Interior, Bureau of Education, "Survey of Negro Colleges and Universities." United States Department of the Interior, 1929.

Accreditation Standards

Accreditation Manual. Forest, VA: Transnational Association of Christian Colleges and School, 2010.
Principles of Accreditation: Foundation for Quality Enhancement. Decatur, GA: Southern Association of Colleges and Schools, 2006.

Standards for Accreditation: Requirements of Affiliation. Philadelphia, PA: Middle States Commission of Higher Education, 2009.

Books

Acts and Joint Resolutions of the General Assembly of the State of South Carolina Passed at the Regular Session of 1869–70. Columbia: John W. Denny, State Printer, 1870.

Adair, Alvis V. *Desegregation: The Illusion of Black Progress.* Lanham, MD: University Press of America, 1984.

Alba, D.R. *Ethnic Identity: The Transformation of White America.* New Haven, CT: Yale University Press, 1989.

Albright, Robert Lewis, and George Neely. *Challenges for the Traditionally Black College: A New Look.* Atlanta: Southern Education Foundation, 1987.

Aleman, Ana M., and Kristen A. Renn. *Women in Higher Education: an Encyclopedia.* Santa Barbara, CA: ABC-CLIO, 2002.

Allen, Jennifer M., and Rajeev S. Sawhney. *Administration and Management in Criminal Justice: A Service Quality Approach.* Thousand Oaks, CA: Sage, 2009.

Allen, Walter R., Edgar G. Epp and Nesha Z. Haniff, ed. *College in Black and White: African-American Students in Predominately White and in Historically Black Public Universities.* Albany: State University of New York Press, 1991.

American Association of University Professors. *Historically Black Colleges and Universities: Recent Trends.* American Association of University Professors, 2006.

American Colonization Society. *The African Repository.* Washington, D.C.: American Colonization Society, 1889.

American Council on Education. *Educating Americans for a World in Flux: Ten Ground Rules for Internationalizing Higher Education.* Washington, D.C.: American Council on Education, 1995.

_____. *Minorities in Higher Education.* Washington, D.C.: American Council on Education, 1988.

Anderson, Charles. *International Studies for Undergraduates.* Washington, D.C.: American Council on Education, 1988.

Anderson, Eric, and Alfred A. Moss Jr. *Dangerous Donations: Northern Philanthropy and Southern Black Education, 1902–1930.* Columbia: University of Missouri Press, 1999.

Anderson, James. *The Education of Blacks in the South, 1860–1935.* Chapel Hill: University of North Carolina Press, 1988.

Andrew, Rod. *Wade Hampton: From Confederate War Hero to Southern Redeemer.* Chapel Hill: University of North Carolina Press, 2008.

Arsenault, Raymond. *Freedom Riders: 1961 and the Struggle for Racial Justice.* New York: Oxford University Press, 2006.

Association for International Education. *Americans Call for Leadership on Internal Education.* Washington, D.C.: NASFA, 2006.

Baird, David W., and Donnie Goble. *Oklahoma: A History.* Norman: University Oklahoma Press, 2008.

Barber-Scotia College Catalog, 1993–1998. Concord, NC: Barber-Scotia College, 1993.

Barry, John M. *Rising Tide: The Great Mississippi Flood of 1927 and How it Changed America.* New York: Touchstone, 1997.

Bates College. *General Catalog of Bates College and Cobb Divinity School 1863–1915.* Lewiston, ME: Bates College, 1915.

Bensimon, Estela M., Anna Neumann, and Robert Birnbaum. *Making Sense of Administrative Leadership: The "I" Word in Higher Education.* Washington, D.C.: George Washington University, 1989.

Bergeron, Paul, Stephen V. Ash and Jeranette Keith. *Tennesseans and Their History.* Knoxville: University of Tennessee Press, 1999.

Blackwell, James E. *Mainstreaming Outsiders: The Production of Black Professionals.* New York: General Hall, 1981.

Blake, R.R., and J.S. Monton. *The New Management Grid.* Phoenix, AZ: Gulf, 1978.

Bond, Horace Mann. *The Education of the Negro in the American Social Order.* New York: Octagon, 1966.

_____, and Julia W. Bond. *The Star Creek Papers: Washington Parish and the Lynching of Jerome Wilson.* Athens: University of Georgia Press, 1997.

Brazziel, Marian. *Black Colleges and Universities: How They Started and What They Do.* Atlanta: Marian Brazziel, 1987.

Brown, Christopher, and Kassie Freeman. *Black Colleges: New Perspectives on Policy and Practice.* Santa Barbara, CA: Greenwood, 2004.

Buller, Jeffrey L. *The Essential Academic Dean: A Practical Guide to College Leadership.* San Francisco, CA: John Wiley, 2007.

Bullock, Henry. *A History of Negro Education in the South from 1619 to the Present.* New York: Praeger, 1970.

Burke, Dawne Raines. *An American Phoenix: A History of Storer College: From Slavery to Desegregation, 1865–1955.* Pittsburgh: Geyer, 2006.

Burke, Lewis W., and Belinda F. Gerel, ed. *Matthew J. Perry: The Man, His Times and His Legacy.* Columbia: University of South Carolina Press, 2004.

Butler, Addie Louise. *The Distinctive Black College: Talladega, Tuskegee and Morehouse.* Metuchen, NJ: Scarecrow, 1977.

Caliver, Ambrose. *Postwar Problems of Negro Colleges.* Raleigh: North Carolina Negro Conference Proceedings, 1943.

Carter, Vertie. *Arkansas Baptist College: A Historical Perspective, 1884–1892.* Houston: D. Armstrong, 1981.

Chafe, William H. *Civilities and Civil Rights: Greensboro, North Carolina and the Black Struggle for Freedom.* Oxford: Oxford University Press, 1980.

Chait, Richard, Thomas P. Holland, and Barbara E. Taylor. *The Effective Board of Trustees.* Westport CT: Oryx, 1993.

Clark, C. *The Conditions of Economic Progress.* New York: Macmillan, 1957.

Clark, Kenneth, ed. *Impact on Leadership.* Greensboro, NC: Center for Creative Leadership, 1992.

Cobb, Charles E. *On the Road to Freedom: A Guided Tour of the Civil Rights Trail.* Chapel Hill, NC: Algonquin, 2008.

Cozart, Leland. *Venture of Faith.* Ann Arbor: University of Michigan Press, 1967.

Curtis, Nancy C. *Black Heritage Sites: An African-American Odyssey and Finder's Guide.* Chicago: American Library Association, 1996.

David, Leroy, Sr. *Still Striving: What HBCU Presidents Need to Know About SACS Accreditation.* Atlanta, GA: Southern Education Foundation, 2007.

Davis, K., and J. Swartz. *Increasing Black Students in Predominately White North Carolina Colleges and Universities.* New York: College Entrance Examination Board, 1972.

Drewy, Henry N., and Humphrey Doermann. *Stand and Prosper: Private Black Colleges and Their Students.* Princeton, NJ: Princeton University Press, 2002.

DuBois, W.E.B. *The Autobiography of W.E.B. DuBois: A Soliloquy on Viewing the Last Decade of Its First Century.* New York: International, 1968.

_____, and A.C. Dill. *The College Bred Negro American.* Atlanta: Atlanta University Press, 1910.

Dyson, Walter. *Howard University, the Capstone of Negro Education: A History 1867–1940.* Washington, D.C.: Howard University, 1941.

Ehrle, Elwood B., and J.B. Bennett. *Management the Academic Enterprise.* New York: Macmillan, 1988.

Ehrlirch, H.J. *Campus Ethnoviolence and the Policy Options.* Washington, D.C.: National Institute Against Prejudice and Violence, 1990.

Ellison, Ralph. *Invisible Man.* New York: Vintage, 1972.

Elon University Fact Book. Elon, NC: Elon University 2006.

Fairclough, Adams. *Race and Democracy: The Civil Rights Struggle in Louisiana, 1915– 1972*. Athens: University of Georgia Press, 1995.

Farmer, J. *Lay Bare the Heart: An Autobiography of the Civil Rights Movement*. New York: Arbor House, 1985.

Favrot, Leo Mortimer. *A Study of County Training Schools for Negroes in the South*. Charlottesville, VA: John F. Slater Fund, 1923.

Fisher, Miles Mark. *The Historically Black Colleges and Universities: A Critical Resource*. Washington, D.C.: Howard University Press, 1978.

Fleming, Jacqueline. *Blacks in College: A Comparative Study of Students' Success in Black and White Institutions*. San Francisco: Jossey-Bass, 1984.

Foster, Gerald. *Are Black Colleges Needed? An At-Risk Prescriptive Guide*. Kearney, NE: Morris, 1996.

_____. *Is There a Conspiracy to Keep Black Colleges Open?* Dubuque, IA: Kendell/Hunt, 1964.

Frankenberg, E., G. Siegel-Hawley, and G. Wang. *Choice Without Equity: Charter School Segregation and the Need for Civil Rights Standards*. Los Angeles: Civil Rights Project, 2010.

Galloway, Oscar F. *Higher Education for Negroes in Kentucky*. Lexington: University of Kentucky Press, 1933.

Garibaldi Antoine, ed. *Black Colleges and Universities: Challenges for the Future*. New York: Praeger, 1984.

Gasman, Marybeth, and Christopher L. Tudico. *Historically Black Colleges and Universities: Triumphs, Troubles and Taboos*. New York: Macmillan, 2008.

Gates, Henry Louis, and Cornel West. *The African-American Century: How Black Americans Have Shaped Our Country*. New York: Touchstone, 2000.

Gibson, Arrell Morgan. *Oklahoma: A History of Five Centuries*. Norman: University of Oklahoma Press, 1981.

Gore, Blinzy L. *On a Hilltop High: The Origin of Claflin College to 1984*. Spartanburg, SC: Reprint Company, 1994.

Green, Madeleine, Dao Luu, and Beth Burris. *Mapping Internationalization on U.S. Campuses: 2008 Edition*. Washington, D.C.: American Council on Education, 2008.

Grose, Philip G. *South Carolina at the Brink: Robert McNair and the Politics of Civil Rights*. Columbia: University of South Carolina Press, 2006.

Gurin, Patricia and Edgar Epps. *Black Consciousness, Identity and Achievement: A Study of Students in Historically Black Colleges*. New York: Wiley, 1975.

Hacker, A. *Two Nations: Black and White, Separate, Hostile, Unequal*. New York: Charles Scribner and Sons, 1992.

Hale, Frank W. *How Black Colleges Empower Black Students: Lessons for Higher Education*. Sterling, VA: Stylus, 2006.

Hamilton, G.P. *Beacon Lights of the Race*. Memphis: E.H. Clarke, 1911.

Harlan, Louis R. *The Booker T. Washington Papers*. Urbana: University of Illinois Press, 1972.

Harrison, Alferdteen B. *Piney Woods School: An Oral History*. Jackson: University of Mississippi, 1982.

Hartshorn, William Newton. *An Era of Progress and Promise, 1863–1910: The Religious, Moral and Educational Development of the Negro American*. Boston: Pricilla, 1910.

Hayward, Fred M. *Preliminary Status Report 2000: Internationalization of U.S. Higher Education*. Washington, D.C.: American Council on Education, 2000.

Haywood-Farmer, J., and J. Nollet. *Service Plus*. Quebec, Canada: Morin, 1991.

Herbold, R.J. *The Fiefdom Syndrome: The Turf Battles that Undermine Careers and Companies and How to Overcome Them*. New York: Doubleday, 2004.

Hewitt, Christopher. *Political Violence and Terrorism in Modern America: A Chronology*. Westport, CT: Praeger, 2005.

Hogkinson, Harold. *All One System*. Washington, D.C.: Institute for Educational Leadership, 1985.

Holland, Jesse J., and J.R. Oldfield, ed. *Civilization and Black Progress: Selected Writings of Alexander Crummell on The South*. Charlottesville: University of Virginia Press, 1995.

Holloway, M.M. *A Daughter's Memento*. Jacksonville, FL: Edward Waters, 1920.

Holmes, Oliver Wendell. *The Evolution of the Negro College*. New York: Teachers College, Columbia University, 1934.

Humes, Edward. *Over Here: How the G.I. Bill Transformed the American Dream*. Orlando: Harcourt, 2004.

Hurst, Rodney. *It Was Never About a Hotdog and a Coke*. Livermore, CA: Wingspan, 2008.

Injay. *Black Colleges and Universities: Charcoal to Diamonds*. Princeton, NJ: Princeton University Press, 1999.

Inscoe, John. *Appalachians and Race: The Mountain South from Slavery to Segregation*. Lexington: University of Kentucky Press, 2005.

Institute on Race and Poverty. *Examining the Relationship Between Housing, Education, and Persistent Segregation: Final Report*. Minneapolis: University of Minnesota, 2007.

Jackson, Cynthia, and Eleanor F. Nunn. *Historically Black Colleges and Universities: A Reference Handbook*. Santa Barbara, CA: ABC-CLIO, 2003.

Jackson, David H., and Canter Brown. *Sound the Trumpet: Selections in Florida's African-American History*. Tampa, FL: University of Tampa Press, 2005.

Jaffee, Abram. *Negro Education in the 1960s*. New York: Praeger, 1964.

Jencks, Christopher, and David Reisman. *The Academic Revolution*. New York: Doubleday Anchor, 1968.

John F. Slater Fund. *County Teacher Training Schools for Negroes*. New Orleans: Tulane University Press, 1913.

Johnson, Charles Spurgeon. *The Negro College Graduate*. New York: Negro Universities Press, 1969.

Jones-Wilson, Faustine C. *Encyclopedia of African-American Education*. Westport CT: Greenwood, 1996.

Jones, Thomas J. *Four Essentials of Education*. New York: Scribner's, 1926.

Jones, Thomas Jesse. *Negro Education: A Study of the Private and Higher Education Schools for Colored People in the United States*. Washington, D.C.: Government Printing Office, 1917.

Keller, George. *Transforming a College: The True Story of a Little Known College's Strategic Climb to National Distinction*. Baltimore: John Hopkins University Press, 2004.

Kerr, Clark. *The Uses of the University*. Cambridge, MA: Harvard University Press, 2001.

Kranz, Rachel. *African-American Business Leaders and Entrepreneurs: A to Z of African Americans*. New York: Facts on File, 2004.

Lambert, Richard. *International Studies and the Undergraduate*. Washington, D.C.: American Council on Education, 1989.

Law, William, and V. Clift. *Encyclopedia of Black Americans*. New York: McGraw Hill, 1981.

Lawrence, R.V. *The Centenary Souvenir, Containing a History of Centenary Church, Charleston, and an Account of the Life and Labors of Rev. R.V. Lawrence*. Charleston, SC: RV Lawrence, 1885.

LeMelle, Tilden J., and Wilbert J. LeMelle. *The Black College: A Strategy for Relevancy*. New York: Praeger, 1969.

Lewis, David L. *W.E.B. DuBois: Biography of a Race*. New York: Holt, 1993.

Lewis, Ronald L. *Black Coal Miners in America: Race, Class and Community in Conflict, 1790–1980*. Lexington: University of Kentucky Press, 1987.

Lincoln, Eric C., and Lawrence H. Mamiya. *The Black Church in the African-American Experience*. Durham, NC: Duke University Press, 1990.

Lomotey, Koffey, ed. *Going to School: The African-American Experience*. New York: State University of New York Press, 1989.

Long, Charles S. *History of the AME Church in Florida*. Philadelphia; AME Book Concern, 1939.

Maslow, A.H. *Eupsychian Management*. Homewood, IL: Richard D. Irwin and Dorsey Press, 1965.

Mays, Benjamin Elijah. *Born to Rebel: An Autobiography*. Athens: University of Georgia Press, 2003.

Mbajekwe, Carolyn Wilson. *The Future of Historically Black College and Universities: Ten Presidents Speak Out*. Jefferson, NC: McFarland, 2005.

McCuistion, Fred. *Higher Education of Negroes*. Nashville, TN: Committee on Approval of Negroes Schools, 1933.

McGehee, Stuart C., and Frank Wilson. *Bluefield State College: A Centennial History, 1895–1995*. Bluefield, WV: Bluefield State University, 2006.

McGrath, E.G. *The Predominantly Negro Colleges in Transition*. New York: Teachers College Press, 1965.

McPherson, James M. *The Abolitionist Legacy: From Reconstruction to the NAACP*. Princeton, NJ: Princeton University Press, 1975.

Mingle, James R. *Trends in Higher Education Participation and Success: Focus on Minorities, Education Commission of the States*. Denver, CO: State Higher Education Executive Officers, 1987.

Minorities in Higher Education. Washington, D.C.: American Council on Education, 1988.

Minutes of the Seventy-Seventh Session of the New England Conference of the Methodist Episcopal Church. Boston, MA: James P. Magee, 1876.

Moore, Winfred B., and Orville Vernon Burton, ed. *Toward the Meeting of the Waters: Currents in the Civil Rights Movement of South Carolina During the Twentieth Century*. Columbia: University of South Carolina Press, 2008.

Morgan, B.S., and T.F. Cork. *History of Education in West Virginia*. Charleston, WV: Moses W. Donnally, 1898.

Moss, Alfred A. *Dangerous Donations: Northern Philanthropy and Southern Black Education, 1902–1930*. Columbia: University of Missouri Press, 1999.

Moton, Robert Russa. *Finding a Way Out: An Autobiography*. Garden City, NY: Doubleday, Page, 1921.

Nasby, Dolly. *Harpers Ferry*. Charleston, SC: Arcadia, 2004.

National Association for International Education. *Americans Call for Leadership on International Education*. Washington, D.C.: National Association for Foreign Student Advisors, 2006.

National Commission on Testing and Public Policy. *From Gate Keeper to Gateway: Transforming Testing in American*. Boston: Boston College, 1989.

Nelson, George. *Elevating the Game: Black Men and Basketball*. New York: HarperCollins, 1999.

Newbould, Nathan Carter. *Five North Carolina Negro Educators*. Chapel Hill: University of North Carolina Press, 1938.

North Carolina Wesleyan College Catalog 2001–2002. Rocky Mount: North Carolina Wesleyan College, 2001.

North Carolina Wesleyan College Catalog 2002–2003. Rocky Mount: North Carolina Wesleyan College, 2002.

North Carolina Wesleyan College Catalog 2006–2007. Rocky Mount: North Carolina Wesleyan College, 2006.

Omolewu, Gabriel Adebayo. *President Rembert Strokes of Wilberforce, 1956–1976*. Bloomington, IN: AuthorHouse, 2009.

Orfield, G., and F. Monfort. *Racial Change and Desegregation in Large School Districts*. Washington, D.C.: National School Boards Association, 1988.

Patterson, Zella Black. *Langston University: A History*. Norman: University of Oklahoma Press, 1979.

Penn, Garland. *The Afro-America Press and Its Editors*. Springfield, MA: Wiley and Company, 1891.

Perry, Gail. *Fired-Up Fundraising: Turning Board Passion into Action*. Hoboken, NJ: John Wiley, 2007.

Porter, Gilbert, and Leedell W. Neyland. *History of Florida State Teachers Association*. Washington, D.C.: National Education Association, 1977.

Principles of Accreditation: Foundation for Quality Enhancement. Decatur, GA: Southern Association of Colleges and Schools, 2006.

Private Negro Colleges and Schools of South Carolina: A Survey Report, Division of Surveys and Field Services. Nashville, TN: George Peabody College for Teachers, 1947.

Provasnik, Stephen, and Linda Shafer. *Historically Black Colleges and Universities, 1976 to 2001*. Washington, D.C.: Government Printing Office, 2004.

Range, Willard. *The Rise and Progress of Negro Colleges in Georgia, 1865–1949*. Athens: University of Georgia Press, 1951.

Ricard, Ronyelle Bertrand, and Lenoar Foster. *Ebony Towers in Higher Education: The Evolution, Mission and Presidency of Historically Black Colleges and Universities*. Sterling, VA: Stylus, 2008.

Rivers, Larry E., and Canter Brown. *Labor in the Vineyard of the Lord: The Beginnings of the AME Church in Florida*. Gainesville: University of Florida Press, 2001.

Roebuck, Julian, and Komanduri S. Murty. *Historically Black Colleges and Universities: Their Place in American Higher Education*. Westport, CT: Praeger, 1993.

Roscoe, Wilma. *Accreditation of Historically and Predominantly Black Colleges and Universities*. Lanham, MD: University Press of America, 1989.

Rudy, Willis. *Building America's Schools and Colleges: The Federal Contribution*. Cranbury, NJ: Cornwall, 2003

Ruppersburg, Hugh. *The New Georgia Encyclopedia: Companion to Georgia Literature*. Athens: University of Georgia Press, 2004.

Ryu, Mikyung. *Twenty-Third Status Report: Minorities in Higher Education, 2009 Supplement*. Washington, D.C.: American Council on Education, 2009.

Savage, Beth. *National Register of Historic Places: African-American Historic Places*. New York: John Wiley, 1994.

Scott, John Irving. *Negro Students and Their Colleges*. Boston: Meador, 1949.

Scott, William R. *African-Americans and the Italo-Ethiopian War, 1935–1941*. Bloomington: Indiana University Press, 1993.

Scholte, Jan A. *Globalization: A Critical Introduction*. New York: Palgrave Macmillan, 2005.

Selden, William. *Accreditation: A Struggle Over Standards in Higher Education*. New York: Harper and Brother, 1960.

Shackel, Paul A. *Memory in Black and White: Race, Commemoration, and the Post-Bellum Landscape*. Walnut Creek, CA: Alta Mira, 2003.

Sheets, William N. *Report of the Superintendent of Public Institution*. Tallahassee, FL: Tallahassee Book and Job Plant, 1899.

Sleeper, J. *The Closest of Stranger: Liberalism and the Politics of Race in New York*. New York: Norton, 1989.

Smith, Donald. *Admissions and Attrition Problems of Black Students at Seven Predominately White Universities*. Washington, D.C.: National Advisory Committee on Black Higher Education and Black Colleges and Universities, 1981.

Smith, Robert C. *Encyclopedia of African-American Politics*. New York: Facts on File, 2003

Sowell, Thomas. *Black Education: Myths and Tragedies*. New York: McKay, 1972.

Statistical Guide of the United Negro College Fund, 1994. Fairfax, VA: United Negro College Fund, 1994.

Statistical Guide of the United Negro College Fund, 1995. Fairfax, VA: United Negro College Fund, 1995.

Statistical Guide of the United Negro College Fund, 1996. Fairfax, VA: United Negro College Fund, 1996.

Statistical Guide of the United Negro College Fund, 1997. Fairfax, VA: United Negro College Fund, 1997.

Statistical Guide of the United Negro College Fund, 2004, Fairfax, VA: United Negro College Fund, 2004.

Statistical Guide of the United Negro College Fund, 2006, Fairfax, VA: United Negro College Fund, 2006.

Stroker, David Augustus. *The New South Investigated.* Detroit: Ferguson Printing Company, 1888.

Swartz, J., and K. Davis. *Increasing Black Students in Predominately White North Carolina Colleges and Universities.* New York: College Entrance Board, 1972.

Talbot, Edith A. *Samuel Chapman Armstrong: A Biographical Study.* New York: Doubleday, Page, 1904.

Talladega College Catalog 2000–2003. Talladega, AL: Talladega College, 2000.

Talladega College Catalog 2003–2008. Talladega, AL: Talladega College, 2003.

Taylor, Quintard. *In Search of the Racial Frontier: African-Americans in the American West, 1528–1900.* New York: W.W. Norton, 1999.

Thelin, John R. *A History of American Higher Education.* Baltimore: John Hopkins University Press, 2004.

Thomas, Gail E. *Black College Students and Factors Influencing Their Major Field Choice.* Atlanta: Southern Education Foundation, 1984.

Thompson, Daniel C. *A Black Elite: A Profile of Graduates of UNCF Colleges.* Westport, CT: Greenwood, 1986.

Thompson, Daniel C. *Private Black Colleges at the Crossroads.* Westport, CT: Greenwood, 1973.

Tucker, Samuel J. *Phoenix from the Ashes: EWC's Past, Present, and Future.* Jacksonville, FL: Convention, 1976.

Walters, Joseph Jeffrey, Garreth Griffiths, and John Victor Singler. *Guanya Pau: A Story of an African Princess.* Orchard Park, NY: Broadview Press, 1891.

Washington, Booker T. *The Future of the American Negro.* Boston: Small, Maynard, 1902.

Watkins, William H. *The White Architects of Black Education.* New York: Teachers College Press, 2001.

Weglinsky, Harold. *Students at Historically Black Colleges and Universities: Their Aspirations and Accomplishments.* Princeton, NJ: Policy Information Center, Educational Testing Service, 1997.

Whitehall, A.R. *History of Education in West Virginia.* Washington: Government Printing Office, 1902.

Whiting, Albert. *Guardian of the Flame: Historically Black Colleges Yesterday, Today and Tomorrow.* Washington, D.C.: American Association of State Universities, 1991.

Williams, Cecil. *Freedom and Justice: Four Decades of the Civil Rights Struggle As Seen by a Black Photographer of the Deep South.* Macon, GA: Mercer University Press, 1995.

Williams, Juan, and Dwayne Ashley. *I'll Find a Way or Make One: A Tribute to Historically Black Colleges and Universities.* New York: Amistad, 2007.

Williams, T.B. *Report on Negro Universities.* Baltimore: John F. Slater Fund, 1922.

Willis, Rudy. *Building America's Schools and Colleges: The Federal Contribution.* Cranbury, NJ: Cornwall, 2003.

Wilson, C.R., and W. Ferris ed. *Encyclopedia of Southern Culture.* Chapel Hill: University of North Carolina Press, 1989.

Wolff, Miles. *Lunch at the 5 & 10.* Chicago: Elephant, 1970.

Wolters, Raymond. *The New Negro on Campus: Black College Rebellions of the 1920s.* Princeton, NJ: Princeton University, 1975.

Wolverton, Mimi, and Walter Gmelch. *College Deans Leading From Within.* Westport CT: Greenwood, 2002.

Woodson, Carter G., and James L. Conyers. *Carter G. Woodson: A Historical Reader.* New York: Garland, 2000.

Woolard-Provine, Annett. *Integrating Delaware: The Reddings of Wilmington*. Wilmington: University of Delaware Press, 2003.
Woolfork, George R. *Prairie View: A Study in Public Conscience, 1878–1946*. New York: Pageant, 1962.
Worth, Michael. *New Strategies for Educational Fundraising* Westport, CT: Praeger, 2002.

Articles

Ahearn, Lorraine. "Greensboro College Puts Up Campus to Back Loan." *Greensboro News & Record*, July 18, 2009.
Ahmed, Z., and F. Krohn. "Internationalizing Business Programs at Non-Accredited Collegiate Institutions." *Journal of Education for Business* 66, no. 2 (1990): 5.
Akomolafe, O. "Africanizing HBCUs: Problems and Prospects of International Education in Historically Black Institutions." *African Studies* 28, no. 1–2 (2000): 1–2.
Allen, Walter, and Joseph J. Jewell. "A Backward Glance Forward: Past, Present and Future Perspectives on Historically Black Colleges and Universities." *The Review of Higher Education* 25, no. 3 (2002).
Allen, Walter R. "Black Student, White Campus: Structural, Interpersonal and Psychological Correlates of Success." *Journal of Negro Education* 54, no. 2 (1985): 28, 29, 135–147.
_____. "The Color of Success: African-American College Student Outcomes at Predominately White and Historically Black Public Colleges and Universities." *Harvard Educational Review* 62, no 1 (1992): 26–43.
_____, Joseph O. Jewell, Kimberly A. Griffin and De'Sha S. Wolf. "Historically Black Colleges and Universities: Honoring the Past, Engaging the Present, Touching the Future." *Journal of Negro Education* 76, no. 3 (2007): 263–280.
Armstrong, Samuel C. "Address Before the 1877 Anniversary Meeting of the American Missionary Association," *Southern Workman* (December 1877): 94.
_____. "Annual Report of the Principal." *Southern Workman* (April 1876): 26.
Asgill. A. "The Importance of Accreditation: Perceptions of Black and White College Presidents." *Journal of Negro Education* 45, no. 3 (1976): 284–294.
Ayman, R., N. Kreicker, and J. Masztal. "Defining Global Leadership in Business Environments." *Consulting Psychology Journal: Practice and Research* 46, no. 1 (1994): 64–77.
Baker, Paul S. "Federal-State Relations." In C.R. Wilson and E. Ferris, ed., *Encyclopedia of Southern Culture*. Chapel Hill: University of North Carolina Press, 1989: 229–250.
Baker, Scott. "Education and Equality: African-American Teachers and the Civil Rights Movement, 1940–1963." In *Beauty is in the Details: A Global View of Persons of Color*. Scarborough, ME: National Association of African-American Studies and Affilates, 2010: 1024–1040.
Barthelemy, Sidney. "The Role of Black Colleges in Nurturing Leadership." In Antoine M. Garibaldi, *Black Colleges and Universities: Challenges for the Future*. Westport, CT: Praeger, 1994: 14–25.
Bartlett, Kellie. "The Changing Role of Faculty in Academe." *Chronicle of Higher Education*, November 26, 2003.
Bell, Derrick. "Black Colleges and the Desegregation Dilemma." *Emory Law Journal* 28 (1979).
Bennett, Lerone. "The Niagara Movement." *Ebony* (May 1976): 130–134.
Billingsley, Andrew C. "Building Strong Faculties in Black Colleges." *Journal of Negro Education* 51, no. 1 (1981): 4–15.
"Birmingham-Southern College Plans 20% Budget Cut, Citing Costly Student-Aid Errors." *Chronicle of Higher Education*, June 15, 2010.

Blight, David W. "The Age of Emancipation." In James Oliver Horton, *A History of the African-American People*. London: Salamander, 1995: 89.

Bollag, B. "Trying Prevention Before Punishment." *Chronicle of Higher Education*, June 2, 2006: A21.

Bolling, L.R. "The Governance of Universities II." *Daedalus* 98, no.4 (1969): 1092–1154.

Bolman, Lee G., and Terrence E. Deal. "Reframing Leadership: The Effects of Leaders' Images of Leadership." In Kenneth Clark, ed., *Impact of Leadership*. Greensboro, NC: Center for Creative Leadership, 1992.

Branson, Herman R. "The Hazards in Black Higher Education: Program and Commitment Needs." *Journal of Negro Education* 56, no. 2 (1987): 129–136.

Brimmer, Andrew. "The Future Outlook of Black Colleges." *Daedalus* (Summer 1971).

Brogue, Jesse P., and Shirley Sanders. "Junior College Directory 1948: Summary of Students 1946–1947." *Junior College Journal* 13 (1948).

Brown, Aaron. "Graduate and Professional Education in Negro Institutions." *Journal of Negro Education* 27, no. 3 (Summer 1958).

Brown, Willis L., and Janie M. McNeal-Brown. "Oklahoma's First Comprehensive University: Langston University, the Early Years." *Chronicles of Oklahoma* 74, no. 1 (1996): 34.

Browning, J., and J. Williams. "History and Goals of Black Institutions of Higher Learning." In C.V. Willie and R.R. Edmonds, ed., *Black Colleges in America: Challenge, Development, and Survival*. New York: Teachers College Press, 1978: 68–93.

Burris, Roddie. "Benedict Struggling Financially." *The State*, July 27, 2009.

Byrd, Shella. "JSU President Defends Black College Unity Plan." *Diverse Issues in Higher Education*, February 1, 2010.

Cabrera, Alberto F., Amaury Nora, Patrick T. Terenzini, Ernest Pascarella, and Linda Hagedorn. "Campus Racial Climate and the Adjustment of Students to College: A Comparison Between White Students and African-American Students." *Journal of Higher Education* 70, no.2 (1999): 134–160.

"Cannonballing to Success." *Pacific Stars and Stripes*, September 1965.

"Capital Financing: Department Management Improvements Could Enhance Education's Loan Program for Historically Black Colleges and Universities." Washington, D.C.: Government Accountability Office, 2006.

Carroll, J.B., and M. Wolverton. "Who Becomes a Chair?" *New Directions for Higher Education* 126 (2004): 3–10.

Casiel, Maureen, and Alison Davis-Blake. "When Accreditation Standards Change: Factors Affecting Differential Responsiveness of Public and Private Organizations." *The Academy of Management Journal* 45, no.1 (2002): 180–195.

Chambers, Fredrick. "Histories of Black Colleges and Universities." *Journal of Negro Education* 57, no. 3 (July 1972).

"CIAA Celebrates Golden Anniversary." *Ebony* (December 1962): 93–98.

"The CIAA Celebrates its 77th Year." *Ebony* (May 1989): 176–178.

"Claflin College is a Private Black College that is Weathering the Economic Storm." *Journal of Blacks in Higher Education*, July 23, 2009.

Clark, Felton G. "The Development and Present Status of Publicly Supported Higher Education for Negroes." *Journal of Negro Education* 27, no.3 (Summer 1958).

"College in Florida Sues its Accreditor." *Chronicle of Higher Education* (March 2005).

Davis, John W. "Land-Grant Colleges for Negroes." *Journal of Negro Education* 21, no. 3 (Summer 1952).

Davis, Mitzi, Yvonne Dias-Bowie, Katherine Greenberg, Gary Klukken, Howard R. Pollio, and Sandra P. Thomas. "A Fly in the Buttermilk: Descriptions of University Life by Successful Black Undergraduate Students at a Predominately White Southeastern University." *Journal of Higher Education* 75, no. 4 (2004): 420–445.

Deskins, Donald. "A Regional Assessment of Minority Enrollment and Earned Degrees in U.S. Colleges and Universities, 1974–1984." In W.R. Allen, et. al., *Colleges in Black and White*. Albany: State University of New York Press, 1991: 17–39.

Dickey, Frank G. "Recognizing and Monitoring Professional and Specialized Accrediting Associations." *Proceedings of the Northwest Association of Secondary and Higher Schools Annual Meeting.* Portland, OR: Northwest Association of Secondary and Higher Schools Annual Meeting, 1973.

Donahoo, S., and W. Lee. "The Adversity of Diversity: Regional Associations and the Accreditation of Minority Serving Institutions." In Marybeth Gasman, Benjamin Baez, and Caroline Sotello Turner, eds., *Understanding Minority Institutions.* New York: State University of New York Press, 2008: 292–310.

Drake, St. Clair. "The Black University in the American Social Order." *Daedalus* 100, no.3 (1971): 846.

Eells, Walter Crosby. "Junior College Directory 1942: Summary of Students 1940–1941." *Junior College Journal* 13 (1942).

Ezzell, Jack, and Alvin Schexnider. "Leadership, Governance and Sustainability of Black Colleges and Universities." *Trusteeship* (May/June 2010).

Fain, Paul. "Birmingham-Southern's President Resign While Trustees Explain College's Financial Meltdown." *Chronicle of Higher Education,* August 11, 2010.

_____. "Tuition Discount Rate Hits Record High, NACUBO Survey Finds." *Chronicle of Higher Education,* March 20, 2010.

_____. "Why Deep Tuition Discounts May Not Spell Financial Doom." *Chronicle of Higher Education,* May 2, 2010.

Fairclough, Adam. "Being in the Field of Education and Also Being a Negro Seems Tragic: Black Teachers in the Jim Crow South." *The Journal of American History* 87 (2000): 65–91.

"Federal Court Halts Move to Deny Paul Quinn College Accreditation." *Diverse* (August 28, 2009).

Fields, Cheryl D. "HBCUs Get Savvy About Fund Raising." *Black Issues in Higher Education,* August 10, 2001, 38–44.

Fleming, J. "Stress and Satisfaction in College Years of Black Students." *Journal of Negro Education* 50, no. 3 (1981): 307–318.

"Florida College Loses Accreditation." *Chronicle of Higher Education,* December 2004.

"Fostering Effective Faculty Governance." *Chronicle of Higher Education,* April 4, 1990.

Frazier, Herb. "South Carolina HBCU Launches Think Tank to Focus on Southern Black History, Culture and Policy." *Diverse Issues in Higher Education* 23, no. 18 (2006): 37.

Garrison, Greg. "David Pollick Resigns as President of Birmingham-Southern College Amidst Turmoil: Mark Schantz Named Interim President." *The Birmingham News,* August 12, 2010.

Gasman, Marybeth. "Accreditation of Black Colleges: Future Success?" *Diverse Education,* July 1, 2008.

_____ and Noah D. Drezner. "Fundraising for Black Colleges During the 1960s." *Nonprofit and Voluntary Sector Quarterly* (April 2010).

Gibbs, J.T. "Patterns of Adaption Among Black Students at a Predominately White University." *American Journal of Orthopsychiatry* 44 (1974): 728–40.

Gmelch, W.H. "The Department Chair's Balancing Act." *New Directions for Higher Education* 126 (2004): 69–84.

Goodenow, Rufus K. "Black Education." In Charles R. Wilson and William Ferris, ed., *Encyclopedia of Southern Culture.* Chapel Hill: University of North Carolina Press, 1989.

Gose, Ben. "Goodbye to Those Overpaid Professors in Their Cushy Jobs." *Chronicle of Higher Education,* July 25, 2010.

Grandison, Kenrick I. "Negotiated Space: The Black College Campus as a Cultural Record of Postbellum-America." *American Quarterly* 51, no. 3 (1999): 529–579.

Green, M.S. "Not for Cowards or Wimps: Leadership in the Post-Heroic Age." *Educational Record* 61, no. 3 (1994): 55–60.

Greenlee, Craig T. "There's a Football Revival Going On: College Football Programs Reappear, Statistical Data Included." *Black Issues in Higher Education,* August 2, 2001.

Gregerson, Hal, Allen Morrison, and J. Stewart Black. "Developing Leaders for the Global Frontier." *MIT Sloan Management Review* 40, no. 1 (1998):21–32.

Griffin, Joye. "The Wal-Mart Foundation Grants $500,000 to UNCF for Institute For Capacity Building." *UNCF News and Media*, May 12, 2010.

Gunn, William. "Benedict Policy May Harm School's Good Name." *The State*, September 24, 2004.

Hacker, Andrew. "Trans-National America." *New York Review of Books* 37, no. 18 (1990): 19–24.

Hamilton, Kenneth. "The Origin and Early Development of Langston, Oklahoma." *Journal of Negro History* 62, no. 3 (1977): 270

Hammond, James T. "Benedict Professors Settle Academic Lawsuit." *The State*, April 17, 2007.

_____. "Early Signal Warned of Benedicts Growing Debt." *The State*, June 30, 2006.

_____. "Stadium Kicks Off a Transformation." *The State*, September 8, 2005.

"Hampton University: Educating for Life in the New Century: Virginia Celebrates 135th Anniversary." *Ebony,* September 1, 2003.

"Hampton University Reaches Goal of $200 Million Three Years Early." *Black Issues in Higher Education*, January 4, 2001.

Harper, Brian. "African-American Access to Higher Education: The Evolving Role of Historically Black Colleges and Universities." *Academic American* 3 (January,= 2007): 113.

Harper, Shaun R., Lori D. Paton, and Ontario S. Wooden. "Access and Equity for African American Students in Higher Education: A Critical Historical Analysis of Policy Efforts." *Journal of Higher Education* 80, no. 4 (July/August 2009).

"Harpers Ferry: Storer College." The National Park Service of the U.S. Department of the Interior. (1999).

"A Harvest of Good News on African-Americans in Higher Education." *The Journal of Blacks in Higher Education* 64 (Summer 2009).

Harvey, William, and Lea. Williams. "History of Black Colleges: Models for Increasing Minority Representation." *Education and Urban Society* 21, no. 3 (1989): 328–340.

Hawkins, Asher, et al. "Private College Financial Rankings." *Forbes*, April 20, 2010.

Hawkins, Denise B. "Doing More with Less: Despite Having Fewer Resources, HBCUs Have Outpaced Majority of Institutions in Producing Black Professionals, but Experts Say Strong Leadership Will be the Key to Their Long-Term Survival." *Black Issues in Higher Education* 21, no. 9 (2004): 44–52.

Haynes, Michael. "The Impact of Financial Aid on Postsecondary Persistence: A Review of the Literature." *NASFAA Journal of Student Financial Aid* 37, no.3 (2008): 30.

"HBCU's Making Major Progress in Curbing Loan Defaults." *Black Issues in Higher Education*, November 2000.

Hemmons, Willa M. "From the Halls of Hough and Halstedt: A Comparison of Black Students on Predominately White and Predominately Black Campuses." *Journal of Black Studies* 12 (1982): 382–402.

Hernadez, Arelis. "HBCUs Explore Ways to Move Beyond Tuition Dependence." *Diverse Issues in Higher Education*, April 15, 2010.

"Historic Mary Holmes College Closes After More Than a Century of Service." *Presbyterian Voice* 16, no.2 (2005).

Humphrey, Joe. "EWC Pushes Its Game Plan, but Football Money Lagging." *Florida Times Union*, January 23, 2001.

Jaschik, Scott. "Threat to Black Colleges." *Inside Higher Education*, November 17, 2009.

"Jesse L. Burns Has Resigned as President of Edward Waters College Amid Reports That He Had Falsified His Resume." *Chronicle of Higher Education*, February 2, 1996.

Johnson, Tobe. "The Black College as System." *Daedalus* 100 (1971): 801–810.

Jones, John B. "Faculty Governance in Difficult Times." *Chronicle of Higher Education*, November 19, 2009.

Jones, Mack. "The Responsibility of the Black College to the Black Community: Then and Now." *Daedalus* 100 (1971): 732–734.

Jones, Sherman, and George B. Weathersby. "Financing the Black College in America." In C.V. Willie and R.R. Edmonds, ed. *Black Colleges in America: Challenge, Development, and Survival.* New York: Teachers College Press, 1978: 313–327.

June, Audrey William. "After Costly Foray into Big-Time Sports, A College Returns to Its Roots." *Chronicle of Higher Education*, May 18, 2007.

_____. "Layoffs at Birmingham-Southern College Highlight a Workplace Paradox." *Chronicle of Higher Education*, July 27, 2010.

Junod, James. "Are Black Colleges Necessary?" *Atlanta Magazine* 27, no. 6 (1987): 78–119.

Kahrl, Andrew. "The Political Work of Leisure Class, Recreation, and African-American Commemoration at Harpers Ferry, West Virginia, 1881–1931." *Journal of Social History* 42, no 1 (Fall 2008).

Kaplin, W. "Judicial Review of Accreditation: The Parsons College Case." *The Journal of Higher Education* 40, no.7 (1969): 543–554.

Keels, Crystal. "Investing in HBCU Leadership: Southern Education Foundation Creates Three-Year Initiative to Facelift HBCU Accreditation." *Black Issues*, September 9, 2004.

Kelderman, Eric. "Black Colleges See a Need to Improve Their Image." *Chronicle of Higher Education*, July 2, 2010.

Lachs, John. "Shared Governance is a Myth." *The Chronicle of Higher Education*, February 6, 2011.

Lamon, Lester C. "The Tennessee Agricultural and Industrial Normal School: Public Higher Education for Black Tennesseans." *Tennessee Historical Quarterly* 32 (Spring 1973).

Lane, David. "The Junior College Movement Among Negroes." *Journal of Negro History* 2 (April 1933).

Laster, Jill. "One-Third of Faculty Members See Dip in Their Salaries." *Chronicle of Higher Education*, March 8, 2010.

"Leaders of Sue Bennett College Say They Were Kept in the Dark On Its Problems." *Chronicle of Higher Education*, September 19, 1997.

Li, Xiaojie. "Characteristics of Minority-Serving Institutions and Minority Undergraduates Enrolled in These Institutions." National Center for Education Statistics, U.S. Department of Education. Washington, D.C.: Government Printing Office, 2007.

Lively, Kit. "Grants Help Black Colleges Build Fund-Raising Capacity Semifinalists in Kresge Program." *Chronicle of Higher Education*, May 7, 1999.

_____. "Hampton U. Campaign Raises $216 Million, Shattering Record for Black Colleges." *Chronicle of Higher Education*, December 5, 2000.

Logan, Frenise. "The Evolution of Private Colleges for Negroes." *Journal of Negro Education* 28 (Summer 1959).

Logan, Frenise. "The Movement in North Carolina to Establish a State Supported College for Negroes." *North Carolina History Review* 35 (April 1959).

Love, Derrick. "Revitalizing Retention Efforts for African-American College Students at Predominantly White Institutions." *Proceedings of the Allied Academies* 15, no.2 (2008): 117–122.

Luzer, Daniel. "Extraordinary." *Washington Monthly* (July 17, 2010).

_____. "How Colleges Spend." *Washington Monthly* (July 10, 2010).

Mallinckrodt, Brent, and William E. Sedlacek. "Student Retention and the Use of Campus Facilities by Race." *NASPA Journal* 49, no.4 (2009): 566–572.

Marklein, Mary Beth, "College Trustees Feel Unprepared." *USA Today*, May 7, 2007.

Maslow, A.H. "A Theory of Human Motivation." *Psychological Review* 50, no.4 (1943): 370–396.

Masterson, Kathryn. "Economy Slows College's Ability to Hire and (Maybe) Retire Too." *Chronicle of Higher Education,* November 19, 2009.

_____. "Howard Assembles Fundraising Juggernaut." *Chronicle of Higher Education*, June 27, 2008.

Mays, Benjamin. "Black College: Past, Present and Future." *Black Scholar* (1974).

McMillan, Lewis K. "Negro Higher Education as I Have Known It." *Journal of Negro Education* 8 (January 1939): 14–18.

McNeal-Brown, Janie M. "Oklahoma's First Comprehensive University: Langston University, The Early Years." *Chronicles of Oklahoma* 74, no.1 (1996).

Meggett, Linda L. "The HBCU Presidential Cooker: Historically Black Colleges and Universities." *Diverse Education,* June 21, 2007.

"Men Struggling to Finish at Black Colleges." Associated Press, March 28, 2009.

Mercer, Joye. "Black Colleges Aim Higher with Fund-Raising Campaigns." *Chronicle of Higher Education*, November 20, 1998.

Miller, D. "What Trustees Must Do, After A.U." *Inside Higher Education* (2006).

Minor, James T. "The Danger of Deference: A Case of Polite Governance." *Teachers College Record* 107, no. 1 (January 2005).

_____. "Dilemma of Decision-Making in Historically Black Colleges and Universities: Defining the Context." *Journal of Negro Education* 73, no. 1 (2004).

"Mississippi Plan to Consolidate Black Colleges Facing Opposition." *Diverse Issues in Higher Education*, November 18, 2009.

Moore, Zena "African-American Student's Opinion About Foreign Language Study: An Exploratory Study of Low Enrollments at the College Level." *Foreign Language Annals* 38, no. 2 (2005): 191–200.

Morgan, Marlor W. "Lemoyne-Owen Closer on Football: Committee Favors Starting in 2012: President, Board Must Approve." *The Commercial Appeal*, October 21, 2010.

Morris, E.W. "The Contemporary Negro College and the Brain Drain." *Journal of Negro History* 41, no. 4 (1972).

"Morris Brow Faces Increased Pressure to Solve Financial Crisis, Pay Back Money." *Black Issues in Higher Education*, November 21, 2002.

Murty, Komanduri. "UNCFSP Global Center Partnerships Evaluation Report." *USAID* (Summer 2003).

Nabrit, S.M. "Reflection on the Future of Black Colleges." *Daedalus* 100, no.3 (Summer 1971): 671.

National Commission on Testing and Public Policy. *From Gate Keeper to Gateway: Transforming Testing in America.* Boston: Boston College, 1989.

"Negro Historian Fired for Attack on South Carolina College System: McMillan Was Warned by President Not to Print Book." *The Harvard Crimson*, June 17, 1954.

Nelms, Charlie. "HBCU Reconstruction." *The Presidency* 13, no.1 (2010): 14–19.

Norton, Ingrid. "International Education Remains A Challenge at Historically Black Colleges." *The Chronicle of Higher Education*, May 30, 2008.

"Notable Minority-Related Grants to Institutions of Higher Education." *Journal of Blacks in Higher Education* 67 (2010): 90–92.

Nyabongo, V.S. "Modern Foreign Language Study in Negro Colleges." *French Review* 20 (1946):153–58.

Offenstein, Jeremy, Collen Morre and Nancy Shulock. "Pathways to Success Lessons from the Literature on Career Technical Education." *The Institute for Higher Education Leadership and Policy* (December, 2009).

Olusoji, Akomolafe. "Africanizing HBCUs: Problems and Prospects of International Education in Historically Black Institutions." *African Studies* 28, nos. 1–2 (2000).

Patton, Adell. "Howard University and Meharry Medical Schools in the Training of African Physicians, 1868–1978."In Joseph Harris, ed., *Global Dimensions of the African Diaspora*. Washington, D.C.: Howard University, 1993: 109–120.

Peeps, Stephen. "Northern Philanthropy and the Emergence of Black Higher Education Do-Gooders: Compromise, or Co-Conspirators?" *Journal of Negro Education* 50, no.3 (Summer 1981).

Pettus, Emily Waster. "Mississippi Governor Wants to Merge State's 3 HBCUs into One." *The Grio*, November 19, 2009.

Phan, Katherine T. "ABHE Announces Newly Accredited Christian Colleges." *Christian Reporter*, February 26, 2009.

Phillips, Ivory Paul. "Shared Governance on Black College Campuses." *Academe* 88, no. 4 (July-August 2002).

Pinkham, Fed O. "The Accreditation Problem." *Annals of the American Academy of Political and Social Science* 301 (1955): 65–74.

Pope, Justin. "Graduation Rates Dismal at Most U.S. Black Colleges." Associated Press, March 29, 2009.

"Professors Take Benedict to Court." *Columbia Free Times* 20, no. 5 (January 31, 2007).

Pulley, John. "New Report Warns of the Danger of Tuition Discounting." *Chronicle of Higher Education*, January 28, 2001.

Qiang, Z. "Internationalization of Higher Education: Towards a Conceptual Framework." *Policy Futures in Education* 1, no.2 (2003): 248–270.

Reagan, Albert B. "The Coronado Expedition." *Southern Workman* 45, no. 11 (1916): 420–22.

Redd, Kenneth. "Historically Black Colleges and Universities: Making a Comeback." *New Directions for Higher Education* 102 (Summer 1998): 35–36.

Rich, Paul B. "The Appeals of Tuskegee: James Henderson Lovedale and the Fortunes of South African Liberalism, 1906–1930." *The International Journal of African Historical Studies* 20, no.2 (1987):271–292.

Rivers, Napoleon W. "A Study of Modern Foreign Languages in Thirty Negro Colleges." *Journal of Negro Education* 2 (1933): 437–493.

Roya, Ayman, Noel A. Kreicker and Jaci J. Masztal. "Defining Global Leadership in Business Environments." *Consulting Psychology Journal: Practice and Research* 46, no. 1 (1994).

Sander, Libby. "Faculty Members Discuss What Role They Play in Governing Athletics." *Chronicle of Higher Education,* October 16, 2007.

Schmidt, Peter. "Governance of Alabama Universities Under Attack." *Chronicle of Higher Education*, April 5, 2002.

"Settlement of College's Accreditation Lawsuit Could Spur Changes in the Process." *Chronicle of Higher Education* (July, 2005).

Sharpe, Shannon A. "Hampton Institute." In Charles R. Wilson and William Ferris, ed. *Encyclopedia of Southern Culture*. Chapel Hill: University of North Carolina Press, 1989.

Smallwood, Scott. "Faculty Group Censures benedict College Again, This Time Over A For Effort Policy." *Chronicle of Higher Education* (January 21, 2005).

Smith, Gina. "Benedict Grading is Under Scrutiny." *The State* (September 18, 2004).

Spivey. Donald "Crisis on a Black Campus." U.S. Department of Agriculture: 433–434.

Spriggs, W.E. "Major Trends Facing Historically Black Colleges and Universities." In National Association for Equal Opportunity in Higher Education, *The State of America's Black Colleges: Expanding Access, Ensuring Success, Promoting Global Competitiveness.* Silver Spring, MD: 2008: 1–6.

Stuart, Reginald. "Ready for Battle." *Diverse Issues in Higher Education*, August 19, 2010.

Stuckert, Robert. "Black Population of Southern Appalachian Mountain." *Phylon* 18, no. 2. (2nd Quarter 1987): 141–151.

"Tisdale Leads Clafin on Journey of Excellence." *Educational Pathways Magazine* 11, no.2 (2007–2010): 48–55.

Tollet, K. "Southern Justice for Blacks." *Ebony* (1971): 60.

"Trends in College Spending: Where Does the Money Come From? Where Does it Go?" *American Institutes for Research* (2009).

"Tribute to an Invincible Civil Rights Pioneer." *Jet* (July 1994): 42.

Trotter, Joe William. "The Formation of Black Community in Southern West Virginia Coalfields." In John C. Incoe, *Appalachians and Race: The Mountain South From Slavery to Segregation*. Lexington: University of Kentucky Press, 2000: 284–285.

Tucker, Mary L., Bernard M. Bass, and Larry G. Daniel. "Transformational Leadership's Impact on Higher Education Satisfaction, Effectiveness and Extra Effort." In Kenneth Clark, ed., *Impact on Leadership*. Greensboro, NC: Center for Creative Leadership, 1992.

"Union Protests Layoffs of 5 Tenured Professors as Florida Atlantic U. Slashes Its Budget." *Chronicle of Higher Education*, June 9, 2009.

"University of South Carolina, Claflin University to Partner on HIV/AIDS Cancer Initiative." *Diverse Issues in Higher Education* 22 (2005): 16.

Veney, Casandra R. "The Ties That Bind: The Historic African Diaspora and Africa." *African Issues* 30, no.1 (2002): 3–8.

Vernon, Carlos H. "A Current History of Black Colleges." *Black World* (February 1973): 26–33.

Walker, Donald E. "When the Tough Get Going, the Going Gets Tough: The Myth of the Muscle Administration." *American Society for Public Administration* 36 (1976): 440.

Wennersten, John. "The Travel of Black Land-Grant Schools in the South, 1890–1917." *Agricultural History* 65, no. 2 (1961): 55–56.

"West Virginia College Closes Dorms After Bombing." *Jet* (December 1968).

White, Neil. "Benedict Kicks Off Again: Officials Hope Revival of Football Will Give Boost to School Spirit." *The State*, June 1, 2005.

Williams, Audrey. "After Costly Foray into Big-Time Sports, a College Returns to Its Roots." *Chronicle of Higher Education*, May 18, 2007.

Williamson, Joy Ann. "This Has Been Quite a Year For Heads Falling: Institutional Autonomy in the Civil Rights Era." *History of Education Quarterly* 44 (2004): 554–576.

Wilson, John S. "America's Historically Black Colleges and Universities and the Third Transformation." *The Presidency* (Winter 2010): 16–17.

Winbush, Donald E. "Spelman Mission Was Not Impossible: How College's Fund-Raising Drive Netted $113 Million," *Diverse*, July 23, 2009.

Woody, Jonathan. "Jonathan Jasper Wright, Associate Justice of the Supreme Court of South Carolina, 1870–1877." *Journal of Negro History* 18 (1933): 114–131.

Wolverton, Brad. "A Costly Move." *Chronicle of Higher Education*, June 22, 2010.

Wright, Jonathan, J. "Associate Justice of the Supreme Court of South Caroline, 1870–1877," *Journal of Negro History* 18 (1933).

Wyche, J.H., and H.T. Frieson. "Minorities at Majority Institutions." *Policy Forum* 31 (1990): 989–991.

Yukl, Gary. "An Evaluation of Conceptual Witnesses in Transformational and Charismatic Theories." *Leadership Quarterly* 10, no. 2 (1999): 285.

Zafar, Ahmed, and Franklin B. Krohn. "Internationalizing Business Programs at Non-Accredited Collegiate Institutions." *Journal of Education for Business* 66, no. 2 (1990).

Zha, Qianq. "Internationalization of Higher Education: Toward a Conceptual Framework." *Policy Futures in Education* 12 no. 2 (2003).

Web Sources

"Academic Freedom and Tenure: Clark Atlanta University," http://www.aaup.org/AAUP/programs/academicfreedom/investrep/2010/clarkatlanta.html.

"Actions Taken by the SACSCOC Board of Trustees, June 23, 2011." http://sacscoc.org/2011%20June%20Actions%20and%20Disclosure%20Statements/11cract%20june.pdf.

"Audit Harsh on Waters College: Internal Report Finds Evidence of Mismanage-ment Under Former President, Who's Still Being Paid." http://www.redorbit.com/modules/news/tools.php?tool=print&id=233465.

Ballard, Currie. "Langston University." http://digital.library.okstate.edu/encyclopedia/entries/1/la021.html.

"Benedict College Enrollment Trends, Academic Year 2008–2009." http://www.benedict. edu/divisions/research/pdf files/statistice/bc research statistics trend data 2008 2009 enrollment.pdf.

"Benedict College Professor Settled Academic Lawsuit." http://www.soutcaroli-nalawyerblog.com/2007/04/benedict college professor set 1.html.

Berry College-Oak Hill and Martha Berry Museum. http://www.berry.edu/oakhill/ history.asp.

Central Intercollegiate Athletic Association. http://en.wikipedia.org/wiki/Central Inter-collegiate Athletic Association.

Civil Rights Act (1964). http://www.ourdocuments.gov/doc.php?flash=true&doc=97& page=transcript.

Claflin University History. http://www.claflin.edu/AboutUs/ClaflinHistory.html.

Consortium for Graduate Study in Management: Anthony David, Vice President for Institutional Advancement. http://www.rpainc.org/closedsearches.html.

David J. Wallace. http://digital .library.okstate.edu/encyclopedia.html.

"Dr. Dorothy Cowser Yancey." http://www.shawuniversity.edu/press_releases/Dr_Yancy. pdf.

Education Pays 2010. http://trends.collegeboard.org/education pays.

Fisk University Staff Listing for the Office of Institutional Advancement, December 2010. http://www.fisk.edu/AlumniAndFriends/.OfficeOfInstitutionalAdvancement/ Staff.aspx.

"Globalization 101: What is Globalization?" http://www.globalization 101.org/.

Handbook of Texas Online, December 10, 2006. http://www.tshaonline.org/handbook/ online.

"Helen M. Stiefmiller." http://digital .library.okstate.edu/encyclopedia.html.

"Historically Black Colleges and Universities: The Development of HBCUs, Academic and Social Experiences at HBCUs." http://www.education.stateuniversity.com/pages/ 2046/Historically-Black-Colleges-Universities.html.

History of Brewton-Parker College. http://www.bpc.edu/administration/institution research/fact books.

Karnasiewicz, Sarah. "Apartheid America: Jonathan Kozol Rails Against a Public School System That, 50 Years After Brown v. Board of Education, is Still Deeply and Shamefully Segregated." http://dir.salon.com/story/mwt/feature/2005/09/22/kozol/index2.html.

Langston University. http://digital.library.okstate.edu/encyclopedia/entries/1/1a021. html.

Little, L. "HBCUs are Still Vital to American Education." http://www.thegrio.com/2009/ 09/seperate-but-equal-the-hbcu.php.

Megett, Linda. "The HBCU Presidential Pressure-Cooker: Historically Black Colleges and Universities." http://diverseeducation.com/article/7686/.

Middle States Commission on Higher Education. "Statement of Accreditation Status." http://www.msche.org/documents/SAS/125/Statement%20of%20Accreditation %20Status.htm.

Minor, James T. "Contemporary HBCUs: Considering Institutional Capacity and State Pri-orities." http://steinhardt.nyu.edu/scmsAdmin/uploads/002/151/MINOR_Contemporary_ HBCU_Report_2008.pdf.

Norfles, N. "Toward Equal and Equitable Access: Obstacles and Opportunities in Inter-national Education." http://www.jhfc.duke.edu/ducis/globalchallenges/pdf/norfles_ abstract.pdf.

Palmiero, P. "Strengthening HBCU Governance for the 21st Century." http://www.goacta. org/publications/downloads/palmieroTougalooRemarks11-1-06.pdf.

"Resume of James Perkins, Former Vice President for Advancement at Talladega College." http://www.jsums.edu/~sst/cset/Resume11_Jim_Perkins.pdf.

Second Morrill Act of 1890. http://www.csrees.usda.gov/about/offices/legis/secondmorrill. html.

Southern Association of Colleges and Schools. "History of SACS." http://www. sacscasi.org/region/history/.

Southern Association of Colleges and Schools Commission on Colleges. "Accreditation Actions and Disclosure Statements." http://www.sacscoc.org/accreditationDisclosure. asp.

"Talladega College Appoints a VP for Institutional Advancement." http://www.talladega. edu/release/showrelease.asp?ReleaseID=18.

Whitmire, Kyle. "BSC Tax Records Show Years of Red Ink." http://weldbham.com/ secondfront/2010/07/26/bsc-tax-records-show-years-of-red-ink/.

"Wilberforce University Needs $3 Million by June." Black America Web, http://www. Blackamericaweb.com/?q=print/news/the state of Black America news/14791.

Unpublished Materials

Boyce, Starita M. "Fund-Raising and Marketing Effectiveness at Historically Black Colleges." Master's Thesis, State University of New York at Albany, 1992.

Carter, M. "From Jim Crow to Inclusion: An Historical Analysis of the Association of Colleges and Secondary Schools for Negroes, 1934–1965." Ph.D. Dissertation, Ohio State University, 1996.

Correla, S.T. "For Their Own Good." Ph.D. Dissertation, University of Chicago, 1993.

Costen, Wanda, Steven N. Waller, and Angela Wozencroft. "Does Race Matter? Understanding the Role of Social Connectedness in Student Retention in Hospitality Programs." International CHRIE Conference-Refereed Trace Paper 7, July 28, 2010.

Davis, J.A. "A Study of Student Attitudes Toward Language Study at Historically and Predominantly Black Institutions." Ph.D. Dissertation, University of Maryland, 1990.

Fairley, Charlestine R. "A History of Claflin College, 1869–1987." Ph.D. Dissertation, University of South Carolina, 1990.

Fels, Michael D. "Assumptions of African-American Students About International Education Exchange." Unpublished Paper, Convention of the Communication Association, Miami, FL, 1993.

Jones, Bronte D. "Restoring Accreditation in Two Private Texas Historically Black College." Ph.D. Dissertation, University of Texas at Austin, 2005.

LeBlanc, H.G. "An Exploratory Study on the Responses to Students' Needs in Foreign Language Instruction in Colleges and Universities Predominately Attended by Afro-American Students." Ph.D. Dissertation, University of Minnesota, 1972.

Lyons, James E. "In the Beginning Faith: Oral History of Barber-Scotia College." Unpublished Paper, Barber-Scotia College, Concord, NC, 1976.

McAdoo, Douglas D. "America's Black Colleges: Survival or Demise: Do They Still Have a Place?" Ph.D. Thesis, University of Massachusetts, 1974.

Meriwether, James Hunter. "The African Connection and the Struggle for Freedom: Africa's Role in African-American Life, 1936–1963." Ph.D. Dissertation, University of California, Los Angeles, 1995.

Miller, Kenneth C. "The Teaching and Learning of Modern Foreign Languages in Colleges for Negroes." Ph.D. Dissertation, Ohio State University, 1953.

Newkirk, Vann. "Barber-Scotia College: A Case for Faith-Based Education." Paper presented to Barber-Scotia College Board of Trustees, October 2005.

Venson, Louis A. "Trends in Black College: Strategies for Improvement of Educational Opportunities in Selected Areas." Ph.D. Thesis, University of Michigan, 1975.

Walters, Ron. "A Cultural Strategy for the Survival of Historically Black Colleges and Universities." Paper presented at the annual conference of the National Council for Black Studies, Atlanta, Georgia, March 1991.

Wesley, Vinetta L. "Leadership at Historically Black Colleges and Universities: Impact on Student Outcomes." Master's Thesis, George Peabody College for Teachers of Vanderbilt University, 1997.

Interviews

Alexander, Edward. Director of admissions at Edward Waters College. Interview by Vann R. Newkirk, 27 December 2010, Jacksonville, FL. In possession of editor, Rocky Mount, NC.

Crumley, Issac. Director of CDEP Program, Fort Valley State University. Interview by Juone Brown, 15 November 2010, Fort Valley, GA. In possession of editor, Rocky Mount, NC.

Faulkner, Belinda. Former vice president for fiscal affairs at North Carolina Wesleyan College. Interview by Vann R. Newkirk, 2 December 2010, Rocky Mount, NC. In Possession of editor, Rocky Mount, NC.

Keese, Wallace. Interview by Vann R. Newkirk, 12 December 2010, Fort Valley, GA. In possession of editor, Rocky Mount, NC.

McLean, Mabel. Former president of Barber-Scotia College. Interview by Vann R. Newkirk, 15 August 2006, Concord, NC. In possession of editor, Rocky Mount, NC.

Newkirk, Vann R. Associate vice president for academic affairs, Fort Valley State University. Interview by Komanduri S. Murty, 29 November 2010, Fort Valley, GA. In possession of editor, Rocky Mount, N.C.

Perry, Eugene. Former vice president for development at Barber-Scotia College. Interview by Vann R. Newkirk, 24 November 2010, Roanoke, VA. In possession of editor, Rocky Mount, NC.

Scipio, Julius. Vice president for academic affairs at Fort Valley State University. Interview by Juone Brown, 29 November 2010, Fort Valley, GA. In possession of editor, Rocky Mount, NC.

Watson, Don. Director of Capital Financing Program. Interview by Vann R. Newkirk, 14 December 2010, Washington D.C. In possession of editor, Rocky Mount, NC.

About the Contributors

Juone **Brown** is an associate professor of education at Fort Valley State University. Her research and teaching interests span two areas: the use of information technology to support teaching and learning, and the role of technology in the decision-making process at historically black colleges and universities. She is the co-author, with Curtis Martin and Kimberly Taylor, of "Standards-Based Reform in the School of Education at Fort Valley State University."

Meigan M. **Fields** is an associate professor of political science at Fort Valley State University. She is the co-author, with Nii Tackie and Arthur Siaway, of "Education of Women as a Contributor to Economic Growth in Africa" *in Women in African Development: The Challenges of Globalization and Liberalization in the 21st Century.* She participated in developing nearly a dozen funded grant projects geared toward improving the disparity of health and education in the African American community.

Dawn J. **Herd-Clark** is an associate professor of history at Fort Valley State University. She has published several book chapters and encyclopedia entries, including "Elizabeth B. Moore, 1878–1932: Education and Community Activism at Georgia's Dorchester Academy" in *The Varieties of Women's Experiences: Portraits of Southern Women in the Post–Civil War Century* and "Reconstruction" in *African Americans in the Nineteenth Century: Perspectives in American Social History.*

Komanduri S. **Murty,** a professor and coordinator of the sociology program at Fort Valley State University, is the author or co-author of five books, including *Historically Black Colleges and Universities: Their Place in American Higher Education*, with Julian B. Roebuck, and has written more than 60 book chapters and articles for books and journals, including the *Encyclopedia of American Prisons, Encyclopedia of Anthropology, Encyclopedia of Great Black Migration, Intimate Violence,* and *The Status of Black Atlanta.*

Vann R. **Newkirk** is the author of *Lynching in North Carolina: A History, 1865–1941,* winner of the Willie Parker Peace History award from the North Carolina

Society of Historians for its contribution to preserving North Carolina history, and *The Greensboro Massacre: Communists, Klan, and Black Relationships.* Newkirk is associate provost/dean of graduate studies and a professor of history at Alabama Agricultural & Mechanical University.

Julius **Scipio** is the author of *A Needs Assessment of Three Participating Partners in Higher Education: Methodology and Major Findings.* He has also published widely in academic journals. Scipio is vice president for academic affairs and an associate professor of education at Fort Valley State University.

Daniel **Wims** is provost at Alabama Agricultural and Mechanical University. He has served in a variety of capacities in historically black colleges including executive vice president and vice president for academic affairs at Fort Valley State University; professor of agricultural sciences at Fort Valley; and assistant vice president for student affairs at South Carolina State University.

Index